SECOND EDITION

Bowling

STEPS TO SUCCESS

Doug Wiedman

HUMAN KINETICS

Library of Congress Cataloging-in-Publication Data

Wiedman, Doug, 1964-
 Bowling : steps to success / Doug Wiedman. -- Second edition.
   pages cm
1. Bowling. I. Title.
 GV903.W48 2015
 794.6--dc23

                              2015015773

ISBN: 978-1-4504-9790-9 (print)

The web addresses cited in this text were current as of June 2015, unless otherwise noted.

Acquisitions Editor: Tom Heine
Developmental Editor: Anne Hall
Managing Editor: Elizabeth Evans
Copyeditor: Annette Pierce
Permissions Manager: Martha Gullo
Senior Graphic Designer: Keri Evans
Cover Designer: Keith Blomberg
Photographs (cover and interior): Neil Bernstein
Visual Production Assistant: Joyce Brumfield
Photo Production Manager: Jason Allen
Art Manager: Kelly Hendren
Associate Art Manager: Alan L. Wilborn
Illustrations: © Human Kinetics
Printer: Walsworth Print

We thank the Purdue Memorial Union's Rac n' Roll at Purdue University for assistance in providing the location for the photo shoot for this book.

Human Kinetics books are available at special discounts for bulk purchase. Special editions or book excerpts can also be created to specification. For details, contact the Special Sales Manager at Human Kinetics.

Printed in the United States of America   10 9 8 7 6 5 4 3 2 1

The paper in this book is certified under a sustainable forestry program.

Human Kinetics
Website: www.HumanKinetics.com

United States: Human Kinetics
P.O. Box 5076
Champaign, IL 61825-5076
800-747-4457
e-mail: humank@hkusa.com

Canada: Human Kinetics
475 Devonshire Road Unit 100
Windsor, ON N8Y 2L5
800-465-7301 (in Canada only)
e-mail: info@hkcanada.com

Europe: Human Kinetics
107 Bradford Road
Stanningley
Leeds LS28 6AT, United Kingdom
+44 (0) 113 255 5665
e-mail: hk@hkeurope.com

Australia: Human Kinetics
57A Price Avenue
Lower Mitcham, South Australia 5062
08 8372 0999
e-mail: info@hkaustralia.com

New Zealand: Human Kinetics
P.O. Box 80
Torrens Park, South Australia 5062
0800 222 062
e-mail: info@hknewzealand.com

E6327

Dedicated to the thousands of students I have enjoyed working with over the years who have made my efforts worthwhile, and to my family who (with no small amount of patience) has shared my passion for playing and teaching the sport of bowling.

Contents

Climbing the Steps to Bowling Success

Welcome to the newest edition of *Bowling: Steps to Success*. This edition retains many of the features that have made the *Steps to Success* series of instructional books so successful. Updated discussions of some of the newer aspects of the modern game make this edition more pertinent and applicable to a wider range of technique preferences. Ideally, both traditionalists and modernists will find satisfaction in the concepts presented.

Bowling: Steps to Success is written to suit the needs of bowlers of many skill levels. People new to the sport benefit from the systematic instruction, which can be adjusted to suit each bowler's rate of development. Experienced players will find that each step isolates a particular element of the game, helping troubleshoot weak spots and guiding them to more advanced techniques. Instructors will find the concept discussions, skill descriptions, and practice drills necessary to develop a course.

Bowling: Steps to Success provides a systematic approach to playing and teaching the sport. Follow this sequence as you work through each step:

1. Read the explanation of the skill emphasized in each step. Understand why the skill is important and how to execute or perform it.
2. Follow the photo demonstrations.
3. Review the missteps, which note common errors and corrections.
4. Perform the drills. Skills improve through repetition and purposeful practice. Read the directions and record your score. Many of the drills appear near the relevant skill discussion, so you can access information more easily if you have trouble with the drill.

Bowling: Steps to Success presents instruction in a specific order. The ordering of the steps for this edition has changed slightly from the previous edition. If you are going on a journey (footwork), it makes sense that you should know the destination (finish position) ahead of time. The discussion of the finish position comes immediately after the discussion of the initial movement. The discussion of the initial movement now merits its own step. Subsequent chapters (footwork, timing, arm swing) expand on the details that connect a bowler's start and his or her finish. The order of the steps more closely represents the order in which skills are developed.

Each skill-specific step discusses principles that influence the nature of the movement, followed by sport-specific descriptions of the movement. Progressive practice drills are included. The order the drills are presented and the evaluation checklist particular to each drill establish a practical and easily understood path to skill development. Illustrations and charts enhance the text to provide a fuller understanding of concepts. Later steps discuss spare-shooting strategies, recognizing and adapting to lane conditions, and developing physical versatility that allows the athlete to learn strategies and techniques to cope with a wide range of performance demands.

A significant feature of this edition is the use of color photographs instead of the line drawings used previously. Drawings exhibit artistic interpretation and may not precisely convey the author's intent. Photos of athletes demonstrating the skills discussed in each step allow readers to better visualize how they should perform the skill themselves.

The goals of *Bowling: Steps to Success* are to facilitate skill development, promote an appreciation of the game, and inspire lifelong involvement. Increased scoring potential and the achievement of personal goals drive an athlete to pursue even higher levels of performance. With the development of knowledge and skill comes a deeper appreciation for the challenges of the game. If doing something is enjoyable, then doing it well goes beyond mere enjoyment—it becomes a satisfying experience. Successful implementation of the concepts discussed gives the reader this opportunity.

The intent of *Bowling: Steps to Success* is to provide the *why* as well as the *how* for the sport. It is hoped that your possession of this book demonstrates a willingness to accept the challenges of the game. With *Bowling: Steps to Success* as your guide, every bowling outing presents a chance to develop skills, conquer the challenges of bowling, and increase your enjoyment of the sport.

Acknowledgments

Throughout life, many sources of information and inspiration contribute to one's success. This is a small sampling of those influences in my bowling life. Those friends and colleagues listed below deserve particular acknowledgement for the help and support in making this book a reality.

Grant Chleborad, former student and teammate: Upon informing me you had listed my name on a coaching website site, you said, "You never know what might come from it." This book is what came from it. Thank you for your respect and your friendship.

Drs. Donald Corrigan, Thomas Templin, William Harper, and Tim Gavin: These are the successive heads of the Department of Health and Kinesiology at Purdue University since 1993, the year I first started teaching the bowling class. I have been granted the opportunity to make a vocation out of my avocation. I consider myself among the lucky few who wake every morning looking forward to the workday ahead.

Tom Taylor, operator of the Triple Crown Pro Shop: For more than 10 years, you demonstrated endless patience answering ball-drilling questions. You gave invaluable help to my family and me concerning bowling equipment, allowing all of us to enjoy a measure of success at this game. Additional thanks for providing outstanding service to the hundreds of my students who came looking for advice and bowling equipment.

Terry Clayton, assistant director of the Purdue Memorial Union: In the winter of 1993, a chance luncheon meeting at a Fred Borden instructional clinic led to the creation of the bowling course. You recognized an opportunity others had turned their backs on. Every year since has shown just how shortsighted they were. Thank you for your confidence and my career.

Bowlers Journal International: As a history major, I appreciate your effort to preserve the legacy of the sport of bowling. Many of your articles (particularly those by J.R. Schmidt) provide excellent reading, highlighting the history and development of the game that is still going on.

Scott Savage, former manager of the PMU Recreation Center: Despite budget cuts and other bureaucratic constraints, the bowling program continues to field a quality team. Your efforts in particular are responsible for the development and the continued success of the intercollegiate bowling team. Go Purdue!

The Sport of Bowling

Welcome to the sport of bowling. Bowling is one of the world's most popular physical activities. Figures indicate that more than 60 million people in the United States bowl at least once per year. Almost 2 million are dues-paying member of the United States Bowling Congress (USBC), and many others participate in independent noncertified leagues. Worldwide participation exceeds 100 million. What accounts for bowling's popularity?

Bowling is a simple game. Roll a perfectly round object on a flat surface at pins that don't move. The equipment is minimal. The basic rules are easily understood. It is one of the most inclusive of all sports. Unlike many sports, bowling grants no advantage to people of a particular size, height, strength, speed, or flexibility. With the availability of bumper bowling installations and ball ramps, the very young and people with physical disabilities are able to participate in the game.

But, don't underestimate the game. Just because it is simple does not mean it is easy. Although it might not favor people with particular fitness attributes, it is still a demanding athletic activity. Success at bowling requires precise movement, subtle physical adjustments, a particularly unique blend of balance and power, and keen observation of constantly changing lane conditions. These challenging aspects of the sport are what inspire participants to a lifelong commitment.

BOWLING'S BACKGROUND

Bowling is an ancient game whose history can be traced back to 3100 BC in Egypt. It has had many forms in many cultures. The most familiar is bowling at wooden pins, which dates back to early medieval Germany (before 1000 AD), where it was initially part of religious activities. Because of the passionate following by its many participants, it is has caused a variety of bans and restriction.

How passionate? Adam Smith, upon his return bearing supplies from England, found the Jamestown colonists busy bowling even though most of them were near starvation. Various medieval kings banned recreational activities like bowling because soldiers were taking too much time from their military duties. Because of its association with gambling and drinking, various communities passed laws against the game; the most famously cited is the early 1800s proscription in Connecticut. Bowling in the United States remained without a consistent set of codified rules and regulations until the formation of the American Bowling Congress (ABC) in 1895.

Throughout bowling's modern era, controversies have arisen. One of the biggest controversies, and one frequently cited for the drop in committed league participation, is that of lane conditions. From the 1960s and onward, marketing emphasized bowling's recreational aspect, making it attractive to a larger customer base by downplaying its competitive aspects. Starting in the late 1970s, allowance for crowned lane conditioning permitted higher scores in the hopes that the average participant would have a more satisfying (if less athletically challenging) experience. By the early 1990s, the governing bodies had abdicated responsibility for controlling the scoring environment under the rationale that lane conditions are a customer service consideration. While yearly recreational participation remains over 60 million, membership in the USBC is less the one-third of what it was in the late 1970s.

Efforts to reverse this decline are being made in a couple of ways:

1. USBC Certified Coaching program—Thousands of coaches have taken official courses to be certified as level I, bronze, silver, or gold coaches. These committed instructors are the vanguard of reasserting the sport aspect of bowling. By giving direction and guidance to willing players, the coaching program allows athletes to receive a consistent program of instruction from the time they first take up bowling until they reach the highest levels of the game.

2. Sport bowling—The USBC recognizes both a recreational approach and an athletic approach to the sport. Lane conditions that meet a standard set of parameters present a true athletic challenge: sport bowling. Almost all collegiate, professional, and serious amateur events are conducted on some form of sport lane condition.

BOWLING LANE AND EQUIPMENT

The sport of bowling is enjoyed worldwide. Through the joint organizational effort of both the USBC and the FIQ (Federation Internationale des Quilleures) the rules, equipment specifications, and scoring system of tenpin bowling are standardized worldwide.

Bowling Pins

Pins are arranged in an equilateral triangle, with the top of the triangle pointing toward the bowler (figure 1). The pins are numbered from left to right; the closest pin, the headpin, is at the top of the triangle as 1. Twelve inches (30.5 cm) is the distance between the center of one pin and the center of any other pin next to it. The entire arrangement makes a triangle 3 feet (1 m) on each side.

- Pins are 15 inches (38 cm) tall, with a diameter at their widest point slightly more than 4.75 inches (12 cm).
- Pins are a little more than 1.5 inches (3.8 cm) at the narrowest part of the neck.

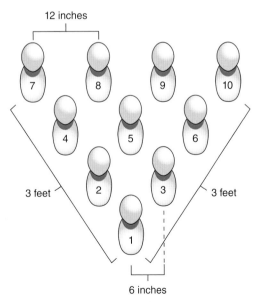

Figure 1 Tenpin triangular setup.

- They stand on a flat base 2.5 inches (6.3 cm) wide.
- Pins weigh from 3 pounds 6 ounces to 3 pounds 10 ounces (1.5-1.6 kg).

Bowling Lanes

The surface of the bowling lane is made of wood or a very hard synthetic material. Lanes are flat to a tolerance of 40/1,000ths of an inch (1 mm), as measured across the width of the lane. Distinctive lane markings guide the player's footwork and serve as targets. A set of seven evenly spaced dots cross the approach 15 feet (4.6 m) and 12 feet (3.6 m) from the foul line. A set of corresponding dots are located a few inches in front of the foul line. These dots are aligned with the seven target arrows arranged about 15 feet past the foul line (figure 2).

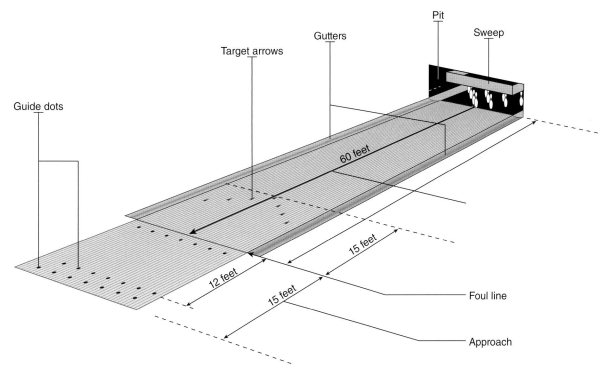

Figure 2   The bowling lane.

The bowler walks on the approach, which is 16 to 17 feet (4.8-5 m) from the beginning of the approach to the foul line. From the approach, the measurements of the lane are as follows:

- From the foul line to the center of the front (head) pin is 60 feet (18.3 m).
- The lane is 41 to 42 inches (104-107 cm) across.
- The depressions on either side of the lane (called *gutters* or *channels*) are about 10 inches (25.4 cm) wide and 3.5 inches (8.9 cm) deep.

Bowling Ball

After the finger holes are drilled into a ball, it is weighed on a dodo scale to highlight imbalances. A *dodo* scale is a special scale that allows the ball driller to measure the weight difference between various halves of the ball. Every ball shares these basic characteristics:

- The circumference is 27 inches (69 cm), and the diameter is 8.595 inches (22 cm).
- Balls are made of solid, nonmetallic material.
- The maximum weight of a bowling ball is 16 pounds (7.3 kg).
- The difference in weight between the top and bottom halves cannot be more than 3 ounces (85 g) (figure 3).
- The maximum imbalance allowed between the left and right halves or the front and back halves is 1 ounce (28 g).

Besides the bowling ball, a few other pieces of equipment are particular to bowling. Well-made shoes promote a smooth approach and a balanced finish while generating power. High-quality bowling shoes have a different sole on each shoe. The sole of the shoe used for sliding is made of smooth leather; the other shoe, used in the power step, has a nonmarking, rubberized surface for traction. Rental shoes have a slide sole on both shoes so they can be used by either left- or right-handed bowlers. The poor traction of rental shoes restricts development of sound footwork and balance; they do not provide good support or a consistent slide. Consider acquiring your own bowling shoes as soon as possible.

Although bowling centers do not generally enforce dress codes, bowlers should use common sense. Wear loose, comfortable clothing. Avoid clothing that is so tight it restricts movement, but do not wear items that are so baggy they get in the way. Bowling is an athletic activity; this is not the time to make a fashion statement. Bowling does not require a lot of intense physical activity, but it does require a large range of motion. Choose clothing that allows you to bend at the knees and make a long, fluid swing.

Bowling gloves are also available, and many types are on the market. Some gloves have a textured or tacky surface, providing a better grip on the ball. Other types of gloves contain hard support pieces to help the bowler maintain proper wrist

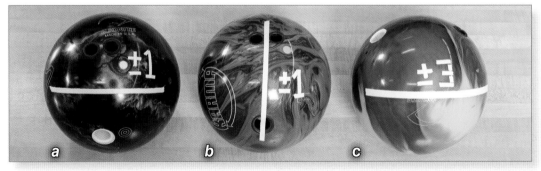

Figure 3   The bowling ball split along three different axes. Imbalance between the front and back halves can be no more than 1 ounce (*a*). Imbalance between the left and right halves can be no more than 1 ounce (*b*) and the top and bottom halves can be no more than 3 ounces.

position. Some gloves support just the wrist, but others support all the way up the hand to the fingers. Certain glove styles allow the bowler to adjust the position of the support for more comfort.

I believe wrist supports limit a bowler's range of motion and inhibit developing strength in the parts of the wrist and hand that contribute to a reliable and versatile release. Wrist supports act as a crutch; use wrist support only if absolutely necessary. If weakness or injury prevents the development of proper release technique, then use a wrist support. For the majority of bowlers, though, it is better to develop wrist strength and release versatility without an artificial support.

RULES OF PLAY AND ETIQUETTE

The basic conduct of play is simple and everyone, even the youngest bowlers, should follow it. A player is allowed up to two throws of the ball with each turn, called a *frame*. The score for each throw is recorded. The goal is to knock down as many pins as possible.

If all 10 pins fall on the first throw of the frame, the second throw is not needed. This is called a *strike*. A strike is indicated by an X. When fewer than 10 pins are knocked down on the first throw, the bowler then attempts a spare. If the remaining pins are knocked down, it is called a *spare conversion*. A *spare* is indicated by a diagonal slash (/) in the upper, right-hand box of the frame. (Strikes and spares are referred to as *marks* because a mark is used to indicate the throw rather than a number. The mark is a reminder that a bonus will be added to the frame containing the mark).

If pins remain standing after the second throw, the bowler is said to have an *open frame*. The bowler is allowed no more throws in that frame. The mechanical *sweep* will remove remaining pins.

Committing a Foul

The end of the approach is indicated by the foul line. No part of the bowler's body may touch any part of the building or lane past the foul line. If there is direct bodily contact past the foul line, the throw is scored a zero. If a foul occurs on the first throw of a frame, the bowler is permitted the second throw. All bowling centers have a device (usually a light sensor that when tripped will light up and give off an audible signal) that indicates when a bowler has fouled. This device is usually turned off during open play, but it must be activated during certified competition. A foul committed without setting off the foul light still must be recorded as a zero for that throw.

Illegal Pinfall

A ball that falls into the gutter before making pin contact is scored a zero. If the ball bounces out of the gutter and back onto the lane, knocking over pins, the pinfall does not count. If this occurs on the first throw of the frame, the machine must be cycled to a full set of pins before the second throw is taken. At bowling centers that use automatic scoring, the score must be changed using the score correction feature because the scorekeeping device cannot tell whether pins have been knocked down legitimately or not.

Pins knocked over by the pinsetter do not count for score. If a pin is moved so that it is outside the range of the pinsetter (referred to as *off spot* or *out of range*) or if it is still wobbling and the pinsetter happens to knock it over, the pin must be reset to its original position. Even if it appears that the pin would have fallen on its own, the pin must be reset before the subsequent throw. A pin standing out of position yet not knocked over by the pinsetter is played where it stands. Pins are only put back on spot if they are illegally knocked over.

Dead Wood

Sometimes pins end up on a part of the lane outside the range off the *sweep*. The sweep is part of the machinery that drops down after each throw to remove fallen pins. Pins that have fallen over but are not removed by the sweep are considered *dead wood*. Do not play the dead wood. A ball that touches dead wood, whether the pin is on the lane or in the gutter, is a dead ball. The throw counts and is scored a zero.

Dead wood (on the lanes or in the gutter hit) struck by a thrown ball can cause damage. The pin may fly off in an unexpected direction, or the rebounding ball may become airborne and damage the ball, pins, or machinery. If you observe dead wood, ask for assistance. These pins must be manually removed by bowling center personnel.

Altering Surfaces

No substance may be put on the ball or the shoes that could alter any playing surface—the ball, the approach, or the lane. Any substance that mars the surface of the ball or lane or leaves a residue behind on the approach is prohibited.

Altering the ball's surface (e.g., by sanding or refinishing) is allowed up until the end of the designated practice time. Balls thrown during the practice time are permitted to be altered. Once competition is declared to have started, no alterations to a ball's surface will be allowed while that round of competition is ongoing. Many serious bowlers have more than one ball. No matter how many a bowler has brought, once competition has started, no ball's surface (even one that has not yet been used in competition) may be altered.

The ball may be wiped clean during competition. The use of mild cleaners is permissible in most circumstances. It is difficult for tournament officials to police the cleaning of balls. Some tournaments have a "dry towel only" rule. Know a tournament's rules before the start of competition.

Lane Etiquette

When crossing a street, it is wise to look both ways; we have been taught this since we were youths. In bowling, it is no different. Before stepping onto the approach, look both ways. Look at the lanes to the immediate left and immediate right.

Part of proper etiquette is to stand completely off the end of the lane while waiting your turn. If a bowler is already on the approach of either of the adjacent lanes, do not step up onto your lane. Wait until the bowlers have completed their throws on both lanes next to yours before stepping up. Stepping up next to another bowler while he or she is preparing is distracting. Don't be rude.

Other Aspects of Bowling Center Courtesy

The simple practice of decency and respect for other participants is all that is necessary for everybody to enjoy the game and the company fellow participants.

- Loud talk and obnoxious, disruptive behavior have no place in the bowling center.

- Do not use somebody else's ball without asking permission. A ball in use, even a house ball, is considered a bowler's private property.
- Courtesy dictates cleaning up the bowling area when finished. Return house balls to the ball rack, and take rental shoes to the control desk. Throw away trash and food items. This prevents clutter and makes it easier for bowlers using the lanes after you.

SCOREKEEPING

Most bowling centers use automatic scoring systems. Yet, knowing how to keep score helps you appreciate the impact that strikes and spares have on the final score (and the detrimental influence of open frames). Additionally, automatic scorers on a rare occasion malfunction, and it is nice to know what the proper score should be so that an appropriate correction can be made.

A game consists of 10 frames. As noted earlier, knocking down all 10 pins on the first throw is a strike; knocking down all 10 pins with two throws is a spare. If the initial throw is not a strike, the pin count of the first throw is recorded in the upper left-hand corner of the frame. In the upper right-hand corner of the frame will be one of three options:

1. An X if the bowler struck on the initial throw
2. A diagonal line (/) indicating the successful conversion of the spare on the second throw
3. The actual pin count of the second throw, if the spare attempt was unsuccessful

The cumulative score of the game is recorded in the bottom half of each successive frame as the bowler completes each turn (see figure 4).

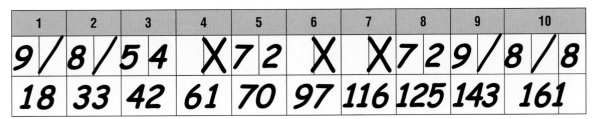

1	2	3	4	5	6	7	8	9	10
9 /	8 /	5 4	X 7 2	X	X	X 7 2	9 /	8 /	8
18	33	42	61	70	97	116	125	143	161

Figure 4 Sample scorecard showing open frames, strikes, and spares.

Bowling is the only game that uses a bonus system of scoring. That is, the value of a good shot is increased by the value of a subsequent shot. In scorekeeping, a bonus is awarded for frames that have marks:

- For a strike, the bowler receives 10 for the frame plus the total pinfall for the next two throws in the subsequent frame or frames.
- For a spare, the bowler receives 10 for the frame plus the pinfall of the next throw of the subsequent frame.
- For an open frame, the bowler receives no bonus and scores only the pin count for the two throws of that frame.

The last (10th) frame is the only one in which a third throw is possible. In the case of an initial strike or spare, an additional throw (or two) is needed in order for those marks to have real value. But, the extra throw has to be earned. When using two throws to make a spare, one additional throw is left. Use one throw for a strike and two throws remain. No strike, no spare: sorry, no extra throw.

SAFETY IN THE BOWLING CENTER

Although not a contact sport, bowlers need to keep safety in mind to prevent injuries in the bowling center. All bowlers should be aware of a variety of safety concerns. These include moisture and dirt, spills of food and drink, proper ball selection, the foul line, keeping hands and ball clean and dry, and other bowlers.

Moisture

Moisture is the number one enemy of safety. The slightest bit of moisture on the slide sole prevents you from sliding properly. Keep bowling shoes clean and dry. Be careful when walking around in your bowling shoes. Keep an eye on the floors: food and drink areas and restrooms are of particular concern. When floors and carpeting are particular dirty or damp, consider taking off you bowling shoes when walking away from the lanes. Put them back on when you get back to bowl. If you have your own bowling shoes, consider buying a shoe covering. These protective sleeves go over the shoes and allow you to walk around without worrying about dirt, dust, or moisture affecting the shoes.

Handling Food

Be careful where you set down food and drink. Be considerate of other bowlers. Clean up after yourself. Ask for assistance if you spill something or see a problem area in the center.

Ball Selection

Select a suitable bowling ball. Having the right ball not only leads to better performance, but it also ensures physical well-being. Don't hurt yourself using a ball of improper fit and weight. In Step 1 Selecting and Gripping the Ball, a more detailed discussion of ball selection can be found. No exact formula determines the proper ball weight. Some people recommend that young bowlers use 1 pound (.45 kg) for every year of age. However, a better method is using the 10-percent rule. The ball's weight should be about 10 percent of the young bowler's body weight.

For adult and young-adult bowlers, athletic fitness has a large influence. Physical maturity and muscular development become important factors. What it comes down to is comfort. Essentially, the ball swings itself, like the pendulum on a large clock, and the bowler merely walks along with the swing. Sound mechanics, such as a fluid swing, evenly paced footwork, and good balance allow a bowler to throw a heavier ball than a less-accomplished bowler would be able to.

Remember, these methods are only guidelines. I knew one young bowler who, although small for his age and barely 115 pounds (52.2 kg), had no trouble using a 14-pound (6.3 kg) ball, as evidenced by a personal-best, three-game series of a 769 and a 190+ average. On the other hand, bowlers have injured themselves or others because of the untimely and misdirected release of a poorly fitting ball.

Foul Line

Be aware of the foul line. The lane is coated with a very thin, nearly invisible film of oil called lane conditioner. Stepping past the foul line is hazardous, frequently resulting in slips and falls.

Staying Dry

Keep the ball and your hands clean and dry. Bowling balls are heavy, smooth objects. The oil on the lanes gets onto the ball. Keep a towel handy. A basic towel (like terry cloth) works well, but microfiber towels work even better. Wipe off the ball and your hands after every throw.

Ball Return

Be careful when picking up the ball from the ball return. Place hands on the sides of the ball, not the front and back, to prevent a returning ball from crushing a finger. When picking up the ball, use both hands and bend at the knees. Do not insert fingers into the holes when lifting the ball. Placing the fingers in the holes is one of the last steps of a preshot routine.

Containing Yourself

Confine movements, gestures, and body English to your own lane. Avoid stepping onto another lane after a throw. Stepping in front of another bowler is not only distracting and rude, but also unsafe—a collision between two bowlers can be dangerous. As soon as your ball hits the pins, walk straight back to the end of your own lane.

Clothing

Clothing is also a safety concern. Tight outfits restrict movement; baggy clothes get in the way. Excessively baggy, and low-sitting pants create a particular hazard. Long, wide pant legs dragging along the floor can easily get under the slide foot, causing a slip and fall. These types of pants also pick up considerable dirt and moisture, especially when worn in inclement weather, creating both a mess and a hazard on the lanes.

PREPARING FOR ATHLETIC ACTIVITY

Many participants (even serious bowlers) fail to prepare for the athletic demands of the sport. This oversight can lead to both acute and chronic injuries. Bowling is an imbalanced activity. Much of the stress (arm swing and release) happens solely on one side. Additionally, the approach finishes on one foot. The body's need to accommodate for the force and counterforce elements of the game, as well as the range of motion of various joints, make preparation imperative. An overall fitness regimen and a specific warm-up routine are as important for bowling as they are for any other athletic activity.

Begin with a good all-around stretching routine. Stretching just before a physical activity is of limited utility, so make a stretching routine part of your normal daily activity. Emphasize the low back and legs (calves and hamstring) during a stretching routine; much of the power of bowling is generated through the leg drive. Groin stretches are also beneficial.

A full range of motion in the swing shoulder is helpful. The longer and more fluid the swing, the less likely muscular tension will pull the swing off target. Stretch out the shoulder over a full range of motion in all directions of movement. Gentle stretching exercises for the wrist and hand prepare the forearm and hand for the stress of the grip and release motions.

While weight training is not a priority, exercises emphasizing hand, forearm, and leg strength can be beneficial. Many people do not have particularly strong forearms. They often cannot keep the wrist position firm enough to allow a proper release. This weakness may require the use of a lightweight ball, limiting the bowler's effectiveness in knocking down pins. Forearm curls and other grip-strength exercises may benefit these athletes.

A good general fitness regimen is all a bowler usually needs. Some professional bowlers run to develop leg strength and endurance. Cycling or swimming gives the same benefits. For the average league bowler who bowls only three games at a time, endurance is not a great concern. Among serious tournament bowlers, who can expect to bowl as many as 8 to 10 games per day, endurance is critical for success.

GETTING INVOLVED

Your local bowling center will have information about leagues, tournaments, and special events in the area. Most leagues and tournaments in the United States require membership in the USBC.

For international bowling, contact the following organization:

Federation Internationale des Quilleurs (FIQ)

Rizal Memorial Sports Complex

Pablo Ocampo Sr. Street

Malate, Manila

Philippines

www.worldbowling.org

For bowling within the United States, you can contact the following:

United States Bowling Congress (USBC): 414-421-6400

College Bowling USA: 800-514-BOWL

USA Bowling: 414-421-9008

E-mail links to each of these organizations can be found at www.bowl.com. The mailing address for all of these organizations is 621 Six Flags Drive, Arlington, Texas 76011. Team USA and the Coaches Association are extensions of the national organizations and can be reached at the same address. For more information, contact each state's bowling association to find information about local high school opportunities.

Selecting and Gripping the Ball

Bowling is one of the few sports in which the player puts the hand into the equipment. Successful bowling requires a smooth, controlled release of the ball. Without ball control, which comes from proper equipment selection, no other skills in the game develop properly.

Get your own bowling ball! Providing house balls to casual bowlers is important for introducing millions of participants to the game. But skill development requires a series of commitments. The first of those commitments is having a properly fitted ball. A poorly fitting ball creates tension in the hand and a loss of confidence in the ability to repeat shots. It may create a cautiousness or tentativeness that affects footwork and the finish position. In short, the bowler's entire mental and physical game can be affected by improperly fitted equipment.

I repeat, the first important element for learning correct bowling technique is to purchase a ball and have it drilled to fit properly. An old adage warns, "You can't outcoach a bad fit." Likewise, bowlers themselves must realize, "You cannot learn your way around a bad fit."

ESSENTIALS OF PROPER BALL FIT

Imagine going to a shoe store and not being able to find a pair of shoes that fit properly. Whether too loose, too tight, or providing insufficient support, the poorly fitting shoes would soon cause considerable annoyance and pain. Like shoes that don't fit, a poorly fitting ball eventually causes pain through cuts, blisters, muscle strain, and so on. A poorly fitting ball interferes with proper swing and release mechanics.

Consider the convenience of having your own ball and not looking for one every time you bowl. Your own ball aids skill development in the short run and prevents injuries in the long run.

The following are the four characteristics of ball fit (figure 1.1).

Figure 1.1 BALL FIT: WEIGHT, HOLE SIZE, SPAN, AND PITCH

1. Ball is the right weight for the bowler's strength.
2. Holes fit fingers comfortably and ball slides onto thumb when fingers are fully inserted.
3. Span is not too short or too long.
4. Pitch is appropriate for the bowler's grip and needs.

Weight

Proper ball weight depends on the bowler's strength and the fit of the ball. Bowlers should use as heavy a ball as they can comfortably swing. The better the fit, the more easily the ball stays on the bowler's hand without additional effort on the bowler's part. A poor fit often forces the bowler to use a lighter ball in order to control it during the swing.

Determining Proper Ball Weight   Extension Test

Hold a ball in the palm of your hand. Do not insert fingers into the holes. Extend the arm forward while taking a step exactly like the initial pushaway movement in a normal approach. Hold the pushaway position for a few seconds. Bring the ball back to the starting position as you step back. Repeat motion. Test balls of various weights. Use the heaviest ball that did not cause you to strain.

Score Your Success

Give yourself 5 points for finding a ball that is the right weight for you.

Your score ___

Once you get to a ball weight that prevents you from extending your arm or causes your wrist to feel like it will give out, then you have reached a weight too heavy for your wrist strength. This extension test gives you an idea of your wrist strength. It is also good practice for learning where the hand should be as you place the ball into the swing.

Hole Size

The size of the finger and thumb holes should allow a smooth, snug fit. The hole should not be so snug that loose skin or the knuckle catches in the hole. If it is necessary to apply force to insert the fingers or thumb, the hole is too tight. A popping or sucking sound (indicating a vacuum effect from trapped air) may indicate a tight fit as well. Sometimes the popping noise is caused by incorrect grip technique. That sound does not always mean the hole is too tight. Many bowlers bend their knuckles inside the gripping holes, which traps air and might cause a popping sound even if the fit is correct.

Learn proper gripping technique: If you feel like the holes are correct, yet your hand won't come free, you may be using improper grip pressure. Imagine squeezing the thumb and fingers together. The long, flat side of the fingers and thumb should press back toward the inside of the holes. There should be more pressure from the finger pressing back than from the thumb pressing forward. The more the fingers support, the less you'll feel an urge to squeeze with the thumb. Grip pressure is distributed along the entire length of the fingers and thumb. Remember, the flat length of the fingers press toward the flat length of the thumb (figure 1.2). Gripping a bowling ball is not like gripping a bar or handle.

Do not allow too much extra space in the holes. Many bowlers make the mistake of choosing holes that are too loose. They worry about the ball sticking on the hand and pulling them down the lane like a scene from a cartoon or slapstick comedy. Overly loose holes force a bowler to squeeze excessively to keep hold of the ball. Excessive grip pressure causes tension all the way up the arm. If the fingers dig into the ball and the knuckles are bending inside the holes, the ball will stick on the hand anyway. Incorrect hole size inadvertently causes the problem the bowler is trying to avoid. Pressure points caused by bent fingers or thumb may hang up the ball at the release (figure 1.3). Over the long run, these pressure points cause pain and injury.

Figure 1.2 Feel as though you are bringing together the surfaces of your fingers and thumb.

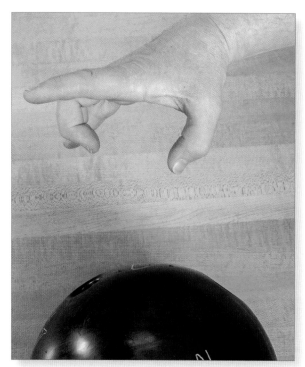

Figure 1.3 Bending the knuckle inside the finger hole will create pressure points.

When the bowler finally relaxes the grip when using a ball with holes that are too loose, the ball barely makes its swing before it falls off with an embarrassingly loud thud. Excessively loose finger holes create a frustrating drop–squeeze release pattern.

MISSTEP

You are able to bend your finger inside the hole, indicating that the finger hole is too large.

CORRECTION

Remember the phrase *fits like a glove*. The holes should be neither too big nor too small. After inserting the thumb completely up to its base, the fingers will feel snug to the appropriate knuckle.

Slight variations in the degree of snugness are a matter of personal preference. However, the ability to insert the finger past the appropriate joint is an obvious indication that the holes are too large. For a conventional grip, the fingers are inserted up to (but not past) the second knuckle. For the fingertip grip, the fingers are only inserted to the first knuckle. The need to force the fingers into the holes so that they reach the appropriate joint is an indicator that the holes are too small.

Span

The span is the distance between the edge of the finger holes and the edge of the thumbhole. After inserting the fingers, the ball slides smoothly onto the thumb. Do not try to stretch the hand to get the thumb into the hole. Proper span opens the hand to allow the ball to rest in the palm.

Sometimes pain in the elbow indicates improper span. With the fingertip drilling in particular, excessive span length may cause pain on the inside of the elbow. Pay careful attention to soreness or bruising near the elbow. Irritation in this area must be dealt with immediately.

Determining Span

To test for proper span, insert the thumb first (figure 1.4). Then, lay the hand out over the surface of the ball without inserting the fingers. For a conventional grip, the crease for the second knuckle will be slightly past the front edge of the finger holes. For a fingertip grip, the front edge of the hole will be about halfway between the creases of the first and second knuckle.

Success Check

- Finger holes are the correct size: not too small, not too large.
- Edge of finger holes aligns correctly with each knuckle of the gripping fingers.
- Fingers and thumb go into the holes up to the correct knuckle.
- After inserting fingers first, the ball easily slides back onto the thumb.
- Webbing at the base of the thumb is not too taut nor too loose.
- Ball feels as though it rests snugly and comfortably in the palm of the hand.

Figure 1.4 Proper span for a conventional grip.

Score Your Success

Give yourself 1 point for properly identifying a span that is too short or too long. Give yourself 5 additional points for correcting the problem by finding a ball with the correct span for your hand.

Your score ___

MISSTEP

There is excessive rubbing and tenderness on the front of the thumb. The webbing between thumb and index finger is taut. The ball hangs up and does not release smoothly.

CORRECTION

These symptoms may indicate an excessive span. Do not overly stretch the hand to insert the thumb. Find a ball that settles comfortably in the palm of your hand when the fingers and thumb are fully inserted.

To put the ball onto the hand properly, insert the fingers first (figure 1.5a), and then gently extend the hand to insert the thumb (figure 1.5b). A need to excessively stretch the hand to insert the thumb fully indicates the span is too long (figure 1.5c). If the span is too long, the bowler will feel considerable pressure on the front of the thumb. The uncomfortable pressure on the thumb, or perhaps the inability to completely insert the thumb, may cause the bowler to struggle with ball control.

Very loose or creased webbing indicates a short span. A short span may cause the front of the knuckles to push into the edges of the finger holes. Bowlers with conventional grips might notice an indentation line just under the second knuckle of the gripping fingers. For some bowlers, this pressure against the extensor tendon near that area of the knuckle is painful. If the ball appears to be propped up on the ends of the fingers and does not settle into the palm, the span is definitely too short (figure 1.5d).

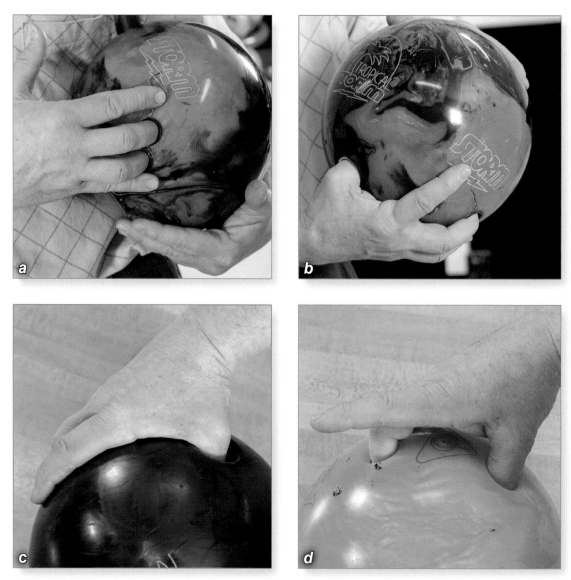

Figure 1.5 (a-b) To put the ball onto the hand insert fingers first and then the thumb. (c) Excessively stretching the hand to insert the thumb means the span is too long. (d) If the ball is propped up by the fingers and doesn't settle into the palm, the span is too short.

MISSTEP

The fronts of the knuckles are bruised or sensitive. The webbing between the thumb and index finger is very loose. Your hand rotates around the ball too early during the downswing, causing the ball to drop off too soon. The ball does not rest in your palm.

CORRECTION

All of these symptoms indicate that the span is too short. Look for a ball that rests easily in the palm of your hand. The natural curve of the hand will fit the curve of the ball. When the span is correct, very little space exists between the hand and the ball surface. This is not necessarily true for fingertip balls.

Rarely are fingertip balls found on house ball racks. And if they are, odds are they will not fit properly. If your game has progressed enough to adopt a fingertip grip, you should already have your own ball. See a trained pro-shop operator to fit a ball for a fingertip grip.

Because the first joint does not bend at as sharp an angle as the second joint, there will be space between the ball and the finger if the ball is drilled for a fingertip grip (see figure 1.9). Be careful how much the hand stretches with a fingertip grip. Old-school drilling advocates using an extra-long span for the fingertip grip with the idea that the finger tension creates more ball revolutions. However, it is a mistake to think that this finger pull creates more lift at the release. In fact, the tension in the hand caused by a long span may restrict the hand's movement around the ball. Excessively long spans have a limited influence on increasing hook, and they may cause injuries. A relaxed hand, up to a degree, creates a faster release motion. Soft hands are fast hands.

Some bowlers prefer a somewhat shorter span than what is considered appropriate for their hand size. A relaxed grip relieves tension, which is helpful for players with conditions such as arthritis or tendinitis. For these bowlers, an increase in the angle of the pitches in conjunction with a relaxed grip may help them hold onto the ball better. A relaxed span might help bowlers unable to rotate the hand around the ball fast enough at the release to generate the side roll necessary for an effective hook. Although, as noted earlier, if the span becomes too short, the release motion frequently starts too early. This early hand rotation may cause the ball to drop off the hand too soon. The inability to control the ball throughout the swing affects accuracy and consistency. Seeing a twirling motion, where the ball looks like a spinning top, means you did not release it correctly.

Proper grip helps develop correct release technique. Release techniques are discussed in step 8.

Pitch

Pitch is the angle at which the holes are drilled into the ball (figure 1.6). The three types of pitches are forward, reverse, and lateral (left or right). A hole drilled toward the geometric center has zero pitch. This is how the holes (particularly the thumbholes) of many house balls are drilled. The finger holes have just enough lateral pitch (left and right) to keep them from coming together inside the ball. While zero pitch may be the most common for beginning bowlers, it is rarely the best one. This

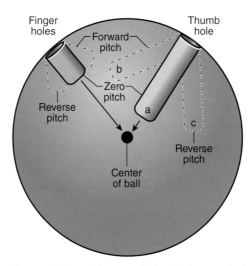

Figure 1.6 Pitches of the finger holes: *(a)* zero pitch, *(b)* forward pitch, and *(c)* reverse pitch.

highlights another problem with house balls. Not only is it likely that the hole sizes and span will be incorrect, but also the pitch angles rarely accommodate the natural strength and flexibility of the most bowlers.

With reverse pitch, the fingers and thumb move away from the palm. In other words, the holes are drilled away from the geometric center of the ball. Reverse pitch allows the hand to release the ball more easily. It is also a way to relieve tension for bowlers who lack hand flexibility.

In a forward pitch, the fingers and thumb move toward the palm. The holes are drilled forward of the geometric center of the ball. Forward pitch allows the bowler to hold onto the ball better. The increase in angle between the fingers and thumb and the palm allows a stronger grip. This is particularly helpful for bowlers with smaller hands or weak grip strength.

For left and right pitches, the holes are drilled toward the left or right, respectively. Left and right pitches of the finger holes are necessary to keep the holes from coming together down inside the ball. Finger holes drilled at an angle toward each other (such as zero pitch) will eventually meet. The holes are said to touch. If this overlap is too great, it creates a weakness (or void) in the ball that could later lead to ball damage.

Left and right pitch also influence the release. For instance, in a ball with a right thumb pitch (right-handed bowler) the thumb will angle toward the palm. This promotes an earlier rotation at the release. The pitch tilts the ball to the inside of the hand earlier in the swing. The opposite is also true. A left pitch opens up the hand, so the bowler can stay behind the ball longer through the release point.

The flexibility of the finger joints and the thumb's range of motion are the most important characteristics to consider when determining the proper pitch angle. The next important factor is the size of the bowler's hand (i.e., the length of the span). The longer the span, the greater the arc being covered around the circumference of the ball and the less likely the holes are going to point toward the center of the ball.

Use caution when pitching the holes. Although slight adjustments may create a different release, it is easy to strain the fingers' joints and tendons if the pitch angles are not appropriate. Seek the advice of a pro-shop professional if you experience any of the following missteps.

MISSTEP

With the fingers properly inserted into the gripping holes, you cannot feel the pads of the fingers or thumb pressing against the inside of the holes.

CORRECTION

The pitch angle is too sharp (forward). Your hand naturally wants to open up away from the gripping surface of the holes. The ball should be drilled so that you to feel the front of your fingers and thumb making contact with the inside of the holes.

MISSTEP

The ball feels as if it will fall off your hand early in the swing. Your arm bends during the arm swing.

CORRECTION

The pitch is too open. Flexing the arm is your body's unconscious response to the sense of dropping the ball. Consider redrilling the holes with more forward pitch.

Drilling techniques can help a bowler. Proper drilling can facilitate the release motion for a bowler who does not have a particularly strong hand action or help maintain control for a bowler who struggles with control during the swing.

Bowlers must go to an experienced, well-trained pro-shop operator. Ask around to learn about the pro shop's reputation. Ask about certifications earned or training courses taken. Given the potential for joint injury, nerve damage, and general aggravation, bowlers should not underestimate the importance of properly trained pro-shop employees. A good ball driller can help take your game to new levels; a bad drilling may limit, or even end, your bowling career.

CHOOSING A HOUSE BALL

Predrilled house balls offer limited options. Typically, as the weight of the balls goes up, the hole sizes and span length increase as well. This does not suit bowlers with short, thick fingers or long, thin ones. It is almost impossible to find a house ball that fits correctly.

Most bowlers use one of two basic grips: conventional or fingertip. Each grip style, to be discussed in more detail in the next section, has fit characteristics unique to that grip. In a conventional grip, the middle two fingers are inserted up to the second knuckle. Most house balls are drilled to accommodate a conventional grip. If you use a fingertip grip, in which the middle two fingers are inserted only up to the first joint, it will be difficult to find a house ball that fits.

House Ball Selection: **Does the Ball Fit?**

Choose a house ball and evaluate it based on the following criteria. If the ball does not score at least 10 points, put it back and try to find a ball that fits better.

- Finger holes offer a smooth, snug fit = 0-2 points
- Thumbhole offers a smooth, snug fit = 0-3 points
- Span is the correct length (hand-placement test, or evaluation of the webbing between the base of the thumb and the index finger) = 0-2 points
- Ball is an appropriate weight = 0-4 points
- Wrist position can be maintained during practice swings = 0-3 points

Success Check

- Evaluate a variety of balls to find the best one.
- Do not let fashion affect judgment. Don't be swayed by colors or styles.
- Choose an appropriate ball based on how it feels in your hand.
- Ask yourself, "Am I confident that I can throw this ball consistently?"

Score Your Success

Your score ___

(Avoid using a ball that scores less than 10 points.)

TYPES OF GRIPS

Before making final decisions about a ball, be sure you know proper gripping technique. Most bowlers use either the conventional grip or the fingertip grip. Each grip style has certain unique characteristics.

For a proper grip (figure 1.7), insert the ring and middle fingers first, and then the thumb. The index and pinkie fingers act as outriggers to balance the ball in the palm of the hand. You are putting the ball onto the hand in reverse order of the way it will come off the hand at the release. Remember, last in, first out. When both fingers are in their holes, it aligns the grip. Once both fingers are positioned snugly, the thumb can enter the thumbhole only one way. Now all that remains is to gently squeeze the fingers toward the thumb. The pressure of the gripping fingers squeezing the ball into the palm and toward the thumb is all that is needed to keep the ball in place throughout the swing.

Inserting the thumb first causes certain problems. The thumbhole is round, so the thumb could be placed into the hole from any position. However, not all positions allow bowlers to properly place the fingers into their holes. Also when people place the thumb first, they have a tendency to set it too deep in the hole. Consequently, when they release the ball, the thumb tends to hang up in the hole. Ball-drilling technique is based on the principle of fingers first, thumb last for putting the ball onto the hand.

Figure 1.7 PROPER GRIP

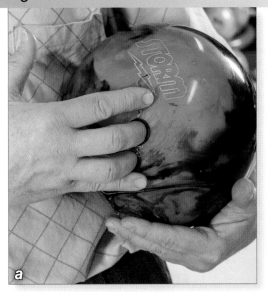
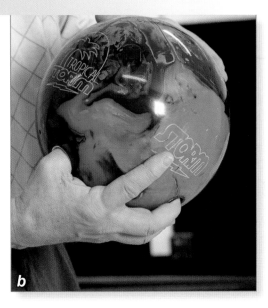

Insert Fingers

1. Fingers are inserted first.
2. Fingers are inserted to correct joint.
3. Middle and ring fingers are inserted.

Insert Thumb

1. Ball rolls back onto thumb.
2. Index finger and pinkie balance ball in palm.
3. Fingers and thumb squeeze together.

Conventional Grip

The main characteristic of a conventional grip is that the fingers are inserted up to the second joint (figure 1.8). Because more of the fingers are in the ball and because the second joint bends at a stronger angle, the bowler has a feeling of better control with the conventional grip.

Figure 1.8 **CONVENTIONAL GRIP**

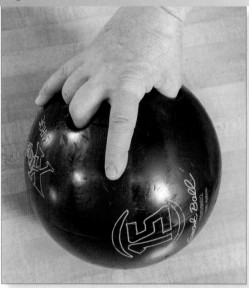

1. Fingers are inserted to second joint.
2. Fingers press ball back toward thumb.
3. Inside the ball, fingers and thumb are flat.
4. Bowler needs a ball with a shorter span than if a fingertip grip is used.

Although we use the term *grip*, think about squeezing the ball rather than gripping it. Ideally the fingers press harder than the thumb. This is true with any style grip. This squeezing technique creates a more even distribution of grip pressure.

Do not grip the ball the same way you would grip a bar or handle. Keep the gripping surfaces of the fingers and thumb flat inside the holes. Less hand tension leads to less arm tension, which in turn leads to a long, smooth, muscle-free swing. Avoid feeling like you are fighting with the ball during the swing.

Do not forget about the outriggers, the fingers not inserted in the ball. The pinkie and index fingers press against the surface of the ball. The pressure from these fingers helps lock the wrist in position and supports the ball throughout the swing. The more support the fingers provide, the less pressure is needed from the thumb. Moderating thumb pressure reduces the chance of the thumb hanging up at the release, enabling a quick, smooth release.

The conventional grip is shorter than the fingertip grip. The finger holes and thumb hole are drilled closer together. Because more of the fingers are inserted (and the second knuckle more easily bends to a sharper angle), conventional drilling provides a stronger grip. Generally, as the hand opens (stretches out), grip strength decreases.

The shorter span may provide a stronger grip, but it also shortens the time between thumb release and finger release. Delaying finger release provides extra leverage. Because a fingertip drilling uses a longer span, the leveraging effect is greater. It puts the fingers more under the ball and allows them to release later in the swing. The torque applied from a late release of the fingers allows more revolutions and side roll, increasing the hook potential of the ball.

This means that a conventional grip potentially limits the amount of hook a bowler can generate. However, proper release technique creates hook, regardless of the grip used. So using a conventional grip does not entirely eliminate the opportunity to create an effective hook.

Semifingertip Grip

Fingertip balls used to be drilled with very long spans so that just the tips of the fingers were placed in the holes. This created a considerable difference in the feel (and the comfort) between balls drilled for a fingertip grip and balls drilled conventionally.

Semifingertip drilling splits the difference between the two extremes. Current drilling technique uses a shorter span for fingertip drilling than what was once common. The current manner of drilling the fingertip grip incorporates many of the ideas behind the old semifingertip style.

Fingertip Grip

For a fingertip grip (figure 1.9), the fingers are inserted up to the first knuckle. This lengthens the grip, allowing more time between the release of the thumb and the release of the fingers. As mentioned earlier, the extra fraction of a second the ball remains on the fingers gives the bowler opportunity to create greater leverage. Some bowlers use the term *lift*. Lift is not the physical upward movement of the hand and fingers during the release. Lift is the finger's resistance to the weight of the ball as the ball accelerates toward the bottom of the swing. When using proper grip and hand position, the fingers initially drive through the back of the ball, then around, and then up the side of the ball. As the swing carries the hand out and up toward the follow-through, the fingertip grip allows the ball to stay on the fingers longer during the extension and turn phases of the release.

With a fingertip grip, you will experience more pressure on the fingers, particularly at the release. Maintain this pressure throughout the swing. Feel as if the fingers were locked in, with the hand firmly supporting the ball all the way to the release. Ideally, this will minimize the urge to squeeze with the thumb. Thumb squeeze is the main cause for feeling "locked up" in the ball and unable to make a smooth, powerful release.

Figure 1.9   **FINGERTIP GRIP**

1. Fingers are inserted to first knuckle.
2. Bowler feels pads of fingertips inside holes.
3. Fingers squeeze toward the thumb.
4. Inside the thumbhole, thumb remains straight, with no bend at knuckle.
5. The span is longer than that of a conventional grip.

When to Use Fingertip Grip

Most bowlers committed to long-term development adopt a fingertip grip. Some coaches have suggested that a ball should be drilled for fingertip immediately. They contend that a properly drilled fingertip ball is not more difficult to throw than one drilled conventionally. I find this to be true most often when bowlers are developing a reliable set of fundamental skills and they are guided in their development by knowledgeable coaching.

I prefer that bowlers use a conventional grip until they have a reasonably consistent physical game. I like to wait until their average is in the 140s or better before considering a fingertip grip.

An affirmative answer to all the following questions may mean you are ready for a fingertip grip:

1. Is your body well positioned and well balanced at the line?

2. Do you have reasonably good control of your swing?

3. Is your hand position at the release consistent and strong enough to create a controllable hook when using a conventional grip?

The fingertip grip provides an advantage in making the ball hook only if both the hand position and the swing movement put the fingers in the correct leveraging position at the release. A fingertip grip is not a cure-all for poor technique. The release is the last element in a chain of events. The bowler must develop the rest of the physical game in order for the release to be effective. If other elements of the physical game are lacking, a fingertip grip does little to increase scoring potential. In fact, it is likely to exaggerate mistakes.

Drilling for a fingertip grip is not a primary step. Although some players seem ready to use a fingertip grip almost immediately, others may not be ready for some time. Physical development varies among athletes. Immediately adopting a fingertip grip fails to take into consideration a bowler's mind-set. The bowler might have seen someone throw a hook and think that a fingertip drilling is the be-all and end-all for throwing a hook without realizing the importance of proper technique regardless of ball drilling.

Few bowlers seek professional coaching. Most bowlers don't get help until after they have trouble with the game. Bad habits are in place and the damage is already done. If they have not yet gone to a fingertip drilling, adding it to their games at this point will provide little benefit.

Claw Grip

Some inexperienced bowlers, not knowing any better, try to bowl using this grip. In a claw grip, the middle and index fingers are inserted into the ball rather than the middle and ring fingers. This creates a weak gripping action and does not center the ball on the hand. Some bowlers use a claw grip because of weakness or injury. Do not use this grip unless it is absolutely necessary.

Two-Finger (Thumbless) Grip

Technically, at the point of release, we are all thumbless bowlers. The thumb should exit the ball before the fingers. The question is how does a swing get to that point and what control does the bowler have over the ball at that point. In the two-finger (or thumbless) grip, the ring and middle fingers are inserted into the ball just as in a regular grip, but the thumb is not inserted. The bowler cups the ball in the palm of the hand, and the thumb stays on the outside of the ball. With the thumbless grip, the bowler doesn't have to worry about whether the thumb exits properly because the thumb is not inserted to begin with.

For many, this grip almost always produces some kind of hook release. Without the support of the thumb during the swing, the hand rotates around the ball to some degree. Many novice bowlers, impressed by the sharp hook, attempt this grip. Many people using house balls experiment with this release. The ease in which they can create a hook motion using this release leads many inexperienced bowlers to rely solely on this technique.

Poor ball selection options limit proper fit, negating the proper release motion. When bowlers cannot find a ball with a proper thumb fit, they often decide not to put the thumb in at all. The thumbless technique offers the following benefits:

1. Generates rotation and a strong hook. Considerable torque can be applied to the ball if the proper hand position and release motion are maintained.
2. Not inserting the thumb puts the ball's weight entirely on the fingers at the point of release.
3. Leaving the thumb out of the ball guarantees the fingers will release later than the thumb.

Some bowlers use a lightweight ball with small finger holes. In this case, they insert the fingers only up to the first knuckle. This gives them the benefit of a fingertip release, plus it is much easier to rotate a lighter ball than a heavier one. Bowlers often adopt the thumbless technique when frustrated at not being able to achieve a proper release motion with the more traditional "thumb in the ball" technique.

The thumbless technique offers considerable shortcomings:

- It is difficult to use this technique without using a lighter ball. First, from the bowling proprietor's point of view, excessive ball damage is an issue. It is easy to crack the shells of lightweight balls. Second, a lightweight ball sacrifices pin carry.
- To maintain support, the bowler must excessively cup the wrist and bend the elbow in order to carry the ball through the swing (figure 1.10). This arm position creates tension in the muscles and restricts the swing.
- The bent arm creates a shorter pendulum, stealing power from the swing.
- It is difficult to keep the ball balanced on the hand throughout the swing.
- "Chicken winging" the elbow out from the body is more likely to occur when the arm is bent.

Figure 1.10 The thumbless grip forces the bowler to bend the arm, creating a shorter pendulum.

- Many bowlers using this technique attempt to generate ball speed through excessive body movement, which not only sacrifices control and accuracy, but may also lead to injuries.
- The thumbless grip lacks versatility because it makes it difficult to throw the ball straight. A release technique that minimizes the amount of potential hook often is preferred in certain spare situations or when bowling on dry lanes.

Bowlers who want a strong hook, are struggling with standard grip techniques, or lack properly fitting equipment might be tempted to use the thumbless grip. To gain the benefits of the thumbless release while minimizing the control issues associated with it, consider the two-handed technique.

Two-Handed Release

The use of this style (figure 1.11) is growing. This technique is a direct outgrowth of the thumbless technique. Many of the shortcomings of the thumbless release can be moderated by using both hands. The growth of the two-handed style and its impact on the game is irrefutable. As stated earlier, at the release we are all thumbless bowlers because at the release point, just before the ball comes off the fingers, the ball is already off the thumb. How a bowler gets to that release point, in terms of swing motion and hand position, is what differentiates one style from another. The two-handed style will be an important part of step 8, which discusses the release in detail.

Figure 1.11   Using the two-handed release.

Developing Grip: Evaluating Proper Grip Technique

It is helpful for a coach or experienced bowler to evaluate your grip technique. Use the following criteria to determine whether your grip technique is sound.

- Middle and ring fingers are inserted before thumb = 1 point
- Middle and ring fingers are inserted to the correct knuckle (second knuckle for a conventional grip, first knuckle for a fingertip grip) = 2 points

- Thumb is fully inserted to the base = 1 point
- Fingers press toward thumb = 1 point
- Finger pressure is greater than thumb pressure = 2 points
- Index and pinkie fingers press against outer surface of ball = 1 point

Success Check

- Have a coach or an experienced bowler evaluate your grip.
- Be sure you are using a ball appropriate for your hand size, style, and strength.

Score Your Success

When your grip earns 6 points or more, you are ready to throw the ball.

Your score ___

SUCCESS SUMMARY

Look carefully for all elements of proper fit. Find a grip style that suits your needs and physical abilities. Stop using a house ball. Having your own ball instills confidence no matter how seriously you pursue the sport. When buying a ball, go to an experienced, well-trained pro-shop operator. Ask other bowlers for advice. Learn about the pro shop's reputation. Look for pro shops that are certified by the International Bowling Pro Shop and Instructors Association (IBPSIA). Ask the operator about other certifications earned or training courses taken.

Review your evaluation scores in this step. Record scores in the spaces that follow and total them.

SCORING YOUR SUCCESS

Determining Ball Weight

Extension Test   ____ out of 5

House Ball Selection

Does the Ball Fit?   ____ out of 14 (minimum score: 10)

Developing Grip

Evaluating Proper Grip Technique   ____ out of 8 (minimum score: 6)

Total   ____ **out of 27**

With a properly selected ball in your hand, it is time to take your position on the lane. Getting into a relaxed, comfortable stance is the first block in building a reliable physical game. The stance is the launching pad for a series of smooth yet powerful movements that take you to the foul line and the ball to the pins. The stance is the topic of the next step.

Establishing a Proper Stance

This step answers two questions about the initial aspect of the game, the stance.

1. Where on the approach should the bowler stand?
2. What does a proper stance look and feel like?

A proper stance, or setup, contributes to important components of an effective throw. One of these is targeting. Where bowlers stand and the direction they face are both fundamental to walking and rolling the ball along an intended target path. Proper positioning creates the correct alignment of the body to the target line. Secondly, the stance establishes the relationship between body position and swing position. The goal is to make a powerful, consistent motion to the foul line without the swing and the body getting in each other's way. A proper stance is essential to making this happen. The bowler is not just standing there. Think of the stance as the launch pad for a smooth, controlled, powerful and accurate movement to the line.

Some bowling terms have multiple meanings, which can lead to confusion. For example, *approach* refers to the physical act of walking and swinging the ball. It also refers to the playing surface the bowler walks on. In other words, you make your approach on the approach.

Starting position is another term with two meanings. In one case, it can mean the position and alignment of the parts of the body. However, most often it refers to where the bowler stands on the approach. If somebody asks "what is your starting position?" they are concerned with where you stand in relation to your intended target. Starting position is part of targeting strategy.

In this book, if I use the term *starting position*, I am referring to where on the approach a bowler stands. When discussing the body itself, I use terms such as *stance, setup,* and *posture.*

PROPER POSITION ON THE APPROACH

Think about where you stand each time you step onto the approach. Only step onto the approach after deciding on an exact starting position, a position based on a predetermined path. The path determines the direction the feet must go and the target line the ball will roll along. Attaining a proper starting position requires determining two things about your placement on the approach: the lateral (left-to-right) placement and the distance from the foul line. If you are not sure where to start, keep it simple.

Place your slide foot (left foot for a right-handed bowler) on the center dot. Place your other foot next to it (figure 2.1). This will offset your arm swing slightly from center.

Next, look at the dot on the approach under your swing-side shoulder. The swing will pass over this dot if you walk in a straight line down the approach. Directly in front of this dot will be an arrow out on the lane. Focus on this arrow, the one in front of the swing-side shoulder, throughout your approach. (If the setup puts the swing-side shoulder between two dots, it means that your visual focus is likely to be between two arrows.) Watch the ball roll over your visual target, then look up to see where it contacts the pins.

Use the arrows on the lane to your advantage. The arrows, at 15 feet (4.6 m) from the foul line, are much closer than the pins. Teach yourself to focus on a target at or near the arrows. It makes targeting easier and allows you to more easily determine errors.

Figure 2.1   POSITION ON APPROACH

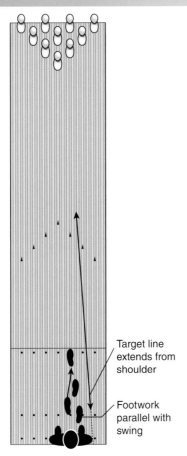

Left-to-Right Positioning

1. Place slide foot on center dot and the other foot next to slide foot.
2. Determine the dot under swing-side shoulder.
3. Focus on arrow directly in front of dot.
4. Visualize ball going over target and contacting pins.
5. Target line runs from strike pocket, through target, to throwing shoulder.

Target line extends from shoulder

Footwork parallel with swing

As mentioned in the introductory step, the approach is marked by dots that run across it. A set of dots is located at the foul line, another at 12 feet (3.6 m) from the foul line, and the last at 15 feet (4.6 m) from the foul line. Each time you step onto the approach, remember where you place your feet. Knowing you position on the approach each time you set up promotes consistency of footwork and targeting. Additionally, a reliable starting position provides a reference point from which strategic adjustments can be made.

To determine the correct distance from the foul line, start by walking up to the foul line and turning your back to the pins (figure 2.2*a*). Place your heels 4 to 6 inches (10-15 cm) from the foul line. Using normal steps, briskly pace off the number of steps you use during your approach (figure 2.2*b*). Don't look at your feet, just walk normally. After the last step, take an additional half step to allow for any slide you might have in your approach. See how far you are away from the foul line (figure 2.2*c*). Repeat the process three or four times. Use the distance from the foul line you reach most often as the starting point for the approach.

Figure 2.2 DETERMINING DISTANCE FROM FOUL LINE

Foul Line

1. Stand at foul line with back to pins.
2. Place heels 4 to 6 inches (10-15 cm) from foul line.

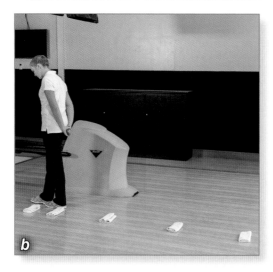

Steps

1. Walk away from the foul line using normal steps.
2. Pace off number of steps used in the approach.

End Position

1. Add extra half stride for slide step.
2. Turn around to see where you are on the approach.

It is important to know exactly where you should start. Most experienced bowlers use the slide foot as a reference point (i.e., the foot in front at the end of the approach). Using the same foot at the beginning of the approach as used at the finish will enable you to connect two reference points for determining the direction of the footwork.

Look at your slide foot when setting up the stance. Some bowlers use the toe; most experienced bowlers use the inside edge of the bowling shoe (the part of the foot closest to the release) as the reference point. Remember the board or dot you started next to. If you have to, write it down. Pay attention to the dots and the individual boards between the dots.

After taking a normal throw, look where the slide finishes. Make note of that also. Keep note of your footwork tendencies, and ask yourself these questions:

- Do I finish left or right from where I started?
- Does putting the ball in various positions affect the direction of the steps?
- Does the direction of the steps change when changing the starting position on the approach or the visual target on the lane?

Consistently missing the visual target is usually a result of physical errors. You simply can't hit what you are looking at. But if hitting on or near the intended target still yields poor results, there is probably a strategic error. You have not yet determined the correct relationship between your starting position and the target on the lane. Trial and error is necessary to work that out.

Many of the physical issues causing target errors are discussed throughout the book, but here is a quick rundown of proper technique:

- Steps are toward the target.
- The slide foot finishes within an inch or two (2.5-5 cm) of a straight line from the starting position at the beginning of the approach.
- At the finish position, the line of the shoulders faces the target.
- The swing follows through straight out from the shoulders toward the target.

MISSTEP

The ball misses the visual target.

CORRECTION

Constantly recheck where the slide finishes relative to where the approach started. Check shoulder alignment and overall body position. Are you facing the target? Monitor arm swing and follow-through. You won't consistently hit a target if the swing is all over the place.

Remember, you are trying to hit the strike pocket in just the right spot from an optimal angle as well. Where is the strike pocket? The strike pocket is an area about 2.5 to 3 inches offset from the center of the head pin. To the right is the strike pocket between the headpin and the 3-pin. To the left is the other strike pocket between the headpin and the 2-pin. If the ball rolls over the visual target but misses the strike pocket, adjust your targeting strategy. There are two basic strategic adjustments. (See step 10 for more detailed adjustment strategies.) One, adjust your starting position on the approach in the direction of the error without changing the original visual target. (If the ball was left of the strike pocket, adjust your starting position to the left. If you missed to the right, adjust to the right.) Walk back to the same visual target. Keep in mind that a change in the starting position while walking toward the same target requires a change in the stance alignment.

Two, find a new visual target. If you are missing right, move the visual target left. If you are missing left, move the target to the right. If the new target is not directly in front of the throwing shoulder, make slight changes in stance alignment and the direction of the footwork.

MISSTEP

The ball rolls over the visual target but misses the strike pocket.

CORRECTION

Move your starting position on the approach in the direction of the error. Change the target.

Trace a mental line from the strike pocket, through the target, and back to the beginning of the approach. The direction of this imaginary ball path determines where the starting position should be.

After deciding on a target line, trace it back to your throwing shoulder. The ball swings from the shoulder; therefore, aim must come from the shoulders, not the eyes. Imagine the head positioned over the throwing shoulder, looking down the arm. This puts the sight line along the arm toward the target. Once you have visualized a target line, you will have an idea of both the direction of the swing and a direction for the footwork.

Position Drill 1   Stringing Them Along

Many bowlers have difficulty visualizing the target line. They think they are aligned with the proper target, but they are not. Sometimes a physical prop is needed. This stance drill requires the help of a partner.

Set up in your preferred starting position. Tape one end of a piece of string to the lane on top of your intended target. (If you are not permitted to go out onto the lane, attach the end of the string to a spot at the foul line close to where the slide foot will finish.) Draw the string back to your throwing shoulder. Practice your setup five times while holding the string in place. After each setup, close your eyes and try to imagine the line to the target.

Once you have a feel for the drill, lay the string loosely on the ground. Set up in your starting position. Your partner brings the string back into position under the throwing-side elbow. Did your setup using a visualized target match the real line determined by the string? Practice this five times. Score 1 point each time your mental line matches the real line.

Score Your Success

Mental line matches real line = 1 point

Your score ___

Position Drill 2   Parallel Tracks

Once you have determined the proper setup for your target line, go ahead and bowl. Retape the string a couple of inches (about 5 cm) away from the intended target. Pull the string tight along the floor. It will lie just outside of the throwing-side foot. Walk along the string without walking on it or away from it. Throw toward the original target. The ball path should be parallel to the placement of the string. Practice five times, checking to see whether both the approach and the ball path are parallel to the line of the string. Score 1 point each time your footwork stays along the string. Score 1 point each time the ball path is parallel to the string and rolls over the target.

Score Your Success

Footwork doesn't deviate from path shown by the string = 1 point

Ball path is parallel to the string's path and rolls over the target = 1 point

Your score ___

A more detailed discussion of targeting strategies for both strike and spare shots are found in later steps of the book. Let's now draw our attention to what constitutes a proper stance. A bowler should feel balanced, comfortable, and ready to make a strong move to the line.

PROPER STANCE

After determining the proper position on the approach, your next order of business is to get in the proper stance. The stance is the preparation for an aggressive, confident movement to the foul line. Because the stance is stationary, it is easy to run through a mental checklist of the components of a proper stance before every throw. Think of it as a preflight checklist. Don't push the launch button until all systems are a go!

When first learning the elements of the stance, practice without a ball. In fact, use shadow bowling (practicing without a ball in hand) every time you first attempt a particular position or movement introduced in this book. Shadow bowling allows you to concentrate on learning a new skill without concerns about the ball or pinfall. Shadow bowling lets you develop a feel for a new skill before concerning yourself with results.

Throughout this book, concern is on technique, not results. When working on a new set of physical skills, forget about the pins. Remember the phrase "process over product." If there were no pins, you would determine the quality of a shot by how it feels.

A gymnast's routine or a diver's performance is not judged solely by the final position. The quality and artistry of the movements determine their score—before they stick a landing or hit the water. That is how you should bowl. Concern yourself with how the movements feel or with the body position. Perfect those things and the scores will take care of themselves.

The primary focus in developing the stance is the throwing side of the body. Our goal is the proper relationship between body and swing. At no point during the approach do the swing and the body to get in each other's way.

One goal of a good stance is, in a small degree, to imitate at the beginning the position the body will be in at the end. So, a bowler will pay attention to both a slight presetting of the body angle as well as to properly positioning the ball.

Because balance is the primary concern, make sure you feel centered over your feet. Get into an athletic, ready-to-move position. With the feet slightly staggered (throwing-side foot back from the other foot) allow 1 to 3 inches (2.5-7.6 cm) between the feet. For most bowlers, this is slightly less than shoulder-width apart.

Position the throwing-side foot 2 to 4 inches (5-10 cm) back from the other foot. Because the movement is front to back, the feet are staggered front to back.

Flex the knees slightly; it is difficult to generate power with stiff knees. Do not march up to the line. To promote footwork that is quick and smooth, keep the knees

Anatomical Position

Let me put an idea in your head. Stand with your face forward, arms to the sides, and palms turned forward. In this position, it is obvious that the elbows are closer to the body than the hands are. Maintaining this elbow-in, hand-out relationship between the swing and the body throughout the approach is a characteristic of an excellent swing. If, after throwing a ball, you find the elbow pointing off to the side or the swing doesn't reach out from the shoulder along the intended target line, you made an error in the swing.

flexed to some degree during the entire approach. Initially flexing the knees in the stance prepares you for the considerable knee bend at the end of the approach.

The hips are in a slightly open position (i.e., the throwing-side hip drops back). Most of the preset hip angle comes from the foot stagger. You are trying to make the body as small as possible. Square hips take up more room, making it more difficult to keep the backswing in line. Preset the hip angle to reduce the area the hips take up. The preset of the lower body matches the preset of the upper body. The upper body and lower body should have the same alignment to the target.

To maintain a comfortable, balanced position, the spine tilt should match the knee flexion, and the back should be straight. (A curved spine decreases balance.) With the knees flexed, the upper body must tilt forward to maintain proper balance. Imagine lowering yourself into a chair. As the knees flex more, you must lean farther forward. If you don't, you will flop back into the seat. The knee flexion in the stance is nothing like the knee bend for sitting down, but the idea is the same. A proper stance promotes an aggressive, ready-to-move position. Leaning back is a passive, slow way to initiate the approach. Because the ball moves forward at the initiation of the swing, the body must be prepared to move forward with it.

For most bowlers, the backswing pulls the shoulders to an open position. Presetting the shoulder angle anticipates some of the additional upper-torso rotation that frequently occurs during the swing. Bringing the nonthrowing hand across the body to a supporting position under the ball not only turns the shoulders to face the target but also accommodates the line of the swing.

Place the elbow at the side of the body, above the hip (figure 2.3). Accuracy starts at the elbow. The body should not get in the way of the swing; keep your elbow at your side. Do not hold the ball near the middle of the chest or tuck the elbow into the belly. These positions interfere with a straight swing. When in the ideal position, you should be able to trace an imaginary straight line from the shoulder through the ball to the target. This establishes the potential swing line. This line should not cross in front of or behind the body at any point.

Earlier we discussed a mental checklist of the elements that create a correct stance. Using this mental checklist accomplishes two things. One, it ensures proper body alignment and ball position. Two, it establishes a mental focus. If you are focused entirely on positioning, other distractions go away. A proper stance routine prepares the mind as well as the body.

The stance checklist contains six items: three for the lower body, three for the upper. Get in the habit of working from the ground up. First set the feet, then the body, then (and only then) position the ball. Until the feet and body are in position, the ball should be cradled in the nonthrowing hand.

Get in the habit of going through the checklist in the same order every time. All good athletes establish a personal routine before performing. A preshot routine

Figure 2.3 Proper lower-body position upper-body position with elbow at the side above hip.

includes a specific set of actions an athlete uses to get into the proper mind-set. For bowlers it might be a set sequence of shoe wiping, ball cleaning, and hand drying. Regardless, consider the way you prepare your stance as an extension of the preshot routine you quite likely started before you stepped onto the approach. See figure 2.3 to establish a proper stance.

STANCE PREPARATION CHECKLIST

☑ Feet—slightly staggered, throwing-side foot back slightly (2-4 in. [5-10 cm])

☑ Knees—slightly flexed, comfortable standing position

☑ Hip—throwing-side hip dropped slightly back (called *presetting the angle*)

☑ Spine—slight tilt forward (10-15 degrees) and straight from hips to shoulders

☑ Elbow—ball-side elbow under shoulder and right next to hip

☑ Ball—swing arm bent until ball is at a comfortable height, everything else still until as ball is brought into position

Do not move the ball to the body. Instead, move the body to the ball. Imagine an arrow sticking out of your shoulder, pointing toward the target. This arrow will point over the top of the ball if it is properly positioned.

Figure 2.4 ESTABLISHING A PROPER STANCE

Lower Body

1. Slightly stagger feet to promote balance and alignment.
2. Flex knees slightly for balance and comfort.
3. Align hips and shoulders toward visual target.
4. Preset the angle of the hips and shoulders.

Upper Body

1. Tilt spine slightly forward to center yourself. Imagine a line dropping straight down from the shoulders, through the knees, and to the toes.
2. Position elbow of throwing arm next to hip.
3. Face palm forward with the hand directly behind ball.
4. Position the elbow directly under shoulder.
5. Bend elbow to bring ball straight up to a comfortable height.
6. Position ball in line with shoulder or center of upper arm.

Support From Nonthrowing Arm

1. Bring nonthrowing hand across front of body.
2. Place nonthrowing hand under ball or slightly off center.
3. Allow nonthrowing hand to take some of the ball's weight.
4. Position elbow of nonthrowing arm comfortably close to the body; avoid contorted position.
5. Adjust ball height to comfortable position; keep ball centered in front of shoulder or upper arm.

MISSTEP

While bringing the ball to its starting position, you also move it inward in front of the chest or stomach.

CORRECTION

Although this inward movement may feel natural, it decreases accuracy. Starting the ball in front of the body forces you to throw the ball around the body. Make sure there is a place for the ball and arm swing and a place for the body; they work side by side. The lateral position of the ball and hand should be somewhere between the inside edge and outside edge of the upper arm.

Other Aspects of the Proper Stance

Keep both hands under the ball. The nonthrowing hand takes some of the weight, which helps relieve tension in the swing arm. Don't feel like you carry the ball into the first step. Let both hands get the ball started; gravity does the work afterward.

Hold the ball at a height that suits your game—a little higher if developing a longer swing. The extra height creates more momentum. Holding the ball higher also helps emphasize the pushaway. A long, slow extension into the pushaway delays the ball's descent into the down drop, which keeps the swing from getting ahead of slower footwork.

To create power from foot speed, try starting the ball a little lower. A lower position helps get the ball into the swing faster, keeping up with those quick feet. Experiment. When you find a position that works well with your footwork, the ball will release from the hand cleanly. Good timing makes for a good release.

Figure 2.5 Proper finish position.

Another function of the stance is to prepare the body at the beginning of the approach for the position it will assume at the end of the approach (figure 2.5). In the finish position, the bowler balances on one foot, with the front knee bent and the leg on the throwing side behind and out of the way.

In an effective finish position, the hips and shoulders are open, the knees are bent, and the spine tilts forward. These are similar to the characteristics of proper stance setup, just to a greater degree than at the start.

A proper finish position is the foundation for the rest of the bowling performance. Ensuring proper placement in the beginning will help you get into the correct position at the end. A properly aligned, well-balanced starting position is the first step toward an accurate and powerful movement to the foul line.

Stance Drill 1   Ball-Toss Practice

This drill is a simple way to emphasize hand position and knee flex. Two bowlers stand 3 to 4 feet (1-1.2 m) apart, facing each other. The catcher is in the stance position: feet staggered, hands cupped in front of throwing arm, and body in a relaxed position. The tosser gently tosses a bowling ball (make sure it is an appropriate weight) to the partner, toward the catcher's throwing-side arm. The partner catches the ball with both hands and slightly flexes the knees to absorb the weight of the ball.

If done correctly, the catcher learns three things:

1. How to position the hands under the ball for proper support.
2. Where the ball position should be relative to the shoulder.
3. How much knee flex and spine tilt is useful for balance and to support the weight of the ball.

Perform the exercise five times per partner. If the ball weight is appropriate for both partners, they can toss the ball back and forth and complete the drill fairly quickly.

Success Check

- Two hands support the ball from underneath when caught.
- The ball's weight is equally balanced between both hands.
- Ball is caught directly in front of throwing-side shoulder.
- Knees flex slightly to cushion the impact of throw.
- Bowler holds ball for a couple of seconds to find a comfortable overall body position.

Score Your Success

Give yourself 1 point for each success check item completed correctly (25 points possible: five items times five practice catches).

Your score_____

Stance Drill 2   Look in the Mirror, Front View

Evaluating your stance in front of a mirror is a great way to develop proper positioning. You get a chance to see what you feel. You can practice the stance setup almost anytime. All you need is a large mirror, preferably full length, or a window you can easily see your reflection in. With a piece of tape, mark a vertical line going up from the floor. This line will be your reference point for proper alignment.

Look at your stance from the front. Stand straight and align your body with the mirror so that the tape line runs up the throwing side of your body past the center of your shoulder. Put body in the proper stance position without moving the shoulder away from the reference line. Remember the three elements for the lower body (feet, knees, hips) and the three elements for the upper body (spine, shoulders, swing arm).

When positioning the ball, also center it on the reference line. Keeping the ball on the line in front of the shoulder helps you learn what proper ball positioning looks like. With enough space, you can practice the entire approach, from setup to finish,

(continued)

Stance Drill 2 *(continued)*

in front of the mirror. When practicing the pushaway and swing, the shoulder and arm stay centered on the reference line throughout your approach.

TO INCREASE DIFFICULTY

- Try to establish the position without looking at the mirror as a reference.
- Practice five setups from the front view without looking at the mirror. After each setup, look at the mirror to see whether each element of the setup is correctly positioned.

Success Check

Look for these five elements of a proper setup:

- Staggered feet, a few inches apart, just enough to promote proper alignment.
- Spacing between the feet. The spacing should only be as much as the bowler needs to feel balanced. The body weight should be evenly distributed onto both feet.

- Position of nonthrowing hand under the ball
- Placement of elbow next to hip
- Alignment of ball in front of shoulder

Score Your Success

Give yourself 1 point for each element correctly positioned without first looking in the mirror (25 points possible: five items times five stance practices). Use the mirror only to confirm positioning.

Your score ___

Stance Drill 3   Look in the Mirror, Side View

Now evaluate your stance from the side. Stand with your throwing side turned to the mirror. Position yourself so that your toes just touch the vertical reference line. Flex your knees until they too appear to touch the reference line. Tilt the upper body forward, keeping the spine straight, until the shoulder touches the line. This is your vertical balance line, the line that runs from the shoulders through the knees down to the toes. Place your elbow above your hip. It will be directly under the shoulder. The upper arm will be parallel to the reference line on the mirror. Position the ball at the preferred height without moving the upper arm.

TO INCREASE DIFFICULTY

- Try to establish the position without looking at the mirror as a reference.
- Practice five setups from the side view without looking at the mirror. After each setup, look at the mirror to see whether each element of the setup is correctly positioned.

Success Check

Look for these six elements of a proper setup:

- Staggered feet, 2 to 4inches (5-10 cm)
- Enough knee bend to position knees over toes
- Hips angled so that ball-side hip is back
- Spine tilted slightly forward and straight
- Shoulders angled so that ball-side shoulder is farther back than other shoulder
- Elbow placed under shoulder (line from shoulder to elbow points to the floor)

Score Your Success

Give yourself 1 point for each element correctly positioned without first looking in the mirror (30 points possible: six elements times five stance practices). Use the mirror only to confirm positioning.

Your score ___

Stance Drill 4   Evaluating the Starting Position

Step onto the approach and assume the starting position. Have a qualified instructor or experienced bowler analyze your stance.

Sometimes it is difficult for new bowlers to analyze themselves without a bit of help. A mirror may not always be available. You might need to rely on the observation skills of a knowledgeable person. The scoring system used here is also useful when performing a self-evaluation.

Score Your Success

Earn points based on the following checklist:

Upper body (hip to head) tilted slightly forward = 3 points

Knees slightly flexed = 3 points

Feet staggered 2 to 4 inches (5-10 cm) = 2 points

Throwing side of the body preset to an open position = 2 points

Elbow of throwing arm directly under shoulder = 4 points

Nonthrowing hand helps support ball = 2 points

Ball directly lined up in front of shoulder = 4 points

Your score ___

SUCCESS SUMMARY

A proper setup is the foundation for the rest of the approach. Before you can even think about putting things in motion, you must have these fundamentals in place:

- Find the correct location on the lane relative to the desired target line.
- Create a stance that best allows the footwork to proceed straight toward the target and the swing to progress unimpeded.
- Be ready to initiate a series of powerful movements with great control and precision.

Carelessness in stance preparation leads to inconsistency. Each element in the stance has a purpose. The feet position and overall posture promote balance while generating a powerful movement. The shoulder and hip alignment, along with ball position, influence swing accuracy. A bowler must feel in control of every throw of the ball. Every time you step up to the approach, have a sense of being comfortable, relaxed, balanced, and ready to move.

Review your drill scores. Record your scores in the spaces that follow and total them. Once you are able to score 90 percent or more of the possible points from all drills, you are ready to put the ball and body into motion.

SCORING YOUR SUCCESS

Position Drills

1.	Stringing Them Along	____ out of 5
2.	Parallel Tracks	____ out of 10

Stance Drills

1.	Ball-Toss Practice	____ out of 25
2.	Look in the Mirror, Front View	____ out of 25
3.	Look in the Mirror, Side View	____ out of 30
4.	Evaluating the Starting Position	____ out of 20
	Total	____ **out of 115**

It seems natural that once you establish a proper position, you will need to get things moving. The next step introduces the initial movement. This is arguably the most important aspect of the game. How the ball and body initially are put into motion together is vital to your chance of success. Everything you do at the end is a product of the actions that came before it. You don't just stroll up to the line. You move with intent. Every step has a purpose. It's in your best interest to make the initial one worthwhile.

Starting Fundamentals

Initiating the swing and steps is the most critical skill in bowling. The quality of the shot you make at the end of your approach is determined by the chain of events that precede it. The starting movement is the first link of the chain. Once something gets a little off, everything that follows is likely to be off as well. If the first link in the chain is weak, the chance of a successful shot is less likely. While a proper start may not guarantee proper execution, it makes executing a satisfactory shot more likely.

Fortunately, the mechanics of the start are simple. First, just start walking. Next, let the ball swing. That's pretty simple. It is natural for the arms to swing while walking. It seems so simple; just push the ball into a relaxed natural swing just as you begin to walk down the approach. In fact, the initial movement seems so simple, one might think it hardly warrants its own chapter in a book. Unfortunately, the ability to correctly perform this one act of synchronized motion eludes a vast majority of untutored bowlers. So, let's identify the essential items of the start.

The start is the relationship between the initial movement of the ball and the initial step or steps of the approach. The following are the essential components of an efficient and repeatable start:

- Timing: The coordination of starting the swing in relation to starting the footwork
- Direction: The lateral movement, left or right, of the steps and pushaway
- Shape: The ways the ball is put into the arc of the swing that complement the bowler's style

TIMING

Timing must be considered from both the beginning and end of the approach. The ball's position in the swing arc at the completion of the first step (or second step for those using a five-step approach) is termed *initial timing*. *Terminal timing* is determined by observing where the ball is in the swing arc as the last (slide) step begins. For experienced bowlers, we don't talk about good or bad timing. The nature of a bowler's timing is most frequently observed from the results (i.e., how the ball was delivered onto the lane). From there we work back, step by step, to the initial starting motion, to see how a bowler's style was established. Timing affects ball roll. With early terminal timing, footwork is just barely finished as the swing gets to the release point. This may cause less finger leverage at the release. Less of the body's momentum transfers into the ball. Often the ball is placed onto the lane early. These are characteristics of the *roller style* of bowling (figure 3.1).

Figure 3.1 Roller-style bowling: *(a)* initial timing, *(b)* swing arc, and *(c)* terminal timing.

Late terminal timing sees the slide starting well ahead of the swing. The ball may still be near the top of the backswing as the slide starts. These bowlers must teach themselves to wait on the swing. More time to clear the back leg allows opportunity for a more dramatic tuck of the swing under the shoulder. What follows is a better chance to work the hand to the inside of the ball. Additionally, the opportunity to load up the wrist position increases, strengthening the finger's leverage position at the release. Late terminal timing is often seen in the *cranker style* of bowling (figure 3.2). The style is often characterized by a more aggressive follow-through, increased ball speed, and a stronger hooking ball.

Figure 3.2 Cranker-style bowling: *(a)* initial timing, *(b)* swing arc, and *(c)* terminal timing.

If bowlers are satisfied with how they perform (i.e., they like the feel of their game), timing may not be their first concern. If overall movement to the line is smooth, the body stays in position and balanced, and the release is repeatable; consider timing adjustments only as a means to add greater degrees of versatility.

A bowler should worry about timing when it negatively affects performance. The following are indicators of timing issues:

- Dramatic changes of body position at the line are often unconscious attempts at making a late swing catch up. Standing up, pulling the shoulder around, or excessive forward lean may be seen at this point (figure 3.3).

• Dropping the ball or general inconsistencies of the release may indicate negative timing issues. With very late timing, bowlers have the urge to let go long before the ball gets to the release point. Conversely, they may feel the need to grab at the ball excessively hard (in an unconscious effort to hold on to it) and then forget to let go.

• With early timing, the ball is so far ahead of the footwork, it reaches the release before the bowler is finished sliding. The ball tends to leave the hand on its own, whether the bowler wants it to or not, usually resulting in a weak, ineffective roll. A further consequence of the swing getting so far ahead is the tendency for the momentum of the swing to pull the shoulder out of position, resulting in the ball missing the target.

Figure 3.3 First step is too short with excessive leaning.

If there are issues at the end, we must first take a look at the start. A key point emphasized in United States Bowling Congress coaching clinics is to change posture by changing timing. If bowlers experience obvious timing issues at the end, they must first pay attention to the initial timing to see whether this is the cause. Of course, other factors may cause timing issues, such as muscular tension inhibiting or accelerating the swing, or changes of footwork speed (sudden rushes or hesitation in the steps).

But, before considering other things, begin the evaluation at the start. If *initial timing* is very late, you are more likely to be late at the end and vice versa. Take care of the basics first, and then, if issues persist, look at other details.

Picture a side view of a bowler in his or her stance. Now, imagine a center line dropping straight down from the shoulder through the knees to the top of the foot. When the first step is complete, the imaginary center line that was in the stance will have moved to a position over the foot. With each step, the bowler remains centered over the foot.

MISSTEP

Foot is ahead of ball when pushaway is complete. The ball needs to be ahead of the foot in order for it to drop into the swing freely.

CORRECTIONS

• Check length of the first step. The first step is a short, soft, smooth weight-transition step. Be sure body is centered over foot. If step is too long, both body and ball will be behind it.

• Check length of pushaway. When being too cautious, there is a tendency to carry the ball. Avoid aiming the swing or guiding the ball into the swing. One should feel as if the ball simply falls forward into the swing. If the pushaway appears to be too short, relax and let the weight of the ball extend the arm forward and down naturally.

Four-Step Versus Five-Step Approach

In this book, everything pertaining to timing and footwork assumes a four- or five-step approach. Almost everything pertinent to a four-step approach also applies to the five-step approach. The only difference is that the five-step approach starts with a weight-transition step (what some instructors call a get-going step) with the foot opposite the throwing side.

Almost all discussions and descriptions assume a four-step approach. When a bowler is walking, the swing moves through four parts (or phases). If the swing has four parts and the bowler use four steps, the steps and the swing start together.

The five-step approach includes an extra initial step with the opposite leg. In this case the swing starts on the second step. The last four steps of the approach match the four parts of the swing. (This is true of any bowler using more than four steps. If taking seven steps, for instance, the bowler uses three get-going steps, and the swing starts when four steps are left.) However many steps a bowler takes, the swing will start when the throwing side leg starts.

MISSTEP

Ball is well ahead (more than 8 inches [20 cm] past the toe) of the first step when pushaway is complete.

CORRECTIONS

- First step is too short. Make it long enough to feel like a real step.
- Bowler is leaning forward excessively as swing starts in an effort to help the ball get started. Bowler must feel a complete weight transition. The entire body from top to bottom (not just head, shoulders, and ball) moves with the step.

If there is excessive push in the pushaway motion, the bowler might be pushing the ball up and out in a straight extension from the shoulder instead of using a smooth, arcing out-and-down motion (figure 3.4). Elbow should not lock out in the pushaway.

Figure 3.4 Excessive push exhibited in the pushaway motion.

Timing Drill 1   Evaluating Standard Initial Timing

The intent of this practice is to reinforce the essential aspects of the initial motion. The focus is getting those parts of the body critical to proper shot execution moving at the correct time in relation to each other.

Success Check

- Everything on the throwing side (body, ball, foot) moves at the same time, in the same direction, and the same distance.
- Ball moves forward into swing arc without creating muscle tension.
- Bowler feels comfortable and balanced at end of initial steps.

Score Your Success

Throwing-side foot and pushaway start together = 2 points

Ball position in swing is 4 to 6 inches (10-15 cm) ahead of foot position at conclusion of initial step = 1 point

As throwing-side foot lands, swing arm is almost fully extended = 1 point

At completion of initial step, the upper-arm muscles of the swing arm disengage to allow the ball to swing freely = 1 point

Everything on ball-side of body moves together: body, ball, and foot = 2 points

Body weight has transferred completely onto foot at completion of the initial step = 2 points

Your score _____

DIRECTION OF START

At this point, when discussing *direction*, we are considering the lateral movement (left and right) of both the initial step and the swing. With a proper start, the swing pushes on a line to the target while being able to get past the throwing side of the body. Our goal is to keep the swing and the body out of each other's way.

As traditionally taught, the first step moves directly forward as the ball moves straight out from the shoulder. The goal is for the line of the footwork and the line of the swing to move along the bowler's target line. This is something for beginning bowlers to think about. It allows novices to emphasize moving everything along a specific line, ideally a line toward their target.

While this might be fine conceptually, mechanically it might not work as planned. Unless the athlete is fortunate enough to have a V-shaped upper body, one in which the shoulders are wider than the hips, it is unlikely that the swing will pass the throwing-side leg unimpeded. Houston, we have a problem. The ball is too wide.

A slight crossover with the initial step is necessary. The modern approach to bowling mechanics helps get the throwing-side leg out of the way of the swing. Instead of trying to move the swing around an initial step that goes straight forward, it is better to move that step out of the way of a straight swing. The throwing-side foot moves in front of the opposite foot as the pushaway starts. The initial crossover is small, just enough to make a couple of extra inches of room for the ball.

If the timing is correct, the ball gets into the down-drop phase as the opposite foot is moving. This provides a stationary throwing-side leg, which is also positioned out of the way as the swing comes by. This is a key to the start of an effective swing. As the swing comes down, it moves into the space where the leg had been.

By the way, the same thing happens at the finish position. The back leg clears to allow the swing to drop next to the hip and under the shoulder. The intent is to fill the gap. The bowler tries to allow the ball to swing into the space where the leg had been both *on the way back* and on *the way through*.

Pay Attention To Hand Position

Some bowlers try to get the hand to a strong inside position very quickly in the swing. Rotating the hand to a stronger position behind the ball during the downswing causes an internal rotation at the shoulder. When the elbow turns in, the forearm may turn out, causing the swing to move away from the body and off-line from the target. To keep the swing on line to the target, the bowler might need to guide the swing inward, closer to the body than normal as the hand turns to a position under and to the inside of the ball. A bowler who uses this style might need to take a longer crossover step to create more room for the change in the initial swing movement.

MISSTEPS

- Crossover is so large, the first step gets in the way of the next step (figure 3.5).
- Opposite foot steps farther off-line in order make it around the foot in front of it.
- Steps move laterally too far from the target line.

CORRECTIONS

- Be careful. A slight crossover is okay, but too much crossover can cause as many problems as too little.
- Imagine walking on a balance beam or tightrope.
- Place initial step of throwing-side leg directly in front of the other foot.

Figure 3.5 Front view of incorrect crossover.

Another common occurrence is swinging the ball around the leg and hips. Bowlers try to avoid the side of the body by changing the direction of the swing, particularly during the pushaway. This decreases accuracy and release consistency. To avoid this looping, side-to-side swing, a bowler needs to understand the effect of anatomical position on a proper swing.

UNDERSTANDING ANATOMICAL POSITION

Bowlers want to keep the swing in line with the shoulder while letting it pass under the shoulder as close to the body as possible to avoid feeling that the ball getting away from them. This close swing position increases the sense of control. A bowler can ensure a straighter swing path by keeping everything in correct anatomical position.

What is meant by *anatomical position*? Stand with your hands hanging down at your sides. Turn the palms to face forward. Notice something? The elbows are closer to the body than the hands are. A bowler should strive to keep this relationship between the hand and the elbow throughout the swing.

Swing Drill 1   Anatomical Swing Practice

With a ball in your hand, let it hang under your shoulder with the palm of the hand facing forward. Keep the elbow close to the hip. Try swinging a ball this way. (You might need to move the throwing-side leg out of the way.)

TO INCREASE DIFFICULTY

Hold ball in starting position, rather than in hanging position. Feel swing-side elbow next to body. Without steps or body motion, make a complete swing motion. The ball should return to its original start position at the end of a full swing.

Success Check

- A correct swing line helps get the hand in a position behind the ball. The hand is more likely to stay in an effective release position throughout the swing.
- Keep the swing-side elbow close to the hip.
- Upper body should not sway as swing moves back and forth.

Score Your Success

Elbow brushes throwing side hip as swing passes back and forth = 2 points

Hand does not change position behind ball = 1 point

Swing makes a smooth, pendulum motion = 2 points

Your score____

Swing Drill 2   Opposite-Hand Pushaway Practice

The opposite hand plays a large supporting role in the stance. It also plays a supporting and guiding role during the pushaway. The opposite hand releases from the ball and moves out to a counterbalancing position as the swing moves to the dropaway phase. The other elbow should also stay in close. If the elbow of the other arm points out during the pushaway, the consequential inward turn of the opposite hand might push the swing off-line.

Success Check

- Elbows of both arms stay close to body during pushaway.
- Weight of ball is felt in both hands until ball starts to drop down into swing.
- Swing stays close to throwing-side hip.
- Swing-side elbow is closer to body during the swing than the ball is.

Score Your Success

Both hands support the weight of the ball in the stance = 1 point

Both elbows close together as the pushaway starts = 1 point

Both hands initially guide the ball along the intended target line = 2 points

As swing moves back, other arm moves forward = 1 point

Your score____

INITIAL SHAPE OF THE SWING

The direction the ball moves during the swing is called the initial shape of the swing. Being able to make adjustments to the shape adds versatility to your game. A bowler can get the ball to the correct spot at the correct time even when adjusting ball speed or the tempo of the footwork. Bowlers also adjust the shape of the swing to fit their mental approach to the sport. Athletes frequently reflect their general personality traits in their style of game. Characteristics of their performance (speed, tempo, release) are the outward manifestation of their internal state of being. Whether aggressive or passive, methodical or freewheeling, bowlers can develop a suitable, individualized starting motion that matches their personality and keeps them in their mental comfort zone without sacrificing proper mechanics. The initial swing movement can take one of three basic shapes: the up-push, the swingaway, and the dropaway (figure 3.6).

Figure 3.6   **SHAPE OF SWING**

Up-Push

Ball moves up and out before it swings downward.

Swingaway

Ball moves out and down into the swing. This is the standard shape.

Dropaway

Ball hinges down from elbow with little forward movement.

As for mechanics, the *up-push* is used primarily for two reasons. One, it delays the swing's arc into the down-drop phase to accommodate slow initial steps. It is used by bowlers who prefer a slow, methodical start. Two, it generates extra swing momentum. Pushing the ball to a higher point gives it more potential energy. Starting the ball in a higher position in the stance serves the same purpose, but not all bowlers are comfortable with a high start position.

An additional aspect of the up-push technique is the sense of free fall it provides. The bowler gives the ball its slight upward push and then completely relaxes the shoulder. The ball then swings smoothly and effortlessly into the backswing. Pushing the ball up and letting it fall is a way to break the habit of trying to aim or guide the ball into the swing. To visualize this technique, imagine a bar in front of your chest. Start the pushaway by trying to move the ball over the imaginary bar. This "over the bar" technique has been popular with instructors for many years.

The *swingaway* is the traditional shape, the standard technique for starting the swing motion. All new bowlers should learn this starting motion first. The ball's movement is out and down. The out movement is caused by extending the upper arm away from the body, and the shoulder muscles are briefly engaged. At the same moment the arm is extending forward, the biceps relax, allowing the ball to swing down. This results in a smooth, arcing motion. There is no abrupt change in direction, no push-and-pull motion. Simply extend the arm far enough to move the ball past the foot, and gravity takes over from there. Imagine tracing a semicircle with the ball. The ball follows a curved path the entire time.

Many advanced bowlers prefer the *dropaway* technique. These bowlers use styles that feature high backswings and open shoulders at the top of the backswing. The swing path is much longer than in a traditional pendulum-type swing. This style of bowling requires getting the ball into the backswing quicker to allow time for the longer swing path. The ball moves into the down-drop phase almost immediately with little or no outward movement at the elbow. The upper-arm muscles relax and allow the ball to swing from the elbow. The elbow is a *hinge joint,* and the weight of the ball opens the hinge, and the arm extends into the down drop with no hesitation.

Ball Height in Stance

The height of the ball's position in the stance influences the choice of initial swing shape. No matter which style a bowler uses, all bowlers strive to get the ball to a position slightly forward of the throwing-side leg as the first step is complete.

If the ball is held high in the stance, it has farther to go to get to that position. There is no time to push the ball out or up. The hinge technique lets the ball fall into position quickly and is preferred by bowlers who start the ball higher.

If the ball is in a standard position, between chest high and waist high, the bowler has options. This is why a moderate starting height is suggested for most bowlers. A standard starting height allows room to move the pushaway in whichever direction best matches the swing shape to the athlete's natural tempo. The initial shape can be adjusted up, forward, or down to suit the bowler's style.

An aggressive, hard-charging bowler who uses a fast tempo might emphasize the down aspect of the shape. A slower, more relaxed or methodical bowler might prefer to emphasize the forward (or even a little bit of the up) motion of the start.

What about a lower starting position? A lower starting position is appropriate for bowlers who have very fast feet. These bowlers generate most of the ball velocity with their legs. This means they need less help from the swing. A low ball position, assuming there is no exaggerated up-push, creates a shorter swing arc. Some bowlers prefer the sense of control they get from a short, compact swing. Bowlers who lack the flexibility to swing the ball through a long arc might choose a lower starting point out of necessity.

Initial Movement Drill 1   Foot Placement

Using a guide can help you practice the appropriate crossover step. In this case, the guide is a small towel placed directly in front of the throwing-side foot. The distance from the foot to the towel is the same as the length of your first step. As the pushaway starts, step with the throwing-side foot to the inside of the towel. The foot will land to the left of the towel for a right-handed bowler.

TO DECREASE DIFFICULTY

- Do not use a ball. Practice only the arm motion and step position.
- Watch yourself make the initial step. Look at your feet as you step next to the towel.

Success Check

- Perform only the initial step and push (the first two steps for a bowler using a five-step approach). After the first step, let the ball swing freely once and allow it to swing back to its start position.
- Practice 10 step-and-pushaway motions. Each time the foot lands in the correct location, score 1 point.

Score Your Success

Score a half-point bonus on each step and pushaway in which the pushaway moves at the correct time (15 points possible).

Your score _____

Initial Movement Drill 2   Partner Help

This drill has been an essential part of bowling instruction for a long time.

The bowler stands facing a partner who is far enough away that the bowler can fully extend the arm during the arm swing with the first step. The partner's hands are cupped to catch the ball and positioned in front of bowler's throwing-side shoulder and level with the bowler's waist. Bowler practices initial swing motion by extending ball into partner's hands. Bowler also takes initial step with pushaway practice. The entire weight of the ball rests in partner's hand so that the bowler's arm can relax. Bowler does not let go of ball to hand it to the partner. Grip on ball remains firm. (The arm relaxes, not the grip.)

TO DECREASE DIFFICULTY

- A partner or instructor stands next to bowler and gently grips the bowling arm.
- The partner guides the arm (both direction and timing) as bowler takes initial step.

Score Your Success

Practice 10 step-and-pushaway motions.

Score 1 point for each correct extension (firm grip, relaxed arm) that lands directly in your partner hands.

Score a half-point bonus each time you use correct crossover step with pushaway.

Your score _____

Initial Movement Drill 3 Weight Transition

I first heard of this drill from Fred Borden, internationally known instructor and former head coach of Team USA. It promotes full body-weight transition on the initial step and swing motion. This practice incorporates a small, almost imperceptible, back-and-forth hip slide. Gradually shifting the weight from back to front helps the bowler move the body forward as the ball is ready to move forward into the pushaway.

Assume a normal stance position with feet slightly staggered and knees slightly flexed. Hold ball at a comfortable height. Very gently shift weight onto back heel by sliding the hips back. Shift weight forward to the ball of front foot by sliding hips forward. Gently feel hips shift back and forth four times. On the fourth forward shift, allow body weight to continue past front foot. As weight shifts in front of feet, make initial step. (Once weight has moved in front of stance, you will feel the need to step. You should feel as though the step catches the body.) Practice proper pushaway movement when taking first step.

TO DECREASE DIFFICULTY

- Put hand behind back and practice shifting body weight into initial step only.
- Practice shifting body weight and pushaway without ball.

Success Check

- Transfer weight smoothly from back heel to front toe.
- Move upper and lower body together.
- Transfer weight smoothly past front toe on the first step.
- When first step is firmly planted, balance body weight over foot.

Score Your Success

Practice full procedure 10 times.

Score 1 point each time body-weight shift and ball-weight shift are simultaneous and smooth.

Score half a point if step and swing motion are in correct direction.

Your score _____

Variation of Weight-Transition Drill   *Five-Step Approach*

One of the benefits of the five-step approach is that the first step automatically leads to a weight transition. Instead of merely shifting onto the front foot, the bowler actually steps with that foot. The body weight gently moving forward with the first small step creates a seamless continuation of the weight shift onto the second step. This weight transition includes the movement of the ball.

Assume a setup stance with the feet slightly staggered. Slide the hips back until the weight is over the heel of the back foot. Smoothly slide hips forward until the weight is past the toe of the back foot. Weight is now over front foot of staggered position. Slide the foot opposite the throwing arm forward. Body weight transfers forward to the opposite foot as the step is taken. As the body weight moves past the opposite foot, take a small step with the throwing-side foot. The ball moves forward into the pushaway just as the throwing-side foot moves for the second step. When the second step is firmly planted, the body weight is centered over the throwing-side foot.

Practice the weight transition with the first step 8 to 10 times before incorporating the second step and pushaway. Once comfortable with second step-and-pushaway motion, score success the same way as in the previous drill.

SUCCESS SUMMARY

You should now have a clearer picture of how critical the start is to a sound game and how it contributes to developing versatility. While every athlete prefers a particular style of game, the more skillful bowlers make adjustments as needed.

A simple adjustment in the pushaway shape helps coordinate the swing with the footwork. An extended outward push delays the ball falling into the swing for bowlers with a slower start, while a quickly descending hinge motion accommodates faster foot speed or bowlers who prefer a higher backswing. The swingaway motion blends both the outward and downward aspects, creating a smooth, arcing initial movement. Many bowlers prefer the swingaway starting technique, and it is the best option for people new to the game.

The initial movement should be simple and easy to repeat. Find the rhythm and speed that falls into your comfort zone. Determine which shapes and speeds fit your game. Experiment with different ball positions and pushaway shapes. Then, practice enough to expand your mastery of various techniques. You are trying to hone a precise game. Be diligent in your efforts.

A bowler must commit to either the four- or five-step approach before conducting the drills. If you choose the five-step approach, substitute the weight transition variation for your grading. Score yourself based on how many steps you have decided to use.

SCORING YOUR SUCCESS

Timing Drill

1. Evaluating Standard Initial Timing   _____ out 9

Swing Drills

1. Anatomical Swing Practice   _____ out 5

2. Opposite-Hand Pushaway Practice   _____ out 5

Initial Movement Drills

1. Foot Placement   _____ out of 15

2. Partner Help   _____ out of 15

3. Weight Transition   _____ out of 15

   Total   _____ **out of 64**

This chapter has introduced the elements of a proper start. At this point you should have a good idea of where to start, what a balanced stance feels like, and the proper way to get the ball in motion. These steps are only the start of the journey, but, there is no sense in getting started if you don't know where you are going. The finish position is where everything ends up. Every bowler must be aware of how to achieve a proper finish position. Bowlers must understand for themselves how the elements of swing alignment and body position established in the beginning apply to a balanced, well-aligned finish.

By rigorously working at developing a solid finish position, the bowler will be able to control how all the elements of power and accuracy come together at the end to produce an outstanding shot. Learning what goes into an excellent finish position is the topic of the next step.

Finishing Fundamentals

The finish position is the point of stability. The force of the swing and the momentum gained through the footwork come together at the finish. The finish position determines the alignment of the body to the target and serves as the anchor point of the swing. To control the swing it is critical that the body reaches a controlled finish.

A solid finish depends on the alignment of movement during the approach, not just at the end. If the body and the swing are too far out of line from each other, it is difficult to recover and establish a balanced finish position. Other steps in this book emphasize footwork and swing. This step focuses on what to expect when the progress to the foul line is complete.

Create a mental image that guides you to your finish position. This reference image is called a *visual template*. A template is a standard form of an image used to re-create that image (e.g., plastic templates for making circles, triangles, engineering symbols, or flowchart symbols). When the template is placed on paper, the correct form can be traced and accurately re-created. The visual template is the picture in your mind of the body's perfect position, the standard against which the finish position will be compared every time you throw a bowling ball.

VISUALIZING AND BUILDING THE FINISH POSITION

Use a visual template to determine how closely the actual finish matches the ideal finish position. In your mind's eye, see yourself repeat the image, molding your body into the template position, throw after throw.

The visualization process starts with a clock face. Picture yourself within the clock. Your head points up to 12:00, and your feet stand on 6:00. For a right-handed bowler, the follow-through extends to 1:00, while the back leg kicks around to 7:00.

Draw a line straight down from the head to the slide foot. This line running from 12:00 to 6:00 is the *static balance line*. The body is centered over the slide foot. When the center of gravity is positioned over the base of support, static balance is achieved.

To hold this position at the finish, all weights and forces must be equal on both sides of this line. The forces cannot be so imbalanced as to pull the body away from the base of support.

Because the force of the swing (i.e., momentum of the ball weight as it swings) is considerable, a comparable counter-force (kicking the back leg behind) is necessary. The line drawn from 1:00 to 7:00 is the force–counterforce line.

We have now established image lines. The basic image of the visual template consists of only two lines: a static balance line and a force–counterforce line (figure 4.1). This image is the same whether viewed from the side or from the back (figure 4.2). The perfect finish position can be built by using this template.

The static balance line is set in the stance and does not change from start to finish. The static balance line is maintained through every step of the approach. At the beginning of the approach, center the body over the feet, and keep it centered over the feet on every step. The position of the upper body is established in the stance. Eliminating extraneous movement—no twisting or turning, no leaning or pulling—is important for overall balance of the body. The more controlled the movement during the approach, the more likely it is that a well-balanced finish will be achieved at the end of the approach.

The main difference between the starting and finishing positions is the knee bend. Bending the knee at the finish lowers the swing toward the lane. The knee is the body's shock absorber. It must be ready to receive the body weight plus the force of the downswing as you enter the slide. If the front knee is locked straight, there will be nothing to absorb the momentum of the approach, and you will need to redirect your energy in a different direction to keep from falling over the foul line. Some

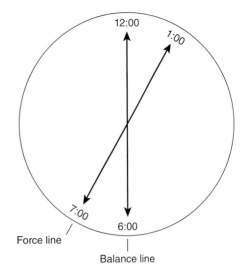

Figure 4.1 The visual template consists of a static balance line and a force–counterforce line.

Figure 4.2 Use the visual template to build the perfect finish position.

bowlers redirect the force vertically (referred to as standing up at the line) or laterally (spinning away from the swing) or by taking an extra step (stepping out of the shot).

MISSTEP

You lock your front knee.

CORRECTION

Bend your front knee as you follow through on the swing. It may help if you keep your back toe on the ground. This promotes a better knee bend as the back leg counterbalances the swing.

Be sure to sufficiently bend the knee of the back leg as well. Because the leg is extended behind, the bend of the knee may not be as dramatic as the front knee. However, both knees bend to some degree so that the hips can descend into the finish position. Keeping the toes of the back foot on the ground after the push-off of the drive step (or *power step*) promotes a better knee bend and ensures the leg counterbalances the swing. Remember these two bowling phrases:

1. Head up, hips down.
2. Drop and drive.

Imagine two parallel lines, one for the footwork and another for the swing (figure 4.3). Both lines are oriented toward the target. When the ball is put in motion toward the target, the bowler walks parallel to the swing. The less a bowler deviates from the straight line to the target, either with the swing or the footwork, the better. This requires the bowler to pay attention to the footwork leading up to the finish. Because the swing itself can pull the bowler off balance, additional movement away from the swing causes even more problems.

Unfortunately, many bowlers tend to walk away from the swing. This is particularly noticeable at two points. The first is as the ball drops down toward the bowler after the pushaway. The second is when the ball comes forward in the downswing. If the steps move the body away from the swing, it is difficult to recover to a balanced, accurate finish position. The results violate bowling's basic tenets—walk straight, swing straight, and stay on line to the target.

As the ball comes forward in the downswing, many bowlers step away because of an subconscious tendency to avoid hitting themselves with the ball (figure 4.4). Stepping to the side as the bowler enters the slide dramatically affects the balance position. Make an effort to center the slide foot under the body.

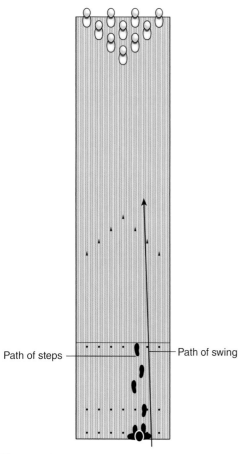

Path of steps ───── ───── Path of swing

Figure 4.3 Both the path of the swing and the path of the steps are directed toward the target.

If the slide step is going one direction and the pull of the swing is going another, the bowler loses balance at the release (figure 4.5). The release takes place at the bottom of the swing, when the momentum of the ball is greatest. It is at this point, the swing exerts the most dramatic unbalancing effect. Proper positioning counters the swing weight. The placement of the slide foot is a key element of proper position.

One of the best ways to ensure a balanced finish is to take a slight crossover step. The goal is to work the slide foot under the center of the body. To initiate this movement, turn the heel slightly inward as the foot enters the slide. With the slide leg moving in front of the push-off leg, the push-off leg will not have as far to go to counterbalance the swing.

The force of the swing on one side of the balance line requires the action of a counterforce on the other side of the balance line. The sweep of the back leg provides the counterforce. Extending the nonthrowing arm aids balance. Now we have a good picture of the finish position (figure 4.6).

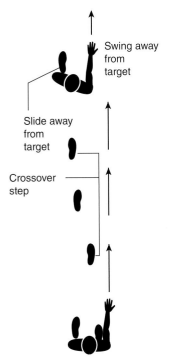

Swing away from target

Slide away from target

Crossover step

Figure 4.4 Stepping away from the swing decreases accuracy. Center the slide foot under the body.

Figure 4.5 Losing balance after releasing the ball.

51

Figure 4.6 FINISH POSITION

1. Upper body is slightly tilted forward (enough to put shoulders over slide foot).
2. Knee is flexed to about 45 degrees.
3. Body is centered over slide foot.
4. Nonthrowing hand extends from the shoulder out to the side.
5. Follow-through extends from throwing shoulder in the direction of the target.
6. The line of the shoulders and line of the swing create a 90-degree angle.
7. Back leg is positioned opposite the throwing side.

For a right-handed bowler, the throwing hand should follow through at 1:00, and the balance leg is at 7:00. For a left-handed bowler, the throwing hand should follow through at 11:00, and the balance leg is at 5:00. Fit your form within the template as closely as possible. The swing leg and throwing arm are on the opposite sides of the dial; the rest of the body is centered over the slide foot.

The nonthrowing arm is the rudder that steers the upper body; the back leg steers the lower body. Avoid oversteering. The arm should extend out from the shoulder, with the hand somewhat below shoulder level but above waist height. Placing the arm to the front or back modifies the shoulder's alignment with the target. The arm will be slightly back (closed) if the target is inside the shoulder line and slightly forward (open) if the target is outside the line (figure 4.7).

When swinging the back leg out of the way, do not pivot on the front hip. Freely swing the back leg. The rotation should occur only at the non-weight-bearing hip joint (figure 4.8a). If the front hip pivots, the line of the hip will turn away from the target (figure 4.8b). Additionally, with the heel turning in at the slide, any outward rotation of the weight-bearing hip puts tremendous strain on the knee.

Many bowlers have difficulty maintaining balance. Some of the drills at the end of this step emphasize proper positioning from a stationary position. This teaches bowlers what to expect (and what to work toward) during an active approach.

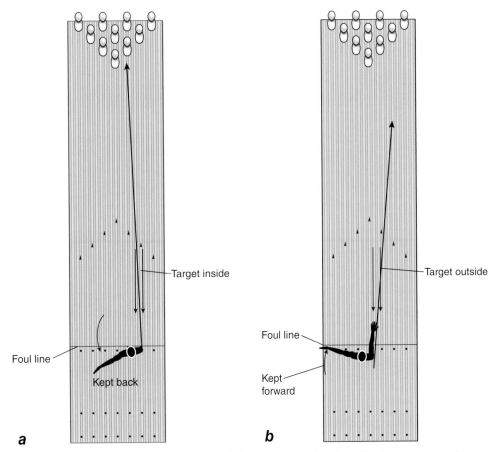

Figure 4.7 *(a)* Arm is closed when target is inside shoulder line. *(b)* Arm is open if target is outside shoulder line.

Figure 4.8 *(a)* Correct rotation occurs at the non-weight-bearing hip joint only. *(b)* The line of the hip turns from target if the front hip pivots.

MISSTEP

You can't keep your balance in the finish position.

CORRECTION

Keep your feet under your body. Use the crossover step to bring your slide foot under your body. Have a coach or trained bowler look at your entire approach from behind and from the side. Do the steps veer away from a centered position? Does the body lean forward or pull back from a position over the slide foot? A balance issue early in the approach can become a problem at the finish.

DRILLS FOR THE FINISH POSITION

The drills for the finishing position cannot be overemphasized. These drills reduce the game to its most fundamental elements. By eliminating concern for footwork and the timing of the initial movement, you will be able to make the game as simple as possible when you get to the foul line. Simplifying the movement allows you to isolate any aspect of the sport that causes concern.

Each of the following practice drills can be completed at five challenge levels. Whenever practical, complete each of the finish-position drills 10 to 15 times at each challenge level. (Not all challenge levels apply to all drills described.)

- Level 1: Practice without a ball.
- Level 2: Practice while holding the ball in front, both hands cupped under ball.
- Level 3: Practice while incorporating full swing without ball.
- Level 4: Practice while incorporating full swing with a ball.
- Level 5: Practice while performing a full swing and releasing ball toward the pins.

Each level adds a measure of complexity (more motion) or an unbalancing effect (caused by weight of ball and force of swing). The last level helps you learn to accommodate for the weight of the ball on the side of the body and for the momentum of a swing. Even though not all challenge levels apply to all the drills, be sure to follow a sequence of increasing weight and complexity as you work your way through a practice regimen.

Finish-Position Drill 1   Finding Your Balance Point

Try to get a sense of what this position feels like without distractions or visual reinforcement. Notice the tilt of the spine and the flex of the knee. What is the most comfortable placement for the back leg? Your goal is to fully investigate what your balanced position feels like. Once fully aware of the finish position, remember the sensation. Strive for this position after every throw. If you don't feel the ideal finish at the end of a throw, something likely went wrong.

From a normal standing position, step forward with your slide foot. Shift all weight forward onto the slide leg.

Raise back leg slightly off ground (2-6 inches [5-15 cm]). Position back leg according to the visual template (7:00, if right handed). Bend the front knee until the back toe touches the floor. Lower hips until reaching comfortable knee bend (approximately 45 degrees). Fully extend opposite arm out from shoulder, positioned slightly below shoulder. Close your eyes and hold the position for 8 to 10 seconds.

TO DECREASE DIFFICULTY

- Keep your eyes open as you hold the finish position.
- Do not use ball until completely comfortable holding this position.

TO INCREASE DIFFICULTY

- Practice the drill at levels 2 through 5.

Success Check

- Front knee is bent.
- Balance foot is touching floor behind slide foot.
- Body is centered over slide foot.
- Spine is straight and angled slightly forward (20 to 25 degrees, depending on knee bend).
- No weight is on back (balance) foot or back toes (figure 4.9).

Figure 4.9   Finish-position balance practice.

Score Your Success

Evaluate your finish at challenge level 4 (ball gently swinging by your side).

Opposite arm moves minimally = 2 points

Knee flex angle is steady, no upward push (straightening) = 1 point

Balance leg is steady, no side-to-side shift = 2 points

Toes of balance leg remain on floor = 1 point

Spine tilt is steady, no swaying forward = 2 points

Body stays centered over slide foot, no sway left to right = 3 points

Your score ___

Finish-Position Drill 2 One-Step Practice

This drill is the most fundamental to the sport of bowling. It is the premier isolation drill. The movement is so simple, it allows a player to focus on any aspect of the game, making it easy to modify to apply to any particular concern. Yet, it generates enough momentum through the drive of the leg and the swing of the ball to replicate real performance sensations.

During this drill, emphasize the weight transfer from the drive leg to the slide foot. The drive leg is the throwing-side leg in the act of pushing off just as the bowler enters the slide. This leg makes a strong push-and-clear motion. The position and knee flex of the power step is actually part of the footwork discussed in another step. But, it needs to be discussed here, as well. As the throwing-side leg drives the body forward, it clears to its counterbalance position, making room for the swing. This motion is critical for balance and accuracy.

Regardless of whether you use this drill to emphasize release, swing, timing, balance, or footwork, the drill uses the same preparation sequence. This is a one-step practice, so take just one step, the slide step. The preparation sequence is as follows:

- Put all weight on the ball-side leg (drive leg).
- Flex knee of ball-side leg (same degree of flex as slide leg's knee at finish).
- Bring slide leg next to other leg.
- Make sure only toe of slide foot is touching ground.
- Feel for tension in thigh of drive leg (drive leg is loaded).
- Use strong spine tilt to bring shoulders slightly ahead of drive foot.

From this position, you have a couple of options. If concerned with the upper body, pay attention to how the hips move forward or how the upper body moves. For the lower body, emphasis is on knee bend, back-leg position, back-foot position, strength of the push-off, or position of slide foot. For this evaluation, perform the practice at challenge level 5, full swing and release of ball.

- The ball will swing back and forth three times.
- At the top of the third backswing, start the slide step.

TO INCREASE DIFFICULTY

Complete 15 to 20 repetitions for each of the five challenge levels.

Once comfortable with a particular challenge level, try that level with your eyes closed. Each time you attempt a challenge level with your eyes closed, feel the movement of the body match the rhythm of the swing. Strive for a sense of a whole-body shift forward onto the slide foot. After the release, feel the balance position and run through a position checklist. Be sure all of the "parts" have ended up where they should.

Success Check

- Hips move forward (and slightly downward) in a straight line.
- Body weight is firmly planted over drive leg.
- Push-off from drive leg starts when ball reaches top of backswing.
- Slide foot works under center of body directly in front of power-step position.

Score Your Success

Slide foot moves forward as ball reaches top of backswing = 2 points

Arm swings close to hip (in line with shoulder) = 1 point

Slide foot moves in, directly in front of drive foot = 2 points

Drive leg fully extends while pushing off = 1 point

Toe of slide foot makes contact first = 2 points

Heel of slide foot turns in slightly = 2 points

As slide finishes, knee of back leg also bends = 1 point

Back leg sweeps to proper counterbalance position = 2 points

Heel of back foot lowers slightly toward ground = 1 point

Toe of back foot drags along behind bowler, just barely touching floor (no weight on back toe) = 1 point

Balance arm counterbalances swing, moving forward and down as ball swings up and back = 1 point

Balance arm moves back without pulling shoulders off-line as swing comes down to release point = 1 point

Body weight is centered over slide foot = 2 points

Your score _____

Finish-Position Drill 3   Ice-Skater

I call this the ice-skater drill, because you will feel yourself glide along the approach on one foot like a skater across ice. This drill emphasizes the lower body.

Put both hands behind the back. Balance all your weight on the throwing-side leg. Pick up the heel of the throwing-side foot slightly. This places your weight more on the ball of the foot. Feel the toe dig in. As you move the slide foot forward, feel for a strong push-off from the drive leg.

TO INCREASE DIFFICULTY

Go through the sequences with your eyes closed. The goal is to sense the weight transfer as the body moves from a balanced position over the drive foot to a balanced position over the slide foot.

Success Check

- Toe of slide foot makes initial contact.
- Slide foot remains relatively flat to promote a gliding sensation.
- A strong push-off from throwing-side leg generates power.

Score Your Success

Slide foot moves in, directly in front of drive foot = 2 points

Drive leg fully extends while pushing off = 1 point

Toe of slide foot makes contact = 1 point

Feel slide on toe before heel contact = 1 point

Heel of slide foot turns in slightly = 1 point

As slide finishes, knee of back leg also bends = 2 points

Back leg sweeps to proper counterbalance position = 2 points

Heel of back foot lowers slightly toward ground = 1 point

Toe of back foot drags along floor (no weight on back toe) = 1 point

Your score _____

Finish-Position Drill 4   **Full Approach**

Once finished with the one-step practices at all challenge levels, test your finish-position drill as part of a normal approach. If you are inexperienced, don't be overly concerned with the actual approach at this point. Other steps of this text will discuss timing, footwork, and arm swing. Just walk through your normal approach and at the end, evaluate the finish just as you did with the one-step practice.

Take your first few approaches without a ball. Put your hands behind your back and simply focus on walking up to the finish position. Gain confidence in the footwork that brings you to a finished position before adding a ball to the exercise. When adding the ball to the full approach, start by holding it in front of you (challenge level 2). Attain the finish position consistently before attempting the full approach using a normal swing and release. Once you are using your normal bowling motion, focus on the finish position.

TO INCREASE DIFFICULTY

- Hold a ball in front of your body and go through the full approach; close your eyes just before starting the last step. Do not swing the ball (yet!); merely cradle it in front of you. Keep your eyes closed as you finish.
- While using a full swing and approach, close your eyes on the last step. Release the ball as you normally would. Closing your eyes on the last step allows you to rely on the feeling as the body moves to the finish position.
- Performing drills with the eyes closed keeps you from aiming and trying to force the ball toward a particular target. Additionally, practicing with your eyes closed on the last step teaches you to trust the swing. You will get a better sense of the fluid, muscle-free pendulum motion. You will not have the urge to aim the throw if you have nothing to look at.

Success Check

- Finish position is consistently well-balanced.
- Step moves in a smooth acceleration to the finish point.
- The footwork and swing work together without strain or loss of control.

Score Your Success

Slide foot moves forward as ball reaches top of backswing = 2 points

Arm swings close to hip (in line with shoulder) = 1 point

Slide foot moves in, directly in front of drive foot = 2 points

Drive leg fully extends while pushing off = 1 point

Toe of slide foot makes contact first = 1 point

Heel of slide foot turns in slightly = 1 point

As slide finishes, knee of back leg also bends = 1 point

Back leg sweeps to proper counterbalance position = 2 points

Heel of back foot lowers slightly toward ground = 1 point

Toe of back foot drags along (no weight on back toe) = 1 point

Balance arm counterbalances swing, moving forward and down as ball swings up and back = 2 points

Balance arm moves back without pulling shoulders off-line as swing comes down to release point = 2 points

Body weight is centered over slide foot = 2 points

Finish position is held until ball hits pins = 2 points

Your score _____

SUCCESS SUMMARY

Examine your finish position often to be sure it matches the visual template in your mind's eye. The visual template is your reference point for the finish.

Review your drill scores. Record your scores in the spaces that follow and total them. If you score at least 50 points, you are ready to move on to the next step. If you score fewer than 50 points, review the sections that are giving you trouble, then repeat the drills.

SCORING YOUR SUCCESS

Finish-Position Drills

1. Finding Your Balance Point _____ out of 11

2. One-Step Practice _____ out of 19

3. Ice-Skater _____ out 12

4. Full Approach _____ out of 21

Total _____ **out of 63**

These early steps of the book have introduced the beginning and the end of the bowling motion: basically, when everything is stationary. The stance, (just before everything gets into motion) and the finish (just as everything has come together at the end) are the easiest parts of the game to evaluate. The best opportunity to run through a mental checklist to determine if all the "parts" are in their correct places is when nothing is in motion.

However, much happens between the start and the finish, none of it more important than the swing. It is the swing, after all, that sends the ball on its way to the pins. The swing is the topic of the next step.

Refining the Swing

The swing is the essential physical skill in bowling. You will build your game around your swing. Directing the swing line is critical to accuracy, and the swing's pace, rhythm, and speed set the pattern to which you will match the footwork. The largest component of the ball's velocity at release is the velocity it achieves as it falls through the arc of the swing. Your goal is to find the means to adjust speed and direction without giving up accuracy, consistency, and balance. A truly free swing, one that is neither constrained nor manipulated by muscular effort, will be consistent. The swing influences balance, control, and the mechanics of the release.

What is it about the swing that influences the nature of the game? How can you use that knowledge to your benefit? (After all, a swing is not necessary for putting a ball in motion down the lane. You could simply cradle the ball in front of you with both hands, run up to the foul line, and push the ball toward the pins). To generate adequate speed and free the hand for the release, the ball must move to the side of the body. This ball position allows a long, unimpeded swing (like a pendulum), a movement that generates considerable speed in a short time. The unbalancing effect of a ball swinging past your side highlights the importance of footwork and the finish position. The fundamental challenge of bowling can be summarized as follows:

Find a way to counteract the unbalancing effect of a long powerful swing while harnessing that power to generate a strong, accurate roll of the ball.

SWING BASICS

One characteristic of the swing is its pendulum motion. So, let gravity do the work. Gravity is a physical constant. Build your game around this constant. Characteristics of a pendulum provide important benefits.

- Once in motion, a pendulum follows the same swing path. Unless another force acts on it, the swing path is reliable.
- The time a swing takes to complete its full motion is consistent. Without muscular effort accelerating or slowing it down, it will travel along its path at the same rate every time.

Any one characteristic of the swing of a pendulum can be adjusted without disturbing any of the other characteristics. One could, for example, lower its position to reduce ball velocity and not affect direction or tempo. All bowlers should take the time to become familiar with the pendulum motion of their own swing. Knowing what your swing feels like now makes adjustment easier later.

- Subtle adjustment of swing direction helps in playing a particular target line.
- Adjusting the height of the swing allows you to increase or decrease ball speed.
- Adjusting the shape of the initial swing movement lets you synchronize the swing and steps without sacrificing the reliability of the motion of the pendulum during the arm swing.

Keep in mind that the arm is not a true pendulum. The structure of the shoulder's ball-and-socket joint is considerably more complex. The arm has a large range of motion in a variety of directions. If too many muscles are involved in the arm swing, the reliable pendulum motion goes away. With practice you can replicate the characteristics of a pendulum motion. To see a great swing is to observe a beautiful lesson in the graceful, fluid generation of power. As the late John Jowdy (longtime pro-tour instructor and author) put it, "Effortless power through powerless effort."

Tempo is the first aspect of your swing to determine. The length of a pendulum arm determines the amount of time it takes to complete a swing. To a bowler, this means the length of the arm determines how long the swing takes. Height of the swing does not matter. A short swing covering a small arc takes the same amount of time as a much longer swing arc if the arm length is the same.

To the casual observer, it seems logical that the higher the starting point of the swing, the longer it should take. This assumption is wrong. It is true that a higher starting position causes the ball to fall along a longer swing path, it is also true that a higher starting position produces greater acceleration because of gravity. The net result is that the ball travels the path in the same amount of time as it would have had it started from a lower position (figure 5.1).

This leads us to two important bowling elements. First, timing is based solely on when the ball is put into the swing. If the swing is initiated at the correct time and the correct direction in relation to the steps, the timing of the bowler's mechanics need not change even if the bowler is changing the way he or she is trying to throw it.

Second, ball speed can be manipulated by adjusting the starting height of the swing. Unlike muscular effort, which tends to vary among all but the most skilled performers, reliable changes in ball speed can be achieved through the careful selection of ball height.

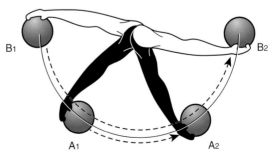

Time of swing

$$B_1 \rightarrow B_2 = A_1 - A_2$$

B₁

B₂

A₁

A₂

Figure 5.1 Long swings do not take more time to finish than short swings.

Timing (discussed in step 7) is the relationship between swing motion and the pace of the steps. Any understanding of timing starts with developing the feel of your own swing. Bowlers must discover the speed of their swing in order to find the appropriate footwork pace.

Ideally, the body momentum generated by foot speed complements the swing's momentum. Recognizing the relationship between the length of a bowler's arm and length of stride is important for determining proper timing. For instance, a tall bowler who has long arms has two choices. One is to use slower footwork than a shorter bowler (who has a relatively short, quick swing rhythm) to avoid running ahead of the swing. The other is to initiate the swing motion quicker relative to the feet so that the swing stays up with the faster footwork.

Avoid using muscular force to either slow or accelerate the swing. Maintain the beneficial qualities of the pendulum by keeping the swing as muscle free as possible. To promote smooth, effortless consistency, follow this general rule:

Fit the steps to the swing, not the swing to the steps.

Because foot speed is an important contributor to ball velocity, circumstances come up in which you need to change the pace of the footwork, either faster or slower. Carefully matching the height and starting motion of the swing to adjustments in the pace of the footwork creates smooth mechanics while minimizing muscular effort.

PARTS OF THE SWING

It seems strange to think of a continuous motion as being made up of parts. Instead, think of the swing as having identifiable positions, or arc segments, through which it passes. The swing has five positions: the pushaway, the down drop, the backswing, the downswing, and the follow-through. We describe the swing this way to more easily coordinate each swing position with a step.

A bowler takes four steps while the swing is in motion. A bowler using a five-step approach does not put the ball in motion on the initial step. After the first step, the swing is put into motion, and then does its work during the last four. For a four-step approach, the initial step and swing movement start at the same time. What about that fifth swing segment? The last segment, the follow-through, is what happens after the steps are completed and the ball has left the bowlers hand.

The pushaway position (figure 5.2a) includes the forward movement of the ball from its stationary position in the stance until it starts to drop down into the swing. The pushaway is something of an outward movement away from the shoulder as the ball drops into the initial arc of the swing. During the pushaway, the swing arm has not yet reached full extension. The ball is not yet in a free fall. The shape and direction of the pushaway and how those elements are linked to the initial steps are bowling fundamentals. Please, review Step 3: Starting Fundamentals.

The down drop position (figure 5.2b) includes the downward movement of the ball after the pushaway until it reaches the bottom of the swing arc. It is the ball's free fall to the bottom of the swing as it passes by the throwing side of the body. Maintain the free swing of the pendulum while keeping the swing on line. The swing passes directly under the shoulder at the bottom of the arc.

The backswing position (figure 5.2c) includes the upward movement of the swing from the lowest point of the down-drop arc until it reaches its highest point behind the bowler. As the ball clears the hip, it continues to a point at least as high as the initial starting position. If the starting height and backswing height are not similar, there is muscular interference. At the top of the backswing, the ball should be in line with the shoulder. A backswing position away from the body or well behind the back indicates that lateral movement has taken the ball off its ideal swing line.

The downswing position (figure 5.2d) includes downward movement of the swing from the top of the backswing until it reaches the release point at the bottom of the forward swing arc. The ball comes off the hand at, or just after it passes through, the bottom of the downswing. Ideally, it will feel as if the ball is freely falling. This sense of a free fall contributes to a muscle-free swing.

The follow-through position (figure 5.2e) includes the swing motion that extends from the shoulder after the ball is released. The bowler feels the swing drive the hand forward through the back of the ball and send it out onto the lane before the swing moves upward. The swing extends out and then up in a long, sweeping motion. The follow-through continues to a point above shoulder height, with the arm bending as the elbow swings up past shoulder height. A stiff, straight arm throughout the follow-through may indicate excessive tension in the swing. The bowler might be trying to aim at a target rather than allowing a free swing from the shoulders.

Troubleshooting the Arm Swing

Many factors influence arm swing. Sometimes the trouble is caused by improper swing mechanics. Other times the swing is influenced by what the rest of the body is doing.

If lack of flexibility keeps the backswing lower than you'd like, adjust your style to accommodate a restricted range of motion. Don't force your body out of position in an effort to create a longer swing arc that may not suit your physical abilities. Other problems can cause a low backswing:

- Too much tension. Learn to let the swing flow. Don't aim the ball. Because the shoulders determine direction, let the ball swing freely from the shoulder.

- Late timing. Timing is late if the last step moves forward to the finish before the ball completes its backswing. The bowler might subconsciously shorten the swing in order to help it catch up.

- Poorly fitting ball. If a free swing seems impossible without feeling a loss of ball control, the ball might not fit properly. An incorrect fit restricts the swing as you fight to hold on.

If the ball fits correctly and the hand position is correct, the momentum of the swing keeps the ball pressed onto the hand. The pressure of the outrigger fingers on the surface of the ball keeps the wrist in a firm position. The ball should not come off the hand until the bottom of the swing.

Significantly bending the elbow, particularly on the downswing, indicates use of upper-arm muscle, otherwise known as grabbing at the ball. Using upward force at the release may cause release inconsistency as well as a swing that pulls off-line.

Figure 5.2 **FULL SWING**

Pushaway

1. Pushaway is straight out from the shoulder toward the intended target.
2. Pushaway makes a smooth arcing motion.
3. Initial movement is usually out and down into the arc.

Down Drop

1. Arm reaches full extension.
2. Swing traces a smooth arc.
3. The true pendulum portion of the swing begins.

Backswing

1. Arm continues past the bottom of the swing on its way back up.
2. Ball is not pulled back; momentum of its drop allows it to swing back on its own.
3. At the top of the backswing, ball is at same height (or higher) as starting position.

Downswing

1. Downswing is a long, smooth arc.
2. The swing is not pulled forward; it falls through the downswing on its own.
3. The elbow bends very little or not at all before the release point.

Follow-Through

1. Throwing hand extends out and up past shoulder.
2. The swing line follows the ball to the target.
3. The momentum of the swing causes it to finish to at least shoulder height.

MISSTEP

- You are forced to loop the swing around your hip during the backswing.

CORRECTIONS

- In the stance, position the ball in line with the shoulder. Improper positioning forces the bowler to redirected the swing around the body as he or she puts it into motion.
- Keep initial direction of the pushaway directly on a line from shoulder to target. Any swing motion away from the intended target can cause a loop in the swing.
- Keep steps and swing working side by side in the same direction. An initial step in the wrong direction may interfere with the backswing because the throwing-side leg is in the way.

If the swing goes back higher than expected, you might be accelerating the backswing. Avoid using a pulling motion. You might also have changed your body position. Leaning forward or turning the upper body into an open position can increase the height of the backswing. When you don't want a higher position, the extra distance covered by the swing changes the swing's rhythm and throws off the timing of the release and finish position.

Some bowlers intentionally rotate the upper body to create a longer swing and might have a backswing above their head! We will discuss this later.

MISSTEP
You lose balance during the swing.

CORRECTIONS
- Keep the swing close to the body. A swing that moves away from the body or steps that move away from the swing might pull you off balance.
- Use the back leg effectively. This leg counterbalances the force of the swing. Bend the knees more and keep the hips low for better stability.
- Extend nonthrowing arm fully from the shoulder. The weight of this arm also helps counter the force of the swing.

Ball Speed and Swing Height

The higher the ball's position in the backswing, the more gravity can contribute to the ball's final velocity (figure 5.3). If the ball is allowed to swing freely, the height of the ball's position in the stance influences how high it goes in the backswing. It follows that one aspect of speed control is the height of the ball in the stance. Subtle variations in the ball's starting position help a bowler develop control at a variety of speeds. Also, consider that the average bowler throws the ball 14 to 18 miles per hour (22.5-29 kph) (about 20 to 26 feet per second [6.1-8 mps]). A long pendulum swing can do much of the work of achieving this velocity (figure 5.4).

For a bowler with slow feet, more extension time delays the ball's drop into the swing. For a bowler with fast feet, the quick extension drops the ball into the swing sooner.

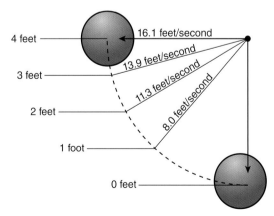

Figure 5.3 Potential speed from various swing heights.

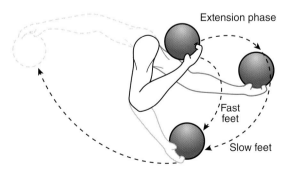

Figure 5.4 Starting position affects the amount of time it takes for the ball to move into the pendulum portion of the arm swing.

UNDERSTANDING THE PUSHAWAY MOVEMENT

Many bowlers struggle to reconcile a change in ball position (as a way to vary ball speed) with the pace of the footwork. For instance, many bowlers use a lower starting position because they have fast feet. They assume the shorter swing takes less time, when in reality, the swing is already significantly extended during the pushaway. The ball does not have far to go to reach the pendulum part of the motion. The lower position places the ball into the swing sooner, keeping the swing on pace with the steps, even though the short swing takes just as much time as a swing from a higher position. But the same thing could be done when using a higher starting position by simply letting the ball fall into the downswing quicker.

This means that ball height does not have to be adjusted to accommodate variations in foot speed. A simple adjustment in the direction of the pushaway coordinates the swing with the footwork without affecting ball velocity. Pushing more outward delays the ball's descent into the swing, while a downward movement quickens it. (If you haven't done so, please review step 3.)

A swing that exceeds a restricted range of motion may cause joint strain or force bowlers into a body position not suited to their game. Bowlers who want to avoid sacrificing proper alignment to the target or are dealing with discomfort can use footwork options to increase ball speed. Other bowlers prefer to use foot speed to alter ball velocity, increasing the speed of the footwork as a means to increase ball velocity. In those cases, the bowler may need to fit the swing to the steps.

Two important factors determine the initial accuracy of the swing: the ball's starting position and the direction of the pushaway. If the ball is aligned directly in front of the shoulder, and the pushaway is straight out from the shoulder, the swing's initial path will be straight. Ideally, the swing moves back and forth smoothly as it passes along the side of the hip (figure 5.5a). The ball swings under the shoulder on the way back and on the way through to the release.

A starting position or pushaway in front of the body causes the backswing to move away from the body on the way back (figure 5.5b). Perhaps it will stay out from the body or it might loop around behind the back (figure 5.5c). In either case, it is not likely to swing along a line that goes to the target.

Outside positioning is a problem for many bowlers. Some bowlers support the weight of the ball by sticking the elbow into the hip or abdomen. Other bowlers simply push the ball away from the body as a matter of habit, perhaps as a subconscious avoidance of the ball. In reality, there is plenty of space between the ball and the body. Another situation causing outward motion is when the bowler overrotates the hand to an open (palm out) position. The swing follows the thumb; as the thumb turns out from the body, the swing follows it to a point outside the shoulder line. Even when aware of the problem, some bowlers have difficulty resisting the urge to move the ball away from the body.

Learn to push the ball straight out from the shoulder. The swing should stay along the target line throughout the swing. The follow-through will finish in a position in line with the shoulder. Feel as if you are reaching out and trying to touch the target on the lane.

The head position, in particular, should be steady; avoid dramatic side-to-side shifts. The head shifting away from the throwing side indicates a pulling from the top, an unnecessary attempt to accelerate the ball into the downswing. Try to maintain upper-body tilt as well. The spine tilt established at the beginning will be fairly steady throughout the approach. For many bowlers, the spine tilts forward more steeply as the ball reaches the top of the backswing. This is a means, sometimes

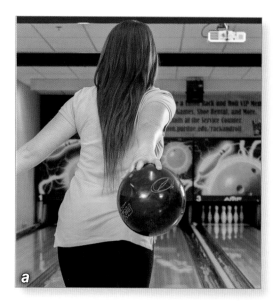

Figure 5.5 *(a)* Straight swing, *(b)* outside swing, and *(c)* wraparound swing.

subconsciously, of raising the swing higher. This frequently is seen in bowlers who open the shoulder to enhance the swing. Regardless of the bowler's style, the spine tilt at the top of the backswing should be maintained until the release is finished.

Be wary of abrupt changes in spine tilt. When a bowler suddenly leans forward on the downswing, the swing gets steeper and changes the ball's trajectory. It may be released into, rather than along, the lane. It is also difficult to achieve a long, smooth follow-through if the spine tilts too far forward.

Excessive forward lean may also cause a loss of balance, adversely affecting position and swing accuracy. Changes in upper-body tilt may indicate timing issues. If footwork and swing are not in sync, the body compensates, to the detriment of shot quality. If the timing is late (the feet are ahead of the ball), a bowler will frequently pull back in an effort to help the ball catch up. When timing is early (the swing is coming down too soon relative to the feet), a bowler may lean forward as a subconscious effort to get the body ahead of the ball.

Pulling the upper body back abruptly accelerates the ball to the release point. The hand may not have time to complete the release motion, and the release occurs too early in the swing arc. Pulling back the upper body also changes the shape of the swing. The swing tends to redirect upward instead of swinging naturally outward. The swing won't always go to the target and the release becomes inconsistent. Remember, the body seeks a balance between the force of the swing and the counterforce of the body position whether or not it is beneficial to your game.

One last thing. Pay attention to the knee bend. As discussed in step 4, Finishing Fundamentals, the knee bend at the start of the last step is maintained throughout the slide. Some bowlers might actually increase the knee bend a little. Remember to drop and drive. As far as the power step into the slide is concerned, start low and stay low. The slide leg should never dramatically straighten. Standing the body up just as the swing comes down is a common fault. Lower the hips on the next-to-last step, and use the power step to drive the hips forward as the swing comes through. You might be surprised at how a good finish improves your swing.

I have seen a few bowlers who get away with straightening the slide leg at the release point. They use the upward drive of the leg as an additional opposing force on the ball as it swings down. While these opposing actions may increase the leverage force, bowlers who do this with any measure of success are few and far between.

How you visualize your target line also affects the swing. Pay attention to how you visualize alignment to the target. Imagine somebody took your head off and repositioned it on top of the throwing-side shoulder. You would be able to look directly down your swing arm. Many skilled bowlers try this. (Well, they don't completely lose their head!) They drop the throwing-side shoulder down and back slightly, and then they slightly shift the head over toward the ball's position in the stance. The result is an alignment of ball position, swing line, and head position with the target line as close as physically possible.

MISSTEP

You look at a target straight ahead and try to swing to that target.

CORRECTION

Your eyes are in the middle of your head. Swinging toward a target directly in front of the eyes causes the swing to cross the body. One way of dealing with an inward pushaway is to first look at a target on the lane directly in front of you. Look at a target in line with the center of your body. Then, shift your line of sight four to six boards over (to the right if right-handed). This moves the eyes to a target in front of the swing instead of swinging to a target in front of the eyes. The pushaway moves along the adjusted line of sight.

SHOULDER POSITIONING: TRADITIONAL AND MODERN SWING

Upper-body rotation, called *core rotation* in sport language, is the most element of bowling that most dramatically separates how the game is now played from how it was traditionally taught. The swing is attached to the shoulder. What the shoulders do, in relation to the swing, has a profound effect on accuracy and power generation.

The emphasis in today's game is on generating speed and ball revolutions. The modern approach to the game emphasizes driving the ball down the lane before it recovers for a strong angle into the strike pocket.

Traditional Shoulder Action: Square to Square

Traditionally, bowlers are taught to minimize shoulder movement. The shoulders become a stable anchor point from which the ball swings. One simply directs the upper body toward the target and remains steady. Ideally, the swing is 90 degrees from the line of the shoulders.

This is still an excellent way to teach beginners. New bowlers should keep the swing and hand position simple, and the steady shoulders provide consistency and control. Therefore the traditional swing works for bowlers whose hand position is directly behind (or under) the ball during the swing and stays in that position until the release. At the top of the backswing the hand is on top of the ball. During the basic release, the hand starts in a neutral position, centered or slightly offset from the ball's center. The hand position changes little during the swing. Because the hand position changes minimally, there is little rotation at the shoulder joint. The shoulder socket acts like an anchor point for a pendulum swing (figure 5.6).

Figure 5.6   Traditional shoulder action.

Modern Shoulder Action: An Open-and-Shut Case

Rotation of the core allows a swing line that puts the hand in a more effective release position. Heed the advice of PBA Hall of Famer Mark Baker. He often states in his television commentary that "amateur bowlers work the outside of the ball, while professional bowlers work the inside." For an effective hook release, the hand position needs to be to the inside of the ball. By *inside,* we mean that the hand position starts left of the ball's center line (for a right-handed bowler) at the point of release.

To get the hand to the inside of the ball, turn the thumb out as the swing goes back. Keep in mind that the forearm does not rotate very far in that direction. The outward rotation is largely accomplished at the shoulder joint. This is where the bowler has to be attentive. As the shoulder rotates outward, the swing tends to bounce outside the line of the body. If the swing moves away from the body, the bowler keeps the swing in line with the target by rotating the upper body. Core rotation brings the swing back around in line with the head and swing shoulder. If upper-body rotation is in sync with the arm rotation in the swing, the swing stays in line (ensuring accuracy) while maintaining the strong inside tuck of the hand to effect a powerful release. The correct way to do this is to let the swing dictate when the shoulders open up (figure 5.7).

There is a difference between a swing-motivated shoulder turn and a shoulder-driven swing. The swing draws the shoulders open. The shoulders don't throw the swing back.

If the shoulders are the motivating force, the swing will inevitably get off-line. If the upper body rotates too early in the backswing, the ball will be thrown behind the body. If the upper body rotates too early in the downswing, it will throw the ball away from the body. Both situations decrease accuracy and release consistency. Let the swing do the work.

I prefer to see a bowler keep the hand in a neutral position until the ball heads toward the backswing. At some point in the backswing the bowler feels tension in the shoulder. When this happens, the shoulder tension is relieved by outward shoulder rotation and by upper-body rotation. Many bowlers try to get to an inside hand position early in the swing, negatively affecting the accuracy of the initial movement. Nothing opens up until the ball passes the bottom of the swing.

This is also true as the ball starts its way down. Let the swing fall into a position next to the hip before anything else unwinds. Efforts to create a strong hand position are wasted if the shoulders close up too early or the release motion starts before the ball reaches the bottom of the downswing. The modern swing can be summarized like this: open at the top; close at the bottom.

Figure 5.7 Modern shoulder action.

TROUBLESHOOTING THE MODERN SWING

Swing errors come about when bowlers attempt, unknowingly, to blend incompatible element of the two swing styles.

Figure 5.8 Error 1: Traditional swing motion with nontraditional shoulder turn.

Figure 5.9 Error 2: Traditional shoulder position with open hand swing.

Error 1: Traditional Hand Position, Nontraditional Shoulder Turn

The swing is square (90 degrees) to the line of the shoulders, but the line of the shoulders is not facing the target. The swing ends up behind the back (figure 5.8). In this case, the bowler is left with two choices:

1. **Attempt for a swing that falls toward the release in a relatively straight line.** Whether accomplished through excessive shoulder drop, extreme kick of the back leg, or a radical shift in the hip position (any of which may allow the swing to go to target and produce an effective shot), consistency becomes questionable. Awkward adjustments cause injuries.

2. **Bring the swing around the body in an outward loop.** Although less likely to cause injury, this option destroys the ability to make a quality shot. When the swing moves away from the body, bowlers may feel they are losing control or grip and might compensate by squeezing harder or tensing the arm. Accuracy is unlikely as the swing moves back and forth across the target line. The whole arm might rotate to a position outside the centerline of the ball, putting the hand into an ineffective release position. Interestingly, bowlers might feel as though they are in a correct release position (firm wrist and finger leverage) and not feel how the arm rotation and swing have taken the hand away from a proper release position.

Error 2: Traditional Shoulder Position, Nontraditional Swing

The shoulder position is square to the target line, but shoulder rotation opens the hand in the backswing (figure 5.9). The swing is likely to drift away from the body as it goes up in the backswing. Once again, the bowler is left with few options, none desirable.

1. **Force a large inward loop of the swing.** This motion is undertaken in an effort to get it back on line before the release. Although some bowlers can do this, it is difficult to repeat.

2. **Allow the swing to stay outside the shoulder line.** Quite likely, the swing will cross in front of the body. Some bowlers, recognizing the tendency to swing across their body, attempt to twist the body outward. They hope that turning the body outward will counteract the pulling motion of the swing, resulting in the ball rolling toward the target. A successful outcome is doubtful at best.

TIMING CONSIDERATIONS FOR THE MODERN SWING

A true pendulum swings to the same height on both sides. It makes sense that a bowling ball would reach the same height at the top of the backswing as the height of its starting position. However, this rarely the case because of transfer of momentum.

Even with a more traditional (steady shoulder position) swing, the ball ends up higher in the backswing than at its starting position. The body has more mass than the ball. As the bowler starts to walk, some of the body's momentum transfers into the ball, accelerating the swing. This scenario assumes two things:

1. The muscles have disengaged, allowing to truly free swing.
2. The swing motion starts at the correct time in relation to the start of the body motion.

An open-shoulder swing does not create a pendulum through all stages. Instead, the ball position at the top of the swing is much higher than at the start position. Most of the additional height is created by upper-body rotation. (Some of the extra height might come from muscular effort as the bowler pulls the ball back. While not ideal, it is common.)

The swing does not follow a true pendulum rhythm: its arc has been artificially lengthened. A bowler can accommodate this extra motion and still be on time at the release by making one of the following simple adjustments (or perhaps a combination of them):

1. **Slow the initial steps.** Give the ball time to get past the throwing side quickly. Technically, the *initial timing* will be early. It has to be. The swing has to feel like it has a head start in relation to the steps because it has farther to go.

2. **Let the ball fall into the swing quicker.** If the pace of the steps is not slower, then the initial drop into the backswing must be quicker. This is where the *hinge start* (with little or no outward pushaway from the body) of the swing is most effective.

3. **Wait for the ball.** Realize that if everything about the start is on time and the pace of the steps is even, a higher backswing position makes the swing late in relation to the slide. While not easy to do, some bowlers have a knack for being able to hit their finish position well ahead of the ball without forcing the swing to catch up. A long slide, which takes more time, is one way to allow the ball to catch up. Lowering the body also positions you to counterbalance the force of the ball as you wait for it to come through.

CORRECT USE OF THE BALANCE ARM: POSITIONING AND MOVEMENT

The nonthrowing arm functions both as a positioning tool and a counterforce to the swing. The opposite arm extends directly out from the shoulder. Imagine a line that goes straight across the chest from the throwing-side shoulder to the opposite shoulder. The opposite arm, once the pushaway is complete, is an extension of this line.

Position of Opposing Arm

New bowlers should pick a spot and aim for it with the opposing arm. After significant practice, the arm will be trained to move in a particular manner. Where should that spot be? That depends on what the bowler wants the shoulders to do.

Bowlers with conservative backswings should find a spot slightly ahead and below the opposite shoulder position. This promotes a slight opening of the shoulders and an opposite hand position that stays relatively low. When the ball reaches the top of a normal swing, the opposite hand should be between shoulder high and waist high. An opposite arm higher than the shoulder creates an off-balance tilt. If the arm is lower than waist high, it might not extend far enough to act as a counterbalance.

I suggest picking a spot at the foul line and a couple of lanes over. Pointing the opposite arm toward the foul line opens the shoulder position early in the approach, which squares up as the bowler approaches the finish position (figure 5.10). Pointing to the foul line provides a simple mental image and a useful practice technique for bowlers trying to develop a consistent opposing-arm motion.

If the shoulders open up, the opposite arm, as an extension of the shoulders, should increasingly point forward and down as the throwing-side shoulder rotates up and back. Bowlers with high backswings might find the opposite arm pointing toward a spot near the foul line of their own lane or to an area on the floor in front of them.

Finishing Movement of Opposing Arm

The arms work in tandem. As the swing moves up and back, the opposite shoulder and arm move down and forward. At the end of the approach, the pattern changes a little. The shoulders stop moving (for the most part) at the end, but the swing continues on to the follow-through. For bowlers with an aggressive follow-through, the opposite arm needs to continue generating an opposing force. As

Figure 5.10 Point the opposite arm toward the foul line to open the shoulder position.

the throwing arm follows through, the opposing arm extends back. Done correctly, the opposing arm will not pull the shoulders off-line.

To keep the opposite arm from pulling the shoulder off-line at the finish, pay attention to the thumb position of the opposing hand. If the thumb points up when the arm is extended, the arm locks into a fixed position that limits the range of motion. If you pull the arm back as a counterbalance, the entire shoulder line moves with it. With the thumb turned downward, the range of motion at the shoulder increases dramatically. Imagine a swimmer's stroke. The hand turns inward as the arm pulls through the water. This is what a bowler's opposing arm should do as well. An aggressive opposing action of the opposite arm can be brought into play if the thumb is turned down to the correct position (figure 5.11).

Figure 5.11 The thumb of the opposite arm is turned down in the correct position.

DRILLS FOR DEVELOPING THE SWING

The following drills follow a particular order. Each successive drill adds more complexity. If you lose your awareness of a smooth, rhythmic swing as you work through the series of drills, you are not progressing properly.

Some of the drills in this text are based on the training regimen created by Dick Ritger. In the 1970s Mr. Ritger, an outstanding professional bowler, was one of the first to develop a complete training system for the sport of bowling. Although the modern bowler is more likely to open the body, drop the shoulders, and so on than those of Ritger's time, the essential aspects of his training regimen are fundamental to bowler training. As one acclaimed instructor noted, "I don't know where I would be without one- and two-step practice drills."

Learn the feel of a pendulum swing by recognizing the rhythm of the swing and the muscle-free motion. Although a gentle, continuous press against the back of the ball during the downswing creates acceleration, use the technique with caution. Avoid using a muscled swing.

Before starting these drills, be aware of a few guidelines:

- Get comfortable with a swing line next to your body.
- Look at where you want the swing to go instead of swinging to where you are looking.
- Because the ball is wider than the arm, positioning adjustments are essential to swing accuracy.

- The *swing weight* (ball weight accelerated by gravity) creates considerable force. Because the swing weight is on one side of the body, a correct finish position counteracts the swing weight.
- During the drills, do not try to throw harder. Try to be smoother. An increase in ball speed is a natural consequence of body momentum working with swing momentum.

Practice should closely reflect real game situations. Focus on a target for most of these drills. Identify the target at which you intend to roll the ball. Your first concern is not aiming, but rather relaxing and letting the swing take the ball down the lane.

Kneeling Swing Drill 1   Swing Isolation

This is an isolation drill. Once in the correct position for the kneeling drill, you will be able to concentrate on different parts of your game because it eliminates the extra body motion and footwork. This is one of the few times you can watch yourself swing and release the ball. For comfort, place padding under the knee.

Use only the swing to send the ball down the lane. The upper body tilts slightly forward. Avoid moving the shoulders side to side. Be steady. Do not sway back and forth with the swing.

Kneel in front of the foul line, with the throwing-side knee on the ground (figure 5.12). Center the foot opposite your throwing hand (what would be the slide foot) in front of the down knee. The toe of the slide foot

Figure 5.12   Swing isolation drill.

is 2 to 3 inches (5-7.6 cm) from the foul line. Place nonthrowing hand on the knee of the front leg. Keep it there. Position the back knee behind the front foot to clear room for the swing line. For balance, bring the back foot (of kneeling leg) around. Grip the ball and raise the throwing shoulder, bringing the ball off the ground. Angle the body to an open position to help direct the swing toward the target. Slowly swing the ball back and forth, lengthening the swing each time. Feel a slight pulling motion on the way back and a completely relaxed swing on the way forward. Do not take more than three swings or you could lose your grip on the ball. Do not stop the swing. Say to yourself, "Back, relax. Back, relax. Back, release."

Success Check

- Keep the throwing shoulder up.
- Do not swing the ball more than three times.
- Swing the ball in a straight line.

Score Your Success

Swing is a smooth pendulum motion = 2 points

Swing line moves back and forth next to the hip = 2 points

Force of swing does not pull bowler off balance = 2 points

Non-throwing hand stays on knee = 1 point

Ball does not hit floor during the swing = 2 points

Ball is release out past the foul line in a smooth roll = 1 point

Your score _____

Kneeling Swing Drill 2 Blind Bowling

Perform the kneeling swing drill with your eyes closed. Concentrate on the feel of the swing.

Score Your Success

The ball feels heaviest at the bottom of the swing = 1 point

The body position does not move = 1 point

The ball comes off hand after lowest part of downswing = 2 points

The swing feels smooth and relaxed = 2 points

Your score ____

Kneeling Swing Drill 3 Partner Help

This drill teaches the feeling of a correct backswing. Some bowlers are so used to the ball swinging behind the back that a proper swing doesn't feel correct. This drill requires a practice partner.

Partner kneels directly behind bowler. From this position, partner can tell how accurate the swing is. Partner places hands behind bowler's swing shoulder. If swing gets off-line, partner stops swing by catching it with both hands (figure 5.13). If partner stops swing, allow partner to

Figure 5.13 Partner catches the ball if the swing gets off-line.

reposition the swing in line with the shoulder. (This helps bowler feel the difference between a good swing and a misaligned swing.) The partner lets go of the ball so that it will swing forward on a straight line.

Success Check

- Swing line stays close to hip.
- Backswing stays in line with the shoulder.

Score Your Success

Practice five sets of three swings. Score 1 point for each swing that touches partner's hand without needing to be repositioned.

Your score ___

Kneeling Swing Drill 4   Swing Past Towel

While in the kneeling position, place a small towel next to the toe of the slide foot. The towel will be under the path the ball swings along. The end of the towel should extend 6 to 8 inches past where the slide-foot toe is placed. If the bowler is positioned very close to the foul line, the end of the towel will extend past the foul line by a couple of inches. With correct swing acceleration and release position, the ball will swing over the towel and land on the lane past the end of the towel.

If ball hits the towel, work on a longer swing or firmer hand position. Excessive shoulder drop may cause the ball to hit the lane early. If you have to, watch the ball swing through the release zone. The proper positioning and swing elements described for the basic kneeling drill should be emphasized.

Success Check

- Finger pressure is sufficient to support weight of ball.
- Wrist position is firm.
- Long follow-through is smooth to target.
- Ball clears towel and contacts lane 4 to 8 inches (10-20 cm) past toe of slide foot.

Score Your Success

Roll the ball eight times. Score 1 point each time ball clears the towel and half a point for each roll that goes toward identified target.

Your score ___

Swing Drill 1   Watching the Arm Swing

This is an opportunity to watch yourself swing the ball. Keep the swing straight. Imagine a line drawn from the shoulder to the target; the swing will follow through directly down that line. The inside edge of the elbow brushes the hip on the way by. Although this is a swing drill, it is also excellent for working on the release.

Score Your Success

Arm is straight throughout the swing motion = 2 points

Wrist does not change during swing = 2 points

Hand position is behind ball throughout the swing = 2 points

Momentum of the swing carries the ball past the foul line at release = 2 points

Follow-through extends directly out from the shoulder = 2 points

Your score____

Swing Drill 2 — Partner-Guided Swing-Line Practice

This drill can be done from a kneeling position, upright in the proper finish position, or as part of a one-step practice. The practice partner is positioned on bowler's throwing side and guides the bowler's swing.

Partner grasps bowler's arm without interfering with the release. Partner grips forearm at the wrist, with thumb positioned under throwing hand (figure 5.14). Bowler swings ball three times and releases ball on third forward swing Bowler executes five throws, and then switches roles with partner.

Success Check

- Execute a smooth, loose swing.

Score Your Success

Partner grades bowler's execution based on the following criteria:

Swing is smooth and partner feels no resistance = 2 points

Swing is straight and partner does not feel the swing pull away = 2 points

Figure 5.14 Partner grips the forearm at the wrist to guide the swing.

Wrist position stays firm; partner does not feel hand flex back = 1 points

Take five practice throws, earning a maximum of 5 points per throw.

Your score ___

Swing Drill 3   Keeping the Shoulder Level

Because of the weight of the ball, it is expected that the throwing-side shoulder ends up slightly lower than the opposite shoulder at the release. Excessive shoulder drop, though, may indicate improper swing technique or improper finish position.

This drill can be performed from either a kneeling position or upright finish position or as a one-step practice drill. Bowlers can also practice it while performing a normal approach.

Place a soft object such as a folded towel, beanbag, or rosin bag on the throwing shoulder (figure 5.15). If the shoulder drops excessively, the object will slide off. Swing two or three times before releasing the ball. Perform five throws of the ball.

Figure 5.15   Keep the shoulder level so that the beanbag doesn't drop off.

Success Check

- Shoulder level stays even throughout the swing.
- Object does not slip from shoulder during the swing.

Score Your Success

Score 2 points for each swing in which object does not fall from shoulder.

Give yourself 1 bonus point if the object remains on shoulder after the release.

Your score ___ (not including bonus)

Swing Drill 4   Keeping Towel Tucked

Towels can be used as simple and useful practice tools. In this drill they help ensure correct swing position.

Tuck the towel in the armpit on the throwing side (figure 5.16). The towel will drop away if the swing moves out from the body. But gently pressing the towel to the body provides a sense of what a straight swing feels like. (With a high backswing it is likely the towel will drop as the ball goes toward the top of the backswing. That's okay. Be concerned if the towel drops during the pushaway or down drop.) This drill works well from a kneeling position, one in which the swing is normally shorter than during a full approach.

Figure 5.16   Towel is tucked under the throwing arm to help practice using a straight swing.

Success Check

- Towel stays in place during swing.
- Arm gently presses into body.
- Swing is smooth and relaxed.

Score Your Success

Take 10 swings from the kneeling position. Score 1 point each time the towel remains in place during the swing.

Your score ___

Swing Drill 5   Weighted-Ball Catch

Play catch with a partner using a weighted ball. Soft exercise balls in a variety of weights (e.g., 3, 5, and 8 pounds [1.4, 2.3, 3.6 kg]) are easily found in sporting goods areas or stores. The lighter weight allows for repetition without fatigue. Throwing to a partner 10 to 15 feet (3-4.6 m) away develops a strong follow-through and helps correct the tendency to release the ball early.

Perform this drill from a kneeling or upright position or using the one-step practice drill. Take the following safety precautions during this drill. Watch out for errant throws. Pay attention to low ceilings, light fixtures, and so on. Makes sure nobody walks between throwers. Do not throw until your partner is ready. The flight of the ball should be a soft arc, not a hard line drive.

Partner puts hands out ready to catch the ball directly in front of bowler's swing-side shoulder. Thrower swings the ball back and forth two or three times before the release.

Success Check

- The swing makes a long, smooth pendulum motion.
- The ball comes off the hand cleanly.
- The swing goes directly toward the catcher's hands.
- The ball reaches the catcher's hands on the fly.

Score Your Success

Throw the ball back and forth to each other 10 times.

Ball makes it to the catcher in the air = 1 point

Catcher does not have to move hands to catch the ball = 1 point

Your score ___

SUCCESS SUMMARY

This step discussed the arm swing, a complex, yet essential, part of the game. Numerous drills were introduced to develop a proper swing. The emphasis on swing line direction, and the momentum gained from a smooth pendulum, helps the bowler establish essential accuracy while still throwing the ball with power. The firm positioning of the hand behind the ball while keeping the strong acceleration that comes from a long, muscle-free swing all cause the ball to release from the hand consistently with a strong rolling motion. Review your drill scores. Record your scores in the spaces that follow and total them.

SCORING YOUR SUCCESS

Kneeling Swing Drills

1.	Swing Isolation	____ out of 10
2.	Blind Bowling	____ out of 6
3.	Partner Help	____ out of 15
4.	Swing Past Towel	____ out of 12

Swing Drills

1.	Watching the Arm Swing	____ out of 10
2.	Partner-Guided Swing-Line Practice	____ out of 25
3.	Keeping the Shoulder Level	____ out of 10
4.	Keeping Towel Tucked	____ out of 10
5.	Weighted-Ball Catch	____ out of 20
	Total	____ **out of 108**

This step focused on those critical items from the waist up. Arm swing motion, shoulder alignment, and upper-body tilt all contribute to a smooth, accurate swing vital to bowling success. But another contributor, and one that poses challenges to bowling success, is the footwork. In some sports, everything is generated from a stationary position, such as a batter in the batter's box, or a golfer getting ready to drive the ball off the tee. In bowling, the athlete is in motion all the way up to the point of release. Footwork (its direction, speed, and position under the body) is critical to performance. The manner in which the steps move a bowler toward the finish position is an interesting aspect of the game. Footwork is the topic of the next step.

Improving Footwork

Bowling consists of just two major movements: the arm swing and the footwork. The feet are the only part of the body in direct contact with the environment while you bowl. Bowlers with poor footwork rarely seem smooth, relaxed, and rhythmic. They never look comfortable.

Footwork serves as the launching pad for a powerful series of movements, and there should be no wasted motion. Until the elements of footwork and the swing are perfectly blended, nothing else—not the release, not balance, not accuracy—will be reliable.

Foot placement, or step elements, are important to stance, the initial movement, and the finish position. Let's review. The stance includes a staggered foot position. The amount of stagger influences both body alignment and the smoothness of the weight transition in the initial step. An important component of the initial movement is the crossover step. The initial step of the ball-side foot moves in front of the opposite foot. The initial step is like walking on a balance beam: one foot lands directly in front of the other.

For the finish position, the opposite foot crosses in front of the power step for balance and direction. Because a bowler finishes on one foot, that foot needs to be centered under the body. The body doesn't chase the foot. The foot is brought back under the body.

This brief review provides important insights into footwork. There are two crossover steps: an early one that moves out of the way of the swing and the last one that crosses back to get under the body. Let's discuss all aspects of footwork in more detail.

FOOTWORK CHARACTERISTICS

The footwork elements discussed in this section were first described by the eminent writer and instructor Tom Kouros in the landmark book *Par Bowling*. As a whole, it all seems pretty obvious. Yet, his insights may be as enlightening for you now as they were those so many years ago.

The six characteristics of footwork are direction, speed, number of steps, stride length (spacing between steps), rhythm (tempo, or beat, of the steps), and contact angle.

Direction

For the new or intermediate bowler, the concern should be walking in a straight line. By that, I mean a straight line toward the target, not necessarily a straight line down the approach (figure 6.1).

The first step is a slight crossover to facilitate the downswing. Every step after that is made side by side until the slide step. The slide step is a crossover back to the original line. Execute a complete weight transition from the power step onto the slide foot. The body does not chase the foot. The slide step must work its way under the body in order to maintain balance.

An important part of direction is knowing where your slide should finish. The slide position is determined by where you would like to release the ball. Where the swing is in relation to the slide foot varies from bowler to bowler. Bowlers need to determine their *lay-down point*. The *lay-down point* is the distance between your slide foot and the center of the ball at release (figure 6.2). Knowing the lay-down point will help you learn where the slide should be in relation to the target. For example, if two bowlers were aiming for the same target, the bowler with a nine-board lay-down point would expect to slide at a different spot then one with a five-board lay-down point.

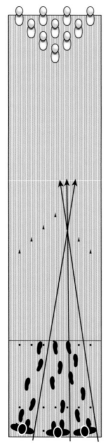

Figure 6.1 Three straight approaches. All align with the same target even though they are not straight down the lane.

Figure 6.2 Lay-down point.

Footwork Drill 1   Determining Lay-Down Point

An observer positioned behind you can easily help determine your lay-down point. For bowlers trying to determine it for themselves, the procedure is fairly straightforward.

You will use the slide foot as the reference point (figure 6.3). For most bowlers, the swing is the same distance from the slide distance on every throw of the ball. If you know where you are sliding, you will also know where the ball is being released from.

When you look down at your slide foot, be sure to use the same point of reference on the foot every time. The part of the foot you use to determine the starting position at the beginning of the approach should be the part you look down at when the slide is finished. Some bowlers use the toe of the shoe. A better reference point is the inside edge of the shoe, next to the big

Figure 6.3   Use slide foot as reference.

toe. That is the part of the shoe closest to the release. For many bowlers, the foot does not point straight ahead on every slide. If the heel turns in or out, the toe points out or in. This makes using the toe as a reference point less reliable.

Success Check

- Complete normal throw of the ball.
- Make sure slide foot is in steady position.
- Hold body in finish position.
- Let swing arm relax and hang down from shoulder.
- Bend knees and lower body until hand touches lane surface.

Score Your Success

Perform this drill three times. Average of all three attempts is your lay-down point.

Identify reference point on slide shoe = 1 point

Identify board number on part of lane directly under middle finger of swing arm = 1 point

Count number of boards between shoe reference point and lane board = 1 point

Your score _____

To see how knowing your lay-down point helps with strategy decisions, let's consider a simple example. A bowler has a six-board lay-down point. The initial strategy is to start and finish the approach on board 16 and release at the 10th board. The bowler uses the second arrow for targeting and decides to move the starting position four boards left while keeping the same target on the lane (second arrow, 10th board).

It is 30 feet (9 m) from the back of the approach to the target arrows. Also, it is 15 feet (4.6 m) from the back of the approach to the foul line (half the distance). If the bowler adjusts four boards left at the beginning, how far over would he or she be at the foul line? Two boards left, half the amount. That means that on the next throw of the ball, the bowler expects to slide on the 18th board, anticipating the release to pass over the 12th board.

Speed

Foot speed influences overall ball velocity. Frequently, the initial step is slower to allow a smooth weight transition and a relaxed start. Once in motion, the bowler then strives for a smooth, continuous acceleration to the line. New bowlers should first determine the quickness of the rhythm of their natural swing, then let the pace of the swing dictate the speed of the footwork. Count out the speed of the swing, and then try to match the speed of the steps to the pace of the swing count.

The ability to adjust ball speed is an important adjustment skill. Adjusting footwork speed is a useful way to vary ball speed. Determining how quickly the ball moves into the swing relative to how fast you choose to walk is an important skill to practice.

Ultimately, how fast you walk depends on your ability to control the stop at the slide. Do not run up so fast you lose control at the finish. Conversely, do not make the approach a slow, mechanical march to the line. The approach is neither a stiff, plodding march nor an all-out sprint. Proper footwork is like a fast dance—quick and smooth, powerful and precise.

To achieve a proper finish, emphasize a good knee bend and a smooth slide. The knee is the shock absorber for the approach, absorbing some of its force. The long, soft slide is the braking action; bring the body to a smooth stop. When using faster footwork, emphasize enough knee bend to maintain balance and expect a longer slide.

Number of Steps

Now things get interesting. The number of steps a bowler uses influences timing. Timing is the relationship between the swing and the steps (and will be discussed in detail in another step). There are four parts to the swing from the start until the release: extension, down drop, backswing, and downswing. (The follow-through is what happens after the steps are done and the ball has been released). To provide enough time for the swing to complete its full motion, it makes sense to have at least four steps in the approach.

How many steps should you use? Do what comes naturally. We are all wired a little differently from each other. If moving the opposite foot first seems natural, you will have a five-step approach. Whenever the initial step and the slide step are on the same foot, there will be an odd number of steps in the footwork. If you prefer the ball-side foot to move first, you'll use four steps. The split between the numbers of bowlers using four steps versus five is pretty even.

On occasion one sees a three-step approach. Bowlers using three steps are almost always better off learning to use five. Why would a three-step approach convert to a five-step more easily? The three-stepper is used to moving the opposite foot first. A five-step approach will allow them to continue to do this.

Stride Length

Some bowlers prefer relatively even spacing, with a relaxed, consistent rhythm from start to finish. This is not necessarily a bad practice. The beginning bowler may find it easier to learn, and it promotes consistent speed. The emphasis is on a relaxed, smooth pace. When all the steps are evenly spaced, acceleration to the foul line may not be strong. The footwork is paced like the "tick, tick, tick" of a watch or metronome.

Most bowlers, though, will vary the length of each step. Earlier, you were reminded of a few aspects of the starting motion and the finish. To promote a smooth, easy weight transition at the start, the first step is usually short. (Maybe not a baby step, but definitely shorter than a normal stride). For the five-step approach, the initial two steps are short. If the finish motion emphasizes a short power step before the slide, we now have a step spacing particular to the sport of bowling. A four-step approach can be described as short, long, short, long (figure 6.4a). A five-step approach is described as short, short, long, short, long (figure 6.4b).

UNDERSTANDING THE POWER STEP

Many bowlers use the next-to-last step as a means to add drive into the finish. This type of step is called the *power step*.

Keeping the power step short keeps the drive foot (the right foot for a right-handed bowler) under the body. This puts the body weight slightly forward, over the ball of the drive foot. From this position, with the knee well flexed, the bowler can push off strongly into the slide step.

The power step is the last opportunity to add body momentum to the overall velocity of the ball. It has to be taken at just the right time. If it is too early, the body launches for-

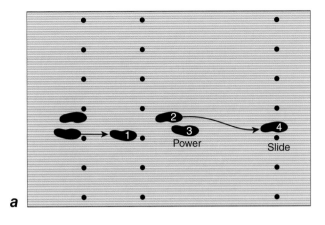

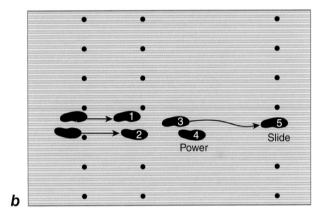

Figure 6.4 *(a)* Stride length for four-step approach and *(b)* stride length for five-step approach.

ward while the swing is still going back; if it is too late, it does not contribute to ball speed.

This leads to the question—when does the power step push off? Although timing will be more fully discussed in another step, we cannot talk about footwork without mentioning timing. If the pace of the steps properly matches the pace of the swing, the ball will reach the top of the backswing at the end of the next-to-last step. At this point, the ball is ready to swing forward, and the power step drives forward with it. The acceleration of the body from the power step starts slightly ahead of the start of the downswing. It will feel as if the swing is following along. The power step is not easy to implement if a bowler has poor timing. While potentially useful for beginning bowlers, other elements of the game must be in place before the bowler can emphasize the power step. Beginning bowlers should focus on a shorter next-to-last step as a positioning tool. They should be concerned first about keeping the hips on line to the target and the body balanced over the foot before the slide.

Another aspect of a shorter next-to-last step is the position of the body relative to the swing. The short power step works with the mechanics of the swing. When the ball reaches the top of the backswing, the leg on the throwing side is forward. You cannot produce a backswing of significant height with a long stride into the next-to-last step. The body is too stretched out. Most experienced bowlers shorten the next-to-last step even if they are not aware they are doing it.

Furthermore, a shortened step allows for a forward position of the body—the foot is under the body instead of ahead of it—which counterbalances the pull of the backswing. By shortening the step, the swing can go higher without creating excessive tension on the throwing side of the body. It puts the body in a stronger position, ready to move forward as the downswing comes forward.

Increasing the ball's speed generates more pin action. Additionally, the technology of bowling balls creates very strong hook potential. That very same technology causes the balls to rapidly remove oil from the lane. Increasing ball speed is one strategy to counteract the extra friction encountered on quickly changing lane conditions. Simply put, the modern bowling game emphasizes power, speed, and hook. Generating ball speed is an important factor for potential success. Two ways to increase ball speed are a higher backswing and faster acceleration of the steps. A short power step helps both of these.

Bowlers do not need to put a lot of power into the power step, however. Sometimes the short step is used only for positioning—getting ready for the finish—without trying to generate extra drive. Practice varying the force of the power step, sometimes driving hard, other times stepping much softer. You may not always need the power, but it's nice to know it is there.

HOW STRIDE LENGTH AFFECTS ALIGNMENT

In the setup, the throwing side of the body is slightly preset to accommodate the swing. Wouldn't it be nice if the hips and the shoulders could keep their preset angle with minimal movement during the approach?

The alternating length of the steps in a short, long, short, long walking pattern helps maintain correct positioning throughout the approach. If the first step is short, the hips will stay in the open position, minimizing awkward forward movement of the throwing-side hip. Two things happen with the longer second step. First, the hips stay open, creating room for the swing to pass by. Second, the longer step takes more time, allowing the swing to pass by the throwing-side hip and leg before that leg starts moving forward into the next step.

The next short step, the power step, has a positioning function as well. Again, the hips stay open. The open hip allows a longer swing. The short step becomes a base for power and balance. If the power step is too long, the bowler may not be able to transfer the weight forward into the slide. Also, the bowler will need to more dramatically kick the leg and open the hip to provide clearance for the swing.

Rhythm

Rhythm is sometimes referred to as cadence. Counting out the beat of the steps is similar to counting out the beat in music. Determine the rhythm of the footwork from the pacing of the swing. The swing has a "one, two, one, two" or "out, down, back, down" beat to it. Feel for the downbeat. The downbeat is felt from the weight of the ball, which feels heaviest at the bottom of the swing.

The swing moves out on a short step, then down on a longer one, back up on a short step, then back down on the long slide step. Although the pace of the steps may have an inherent meter, or timing pattern, do not try to force the rhythm by pausing between beats. The swing is a continuous, fluid movement; the footwork is as well.

Contact Angle

Contact angle is the tilt of the foot when the step lands. It can be heel first, toe first, or flat. The degree of the heel-to-toe gait influences the smoothness of the footwork. The normal walking pattern of heel, toe, heel, toe needs to be slightly modified for bowling.

The bowler does not want to overemphasize either initial heel contact or initial toe contact. During most of the approach, if the heel plants too firmly, the footwork will not be as smooth as it should be. This frequently happens when the bowler's stride is too long and the knees lock out when the leg is fully extended. Conversely, if the toe strikes first, the bowler may tend to lean forward. If the body starts leaning too far forward, the footwork has to be hurried in order to catch up—possibly limiting a chance for a controlled, well-balanced finish. The feet should make full contact with the floor, at least temporarily, to promote balance and control.

Good footwork incorporates a shufflelike step. It is not a true shuffle step—the foot does lift completely off the ground, and the heel does strike the floor a little sooner than the rest of the foot. Imagine a rolling step. The weight rolls onto the heel at contact, then rolls off the toes at release. Attempt to distribute the weight smoothly along the length of the foot during the stride.

Some bowlers have used shuffle steps in their approaches with great success. With a true shuffle step, the foot remains flat. The steps glide along the approach. The stride length for bowlers who use shuffle steps is usually shorter; the feet are under the body promoting a sense of balance. The bowler may be able to generate fast foot speed while still feeling in control.

FOUR-STEP APPROACH

On the first step of the four-step approach, the leg on the throwing side moves first (figure 6.5a). The first step is short and smooth, and the stride should be easy to repeat. The whole body moves forward with the first step. Once the foot is firmly planted, the body is centered over the foot.

If you want a faster approach, use a shuffle step. Quickly transfer your body weight to the ball of the foot. If you want a slower approach, let the heel strike first, and transfer your body weight to the ball of the foot more slowly.

The knee is flexed slightly on the first step. The knees stay slightly flexed throughout the approach. Do not stride out so far as to force the knee to lock out.

The second step of the four-step approach is slightly longer than the first (figure 6.5b). The second step is more like a normal walking step. Again, do not let the stride get too far ahead of the body. Smoothly transfer your body weight from one foot to the other. Maintain a slight flexion at the knees.

The third step is short (figure 6.5c). The foot stays under the body. Again, be sure this step does not get too far ahead of the body. Transfer your body weight onto the ball of your foot. You should feel your body centered over the ball of the foot. The knee is flexed to about 45 degrees. As your body weight passes over the ball of your foot, push off directly forward.

On the fourth step, the toe of the slide foot glides along the approach (figure 6.5d). The slide step begins with toe contact. As the body weight transfers forward, the heel makes contact. Turn the heel inward to guide the slide under the center of your body.

The closer the footwork approaches a heel-to-toe gait, however, the more it will feel like normal walking steps. A walking gait uses an obvious heel strike, foot plant, and toe release. This may be more comfortable for a beginning bowler to learn. The stride may be a little longer, and it will frequently be more methodical. Bowlers preferring an obvious heel-to-toe walking gait are more likely to feel the heel strike, making it easier to count out the rhythm. Each step becomes a beat in the cadence of the approach. This helps a bowler learn timing. He or she can better feel for each position of the swing that coincides with each particular step of the approach.

Figure 6.5 **FOUR-STEP APPROACH**

First Step

1. The leg on the throwing side moves first.
2. Step is short and smooth. The stride should be easy to repeat. The whole body moves forward with the first step, and the weight is centered on the foot at the end of the step.
3. The knee is flexed slightly on the first step.

Second Step

1. This step is slightly longer than the first, more like a normal walking step.
2. Do not let the stride get too far ahead of the body.
3. Smoothly transfer body weight from one foot to the other.

Third Step: Power Step

1. The third step is short.
2. The foot stays under the body. Be sure this step does not get too far ahead of the body.
3. Transfer body weight onto the ball of the foot.
4. Feel the body centered over the ball of the foot.
5. Flex knee to about 45 degrees.
6. As body weight passes over the ball of the foot, push off directly forward.

Fourth Step

1. The toe of the slide foot glides along the approach.
2. The slide step begins with toe contact.
3. As the body weight transfers forward, the heel makes contact.
4. Turn the heel inward to guide the slide under the center of the body.

For some people, the four-step approach feels a little mechanical. As soon as the foot goes forward, the swing starts forward. The start may feel uncomfortably abrupt for some bowlers. Some bowlers feel more comfortable when the body moves before the swing does. These bowlers may prefer the five-step approach.

Varying Foot Speed Through Changing Step Height

Fast feet stay close to the floor, while slow steps are frequently higher. If you know you get to the line too quickly to maintain reasonable control, try raising your steps. Imagine a small object in front of your foot that you must step over. This slight change will do a lot to slow a bowler.

Among bowlers with very quick approach footwork, the difference between initial heel contact and the rest of the foot's contact is often very slight. But, the heel often makes the initial contact with each step. Regardless of whether you are raising the steps to promote a slower, more methodical footwork or keeping the steps low like a rapid shuffle, the slide step is the exception. The slide step is the one step of the approach in which the toe must make contact first. If the toe contacts first, the foot will glide in for a smooth landing. Then as the heel contacts the approach, the bowler will enjoy a smooth, gradual stop. This long, smooth braking action helps the bowler control the body during the release phase of the swing.

An abrupt stop, caused by planting the heel on the approach first, results in two immediate negative effects. First, trying to stop the momentum of the approach too quickly sacrifices balance at the line. The foot will plant, but the body will keep going. A long slide absorbs some of the energy of the approach and allows most of that energy to transfer into the swing. Those bowlers who have

(continued)

Varying Foot Speed Through Changing Step Height *(continued)*

a tendency to stand up at the line or step away from the shot often do so because they plant the heel first on the slide step.

Second, an abrupt stop disrupts the fluid mechanics of the swing. The swing will jerk forward, just as the body jerks forward. Not only will the swing move off-line, but also the release will be less consistent. Consistent footwork leads to a consistent swing and release.

One way to ensure a toe-first slide is to keep the slide foot on the ground when taking the last step (figure 6.6*a*). As the toe of the slide foot moves forward into the last step, glide it along the floor, and then point it into the slide (figure 6.6*b*).

Figure 6.6   *(a)* Don't lift slide foot completely on last step and *(b)* glide to a long approach.

FIVE-STEP APPROACH

The five-step approach isn't much different from the four-step approach. Bowlers who are more comfortable with moving the foot opposite of the throwing arm choose the five-step approach. Many inexperienced bowlers are not aware of which foot they move first; they simply start walking. The first step of the approach is largely unconscious, and it makes no sense to go against natural inclination. If a bowler tends to move the opposite foot first, the approach will start and finish on the same foot. This requires an odd number of steps—five steps instead of four.

Once the throwing-side leg moves, in this case on the second step, the arm swing begins as well. The five-step approach is exactly like the four-step approach except for the extra initial step. This initial step gets the body moving just before the ball starts moving into the swing.

Perhaps the only real advantage of a five-step approach is that the initial step gets the body moving. The transfer of the body weight forward leads into the weight transfer of the ball that comes during the pushaway. This starts everything—the ball, the feet, and the body—moving forward smoothly and consistently.

Figure 6.7   FIVE-STEP APPROACH

First Step

1. Step with foot opposite the throwing arm.
2. Step is short and smooth.
3. Entire body moves forward with step.
4. Body is centered over foot as step is finished.
5. Knees stay slightly flexed.

Second Step

1. Leg on throwing side moves.
2. Step is short and smooth.
3. Stride is easy to repeat.
4. Entire body moves forward with the step.
5. Body is centered over foot once foot is firmly planted.
6. Knees remain slightly flexed.

Third Step

1. Step is slightly longer than first step.
2. Step is more like a normal walking step.
3. Stride should not get too far ahead of the body.
4. Weight transfer from one foot to the other is smooth.
5. Knee is slightly flexed.

(continued)

Figure 6.7 *(continued)*

Fourth Step

1. Next-to-last step is short.
2. Foot stays under body.
3. Step does not get too far ahead.
4. Weight transfers onto ball of foot.
5. Body is centered over ball of foot.
6. Knee is flexed to about 45 degrees.
7. As body weight passes over ball of foot, push-off is directly forward.

Fifth Step

1. Toe of slide foot glides along approach.
2. Slide step begins with toe contact.
3. As body weight transfers forward, heel makes contact.
4. Heel turns inward to guide slide under center of body.

FOOTWORK TROUBLESHOOTING

Fixing footwork problems is not always easy. For many people, the way they walk is as unique as their signature or fingerprints. The unbalancing effect of the swing also influences footwork. Sometimes ball position or swing line may be as much a cause of approach problems as the way a bowler walks. Nevertheless, with patience and diligent practice, a bowler can learn smoother, more accurate footwork.

MISSTEP

The tempo is inconsistent, with hesitations and accelerations.

CORRECTION

Walk at a tempo as consistent as possible and correct obvious changes in the pace of the footwork. Count a rhythm in your head to emphasize proper tempo.

MISSTEP

The steps are choppy or erratically spaced.

CORRECTION

Eliminate short steps or extralong strides. These change the pace of the footwork, causing pauses or accelerations that disturb the smooth progress of the steps. A step that is excessively longer or shorter than any other step often indicates a tempo problem.

Allow for natural acceleration to the foul line. Don't become tentative or tight as you enter the slide step.

The difference in the stride length in the short, long, short, long pattern is not as dramatic as you might think. However, bowlers who are struggling to even out the tempo of their steps may need to work on keeping all their steps about the same length.

MISSTEP

Steps veer dramatically off-line.

CORRECTION

Try keeping the feet together and moving directly forward by brushing the heels of your shoes together as the feet pass each other (figure 6.8). This will keep the feet together and moving in a straight line.

Figure 6.8 Heels brush against each other as the feet pass.

Footwork Drill 2   Isolation Step Placement

After each step you will pause briefly before moving to the next step. Keep your hands behind your back. Do not use a ball or arm swing.

Concentrate solely on the direction, spacing, and balance of each step. Perform 10 to 15 practice approaches. Afterward, slowly increase the pace of the steps until there is no longer a pause. You can still watch your steps, seeing the placement and spacing, while working toward a normal footwork speed.

TO INCREASE DIFFICULTY

- Perform drill with eyes close while keeping hands behind your back. Without visual distractions, the emphasis is on the feel of each step. Concentrate on the position and length of the steps.
- Increase speed of steps. Slowly increase the speed of each practice approach until you can complete the footwork of a normally paced approach with your eyes closed.

Success Check

- Steps are smooth and natural.
- Steps follow short-long pattern if preferred.
- The next-to-last step is short.
- The slide step goes toward the visual target.

Score Your Success

Well-balanced foot placement after each paused step = 2 points

Smooth weight transfer on each step = 2 points

Knees stay slightly flexed during each step = 1 point

Your score _____

The remaining footwork drills follow a specific regimen.

- Do the first drills without a ball.
- Then, practice with the ball cradled in both hands to get used to the weight.
- Do not try a drill using a normal approach and swing and roll of the ball until you have reliably performed the practice without a ball.

The following drills are appropriate for both a four-step and a five-step approach. Enlist the help of an experienced coach or trustworthy fellow bowler. People rarely watch themselves walk. It may be difficult to determine whether effective changes are occurring. An extra pair of eyes is frequently beneficial.

Footwork Drill 3   Walk the Line

Pay close attention to the board on the lane your opposite foot is on in the stance. Place a marker (tape, towel, or piece of paper) in front of the throwing-side foot. Put a second marker 3 to 5 feet (1-1.5 m) ahead of the first one. This should be about where you expect the third step to be. Put third marker at the end of the approach on the same board as the one the opposite foot starts on.

Perform this test without a ball first. Do not use a normal approach or swing the ball until you can consistently score 9 or 10 points on practice footwork.

TO DECREASE DIFFICULTY

- Walk more slowly, feeling for the placement of each step.
- Watch your step. Look down while walking until confident in the step placement.

TO INCREASE DIFFICULTY

- Walk at different angles on the lane by pointing the feet in different directions.

Success Check

- Each step is next to the appropriate marker.
- Body is balanced over feet with every step, with no excessive side-to-side sway.
- Slide step ends in front of predetermined finishing point.

Score Your Success

The first step is to the inside of the marker, not on it = 2 points

Second step is straight forward, moving past the ball-side foot = 1 point

Third step is right next to the second marker, again, not on it = 2 points

Last step (slide) finishes directly in front of third step = 2 points

Your score _____

Footwork Drill 4   Stride-Length Practice

You can practice this drill with or without a partner. Without a partner, you will need to place a marker (towel, pad) on the lane next to where each step should land. You will need one marker for each step you take.

Place the markers at the distance appropriate to the length for each stride. A marker will be to right of each right-foot placement and to the left of each left-foot step. You are boxing yourself in. The position of each marker must be appropriate for the footwork spacing you want to practice.

Make sure your body is centered over your foot after each step. Emphasize the short–long pattern. Watch each step land next to the appropriate marker. On the next-to-last step, feel the drive leg take the body's weight before pushing off. Point the toe of the slide foot to develop a better slide. Practice turning the heel in to develop a slide that moves under the body. Practice 8 to 10 times while watching the feet land next to each marker.

TO INCREASE DIFFICULTY

- Keep eyes focused ahead. Look down only after each step to see whether the feet landed next to the appropriate marker.
- Have a partner watch your approach. Walk through the approach at normal speed. Partner will say "Yes!" each time a step lands next to the proper mark and "No!" each time a step misses. Stop the footwork on the first no. Start over. Repeat footwork until every step is a yes.
- Increase the pace of the footwork.

Success Check

- Steps are smooth and natural.
- Steps follow short–long pattern if preferred.
- The next-to-last step is short.
- The slide step goes toward the visual target.

Score Your Success

Each step lands next to the designated guide = 4 points (1 point × 4 steps)

Drill performed a normal footwork speed = 2 points

Approach has a smooth, rhythmic look from start to finish = 2 points

Slide foot is centered under body at finish = 2 points

Your score ___

Footwork Drill 5   Evaluating Footwork

Ask a qualified instructor or experienced bowler to analyze your footwork while you are bowling normally. Earn points based on the following criteria.

Success Check

- Steps are smooth and rhythmic.
- Body feels well balanced and firmly set over the foot after each step.
- Leg push from power step is strong.
- Slide step moves under body to a center position.
- When footwork done, body is balanced over the slide foot.

Score Your Success

Overall footwork direction is toward target = 2 points

Footwork has a smooth rhythm = 1 point

Initial ball-side step is a slight cross-over = 2 points

Knees are slightly flexed and never lock during a step = 1 point

Steps use a soft heel-to-toe gait = 1 point

Next-to-last step is short, positioned under body = 3 points

Strong push-off into the slide is evident = 2 points

Toe touches the lane first on the slide step = 2 points

Slide step crosses over and finishes under center of the body = 2 points

Your score _____

SUCCESS SUMMARY

The feet stay under the body for balance while driving the body forward for power. This is not as easy as it sounds. Sure, we all know how to walk, but can we learn how to walk with power? Keep a consistent rhythm in the footwork. Make sure every step is toward the target. Think of the footwork as a smooth transfer of energy that brings the body along with the swing.

Review your drill scores. Record your scores in the spaces that follow and total them. If you score at least 40 points, you are ready to move on to the next step. If you score fewer than 40 points, review the sections that are giving you trouble, then repeat the drills.

SCORING YOUR SUCCESS

Footwork Drills

1. Determining the Lay-Down Point   ____ out of 3

2. Isolation Step Placement   ____ out of 5

3. Walk the Line   ____ out of 7

4. Stride-Length Practice   ____ out of 10

5. Evaluating Footwork   ____ out of 16

Total   **____ out of 41**

The proper placement and pace of the steps allow a bowler to generate power without sacrificing consistency and control. A smooth, balanced approach is an important element of the game, but at some point, the bowler needs to throw the ball. The goal of all bowlers is to flawlessly blend the pace of the steps with the rhythm of the swing. Coordinating the motion of the swing with those of the steps is the topic of the next step.

Coordinating the Approach

Coordinating the footwork with the swing effortlessly generates power. Swing momentum combined with body momentum generates the speed necessary for effective pin action. In addition, proper coordination gets the bowler to the line with the correct alignment that produces consistency and accuracy. Coordinating the swing with the footwork is referred to as *timing.*

The preparation of the *stance* as well as aspects of the *start motion* and *initial timing* have been introduced in previous steps. The *finish position* and terminal timing have also been discussed in previous steps. All that is left is tying the beginning and end together. Intermediary timing should come about naturally if other skills of the game are well practiced. This raises the question, "why discuss overall timing at all?"

Much can go wrong between the start and the finish. When steps get off-line or the swing is unreliable, we need to determine the cause. By knowing the proper relationship between the full motion of the swing and all of the steps of the approach, one can better understand the exact point at which things might be going wrong.

GENERATING POWER

Many bowlers have a misconception of how power is generated. Many take what they are familiar with in other sports and try to apply the same movement to bowling. Take, for instance, a baseball pitcher. When throwing a ball, the leg drive leads into the hip turn, which leads into the shoulder turn. The upper body's rotation transfers to the arm, the upper arm in particular. The whole movement terminates with the wrist snap at the release. Ball speed is a result of angular momentum, generated when each segment accelerates the next.

Bowling is a little different. Number one, the bowler's arm and ball swing like a pendulum; the ball is not thrown along a straight line. Number two, the weight of a bowling ball prevents it from accelerating in the same manner as a baseball does. It is impossible to throw a bowling ball like you would a baseball.

Most of a bowling ball's speed comes from two sources: gravity (making the ball fall along the swing) and momentum (where the speed of the body transfers into the ball). There is an interesting concept called *conservation of momentum.* Let's say you are in a car, and the driver suddenly puts on the brakes. What happens to all the passengers? They are thrown forward. That is why we wear seat belts. When a bowler comes to a stop at the end of the approach, the speed of the body transfers to the ball, and the ball accelerates.

Additional power can be generated by rotating the shoulders back and forth, the core rotation mentioned in earlier steps. But, this should make little or no contribution. Rotating the shoulders is a way to get the ball higher, which allows gravity to do more work. The rotation of the shoulder does not accelerate the swing. Forcefully rotating the shoulders to accelerate the ball produces unreliable results.

Do not pull the shoulder back and forth as a means to accelerate the swing!

Let's consider the accuracy requirements of bowling. The strike pocket is only 2 to 3 inches (5-7.6 cm) wide. The center of the ball must drive through that 2- to 3-inch window at pin contact, or a strike will be unlikely. The strike pocket is 60 feet (18 m) from the foul line. This is equivalent to a golfer hitting a 60-foot putt, consistently driving a 250-yard (229 m) tee shot down a fairway 10 yards (9 m) wide, or a pitcher trying to throw strikes over a plate 3 inches wide. The bowler needs to temper the desire for power to accommodate the sport's demand for accuracy.

Power must be delivered with great precision. The movements that create the force must be finely controlled. Synchronizing the footwork with the swing generates force while addressing the need for precision. Timing lies at the heart of bowling success.

TIMING

As the braking action of the slide slows the approach, the body momentum generated by foot speed transfers into the free-moving swing, accelerating the swing toward the release point. If the timing is off at this point, the result is a loss of momentum.

The body momentum is wasted before it can transfer into the swing. When bowlers have *late timing*, they get to the finish ahead of the swing. The momentum of the steps is gone before the swing is in position to come forward. Sometimes the result is a weakly thrown ball that misses wide. Other bowlers attempt to force the swing to catch up by pulling the shoulder through. This forceful effort diminishes consistency as well as accuracy.

When a bowler exhibits *early timing*, the ball gets to the release before the footwork is done. Again, this results in a loss of momentum. The ball is already off the hand before the momentum of the footwork can contribute.

Characteristics of Timing Errors

With ideal timing, the momentum of the swing carries the ball out onto the lane, smoothly rolling it off the hand. With very late timing, the ball frequently falls off the hand early in the downswing.

LATE TIMING

In cases of late timing, the momentum of the body stops before the swing has brought the ball to the release point (figure 7.1). Other signs of late timing include the following:
- Pulling up at the line and using the legs to finish the shot
- Muscling the swing (pulling the swing through)
- A shortened backswing (The later the swing starts in relation to the feet, the less time there is to complete a full, natural pendulum swing.)

Figure 7.1 Late timing causes the slide to finish before the hand is ready to release the ball.

Figure 7.2 In early timing, the ball is ahead of the body and ready to be released before the slide is finished.

EARLY TIMING

With early timing, the ball reaches the release point before the footwork finishes (figure 7.2). The last bit of momentum from the footwork cannot transfer into the swing because the swing finishes before the steps do.

- The swing arrives at the release point before the slide foot moves under the body. The body is often off balance when the release occurs.
- When the body is not in a stable position, the release is ineffective.
- Bowlers with early timing often struggle to hold their finish position. They may even take an extra step after the release.
- A lack of momentum and an off-balanced finish may cause bowlers to drop the ball.
- When the ball arrives at the release point early, it pulls the shoulder forward and down, causing the swing to cross the body.

Athletes feel powerful when they can get their feet under them. A throw is more effective when there is a chance to plant the feet and then drive with the legs and the hips while throwing the ball. Although not as dramatic as a football or baseball throw, there is still a subtle plant-and-throw sensation when bowling. For true power players, the action is decidedly plant and fire.

Other Footwork Elements Affecting Timing

Footwork has a variety of aspects that influence how smoothly a bowler coordinates the pace of the steps with the rhythm of the swing. While initial timing is critical to getting things working together from the very first step, other aspects of footwork must be considered when creating for yourself an effective and repeatable physical performance.

PACING

For perfect step–swing synchronization, consider the pace and size of the steps in the footwork pattern. Swing practice drills will help you develop a sense of the swing's rhythm and pace. Close attention to the footwork is needed to improve step–swing synchronization.

First, the footwork must contain enough steps that the swing can complete its full motion. If the number of steps is even, then the approach starts with the foot on the same side as the throwing arm. If an odd number of steps are used, then the foot on the nonthrowing side starts the approach. Second, in all footwork patterns, the foot opposite the throwing hand must take the last (slide) step. This is essential for balance. Third, the approach usually contains at least four steps. Some bowlers prefer to take five. Fewer than four rushes the swing, forcing it to play catch-up with the footwork. More than five steps makes timing difficult as well.

Finally, with every step of the approach, the body is centered over the feet. At no point is a step too far in front of the body, nor does the body lean out in front of the foot. The balance line established in the stance does not change during the approach. Balance while in motion is a key characteristic of skilled performance.

FOUR-STEP APPROACH

Remember the four phases of the swing? Each phase matches a corresponding step. The last phase of the swing is the follow-through. With proper timing, the footwork stops before the follow-through.

Because the arm swing is made of up four parts, the four-step approach is the most basic step pattern for synchronizing the steps with the swing (figure 7.3). The four steps match the swing phases in this manner:

1. First step—pushaway
2. Second step—down drop
3. Third step—backswing
4. Fourth step (with slide)—downswing

The following are guidelines discussed in previous steps.

- Initiate the approach smoothly without lurching forward.
- Set feet in a staggered starting position.
- Slightly rock back onto the heel of the back foot, and then gently shift your weight forward onto the ball of the front foot.
- As the weight transfers forward, you will feel the need to take a step. Push the ball away as you take that step.

The stride-length pattern for the four-step approach is short, long, short, long. The step pattern matches the rhythm, or beat, of the swing: out, down, back, down. Each long step matches a downbeat in the swing. The first step of the four-step approach is short and smooth and initiates the pattern and the rhythm of the overall movement. If done properly, the first step promotes a relaxed weight transfer of the body synchronized with the weight transfer of the ball.

Figure 7.3   SWING AND FOOTWORK: FOUR-STEP APPROACH

First Step: Ball Starts Into the Swing

1. The initial step is smooth. Glide the foot along the lane. Keep the knee slightly flexed.
2. The extension of the arm is slightly longer than the step; the arm is not fully extended yet.
3. The initial step is long enough to get ahead of the body's center of mass but not ahead of the ball. For a smooth weight transition into the next step, the center of mass will pass over the base of support (the foot) gradually.

Second Step: Swing Brings Ball Down Past Bottom of Swing Arc

1. Use a normal stride
2. The swing comes down and the arm fully extends.
3. Keep head still and upper body steady. Head does not follow the swing.

Third Step: Swing Brings Ball Back to Top of Backswing

1. Take a short third step.
2. Flex the front knee. The throwing-side leg must be in a strong position in order to drive forward just as the swing moves forward. To perform a strong drive into the slide, the knee should bend at close to a 45-degree angle.
3. Feel your hips drop as the body sets up for a drop and drive into the last step.
4. Transfer your weight onto the ball of the foot. Feel the ball of the foot and toes dig in.
5. Swing to the top of the backswing.
6. Maintain the balance line over your foot.

Fourth Step (With Slide): Swing Brings Ball Down to and Through the Release Zone

1. The slide foot works its way under the body.
2. The body maintains balance over the slide foot.
3. The back leg sweeps behind the body, out of the way of the downswing.
4. The downswing starts forward just as the last step begins.
5. The last step touches the floor toe first, slightly ahead of the swing.
6. The slide finishes just before the swing gets to the release point.
7. The body is stable and balanced just before the release.

Because the body is constantly moving, the center of mass should pass over the base of support. The heel should strike just ahead of the center of mass. If the step is too short, the center of mass will be ahead of the base of support, and the bowler will have to hurry the second step to regain balance. As the body moves forward, it will pass over the base of support established by the foot. As the center of mass passes beyond the foot, it is time for another step.

The second step is long, but still smooth and balanced. By long, I mean the step is about as long as a normal walking step. Do not overstride. As the leg on the non-throwing side moves forward, there should be enough time for the swing to pass the throwing-side leg.

With the leg on the nonthrowing side forward and the leg on the throwing side back, the hips are in an open position. This presents a smaller target to swing around.

A bowler with late timing may notice the throwing-side leg is moving forward into the third step before the swing has passed it. Now we have a situation where two things are trying to pass each other going different directions. The swing is going back while the throwing-side leg is stepping forward. Hmm. That ain't gonna work.

The bowler with late timing is left with one of two choices, neither of which is ideal. Cross the third step in front of the body to move it around the swing or change the swing line to avoid bumping into the throwing-side leg. In one case the bowler won't walk straight and in the other he or she can't keep the swing straight. Often, the bowler makes those adjustments without being aware of them.

Learn to evaluate your timing, and try to fix errors before they become too habitual to easily change. Recognize problems and correct them immediately, no matter how uncomfortable or weird the new technique may feel initially.

The first and third steps are the most important in the approach. The first step initiates a smooth, consistent start. The third step sets up a strong finish. Step three is a short power step. A short third step accommodates the stretch from the backswing.

With proper four-step timing, the swing reaches the top of the backswing on the third step. If the third step is long, the leg on the throwing side will be too far forward just as the swing is at maximum extension on the way back. The bowler will feel stretched out.

At this point, many bowlers feel the urge to put something extra into the shot. Resist that urge. Do not ruin the careful preparation and smooth movement by forcing the shot through.

Now you are hitting the landing. With a toe-first contact, the foot will slide smoothly. As the heel contacts the floor, the braking action starts. This is when the deceleration of the slide causes a smooth, yet strong, acceleration of the swing.

The throwing-side leg makes a strong push-and-sweep motion. Keep the hips down as the body drives forward. Because of the knee bend going into the third step (you did bend your knees on the next-to-last step, didn't you?), you will not experience an exaggerated drop into the last step. Let the ball fall through the downswing next to the throwing-side leg.

Remember the most important characteristics of the four-step approach:

- Maintain the short, long, short, long walking pattern.
- The rhythm of the step—a strong one-two-one-two beat—matches the rhythm of in the swing's pendulum motion.
- In general, use a heel-to-toe walking gait. Be careful, though. Do not march up to the line. Keep the knees flexed and the feet fairly flat.
- Think of the approach as a dance. It is neither a lazy shuffle nor a rigid march. The steps are quick, soft, and smooth.

FIVE-STEP APPROACH

The most common variation of the approach is the use of five steps instead of four. Whenever bowlers start and finish the approach with the same foot, they will use an odd number of steps. Some bowlers are more comfortable moving the foot opposite the throwing hand first. A bowler must learn what comes naturally before determining the number of steps or making other adjustments. If you prefer to move the opposite foot first, go with the five-step approach.

There is little difference between the four- and five-step approaches. The five-step approach simply includes an extra weight-transfer step that initiates body movement before the start of the swing. Some instructors call it a *get-going* step. I call it a *cheater* step. The bowler is cheating the body forward, trying to subtly transfer the weight in anticipation of the more obvious weight transfer when the second step and the ball move together. This leaves the last four steps in the approach to match the four parts of the swing. The second step is taken with the leg on the throwing side, and the pushaway begins with the second step. All of the performance aspects of steps two, three, four, and five of the five-step approach are exactly the same as that of steps one, two, three, and four of the four-step approach.

A five-step approach may have a different feel that makes it more appealing to certain bowlers. The four-step approach has, for some, a mechanical, clocklike one-two-one-two rhythm. Some bowlers find this pattern too rigid and cautious. The weight-shift step with the opposite foot in the five-step approach provides a start that feels smoother. Many bowlers prefer the body motion flowing into the swing motion, instead of both of them starting together. This flowing rhythm gives the five-step approach a dancelike quality.

The five-step cadence, is counted as "one . . . two, one-two-three" or as "step... push, three-four-five." If you're a dancer, think of it as "cha . . . cha, cha-cha-cha."

The spacing of the feet must match the rhythm and mechanics of the swing. The first step of the five-step approach is still small. It simply allows a slight weight transfer. Therefore, the walking pattern of the five-step approach is short, short, long, short (power), long (slide).

For a shorter bowler, an extra step helps generate extra momentum. Extra steps may help a very tall bowler achieve a more natural walking gait. Sometimes, tall bowlers trying to cover the entire length of the approach (as much as 17 feet [5 m]) in only four steps. Frequently, their steps are not natural: the momentum is excessive and they look out of control at the finish. An extra step may be just the trick that helps them achieve a more controlled footwork pattern.

TROUBLESHOOTING TIMING ISSUES

Of the components of the approach, the initial movement is the one that causes the most trouble in coordinating the steps and the swing. About 70 to 80 percent of all untutored bowlers experience late timing at the start of the approach. Many players simply will not move the ball when they take the first step. Others may be uncomfortable with the sudden weight shift that occurs when the first step and pushaway move together.

If you have difficulty with the initial movement, try the five-step approach. The body is in motion on the first step, and the swing follows on the second step. Starting the pushaway on the second step of a four-step approach is incorrect, but it is proper for a five-step approach.

If you prefer to stay with the four-step approach, try moving the ball first. Anticipate the hesitation by initiating the swing just before the first step. This may feel uncomfortable at first, but practice the pushaway drills described in step 3, Starting Fundamentals.

Be sure your first step is not too long. If the initial step is too long, the leg will be way out in front, and the body and the ball will hang back. Remember, for a proper initial movement, the ball and the ball-side leg move at the same time, in the same direction, and the same distance.

If struggling with a late start, avoid upward movements during the pushaway. Pushing the swing up and out takes more time than out and down. Women, youth, and smaller bowlers often push the swing up and out, trying to generate more ball speed with a bigger swing. Instead, consider adding power in other ways. Start the ball in a higher position and use a dropaway swing. Walk faster, using the extra momentum and a strong leg drive to create extra speed.

Keep in mind, an up-and-out movement can be useful if performed correctly. Initially, this type of swing is not a true pendulum. If you want to create a bigger swing by using the up-and-out initial movement, you will need to start the swing early. It requires extra time to push the ball up before it falls into the swing. To accommodate the extra time needed for the upward motion, start the pushaway before you start the first step of the four-step approach.

If early timing is the problem, try to extend the pushaway. The up-and-out technique may help bowlers who move the ball into the swing down too soon. Slow feet and a fast dropaway of the swing contribute to early timing. These bowlers might have no noticeable pushaway. These players should work on a smoother (perhaps slower) and more complete swing rhythm. In the case of early timing, imagine pushing the ball over a bar. This creates a better extension into the pushaway, allowing time for the steps.

Timing Drill 1   One-Step Swing Away

This drill helps develop a sense of the swing's movement in time with the first step. While practicing the timing of the movement, try to create a smooth arc in the swing.

Stand in the setup position. Push the ball into the swing. Just as the swing starts, take a short, smooth step with the swing-side leg. Let the ball swing completely back and forth. As the ball swings back to the starting position, catch it and take a step back into the setup position.

If you use a five-step approach, start with the opposite foot in front as if you had already taken the first step. Or take two steps, pushing the ball on the second step. Practice this drill 10 times.

Success Check

- Ball arcs out and down.
- Your step is short and smooth.

Score Your Success

Swing and step start together = 2 points

The ball moves out and down into the swing = 2 points

The swing motion is a smooth arc from start to finish = 2 points

The swing comes all the way back to the start before stepping back = 1 point

Your score _____

Timing Drill 2   Discover the Rhythm

This exercise allows you to feel the "one, two" and "out, down" synchronization of the steps and swing. It is similar to the preceding drill, except you will take the first two steps of a four-step approach. The ball reaches the bottom of the backswing just as the second step lands.

Begin the swing with a smooth, arcing out-and-down movement. Start the first step when the swing begins. Continue to the second step as the swing comes down. Stop footwork after two steps, but continue swing through a full motion. Keep upper body steady without swaying back and forth as the swing moves back and forth. Let the ball swing completely back on its own before returning to the starting position. As the swing returns to the body, take two steps back, returning to the setup position.

As in the previous drill, for bowlers who use a five-step approach, the opposite foot will move forward first. Then the throwing-side leg and swing move together.

Success Check

- Ball moves in a smooth arc, out and down.
- Swing movement does not pull the upper body out of position.

Score Your Success

Practice this drill 10 times, earning up to 7 points each time

Throwing-side leg moves out when swing starts = 2 points

Ball reaches bottom of swing when opposite leg moves = 2 points

Swing creates a smooth, full pendulum arc = 1 point

Upper-body position remains stationary as the swing moves back and forth = 1 point

Your score ___

Timing Drill 3   Side-by-Side Partner Practice

Your partner takes hold of your arm and walks you through the full approach. The goal is to achieve a continuous movement of both the feet and the swing. This is an excellent drill in which an experienced bowler can help an inexperienced bowler develop the skill. At first, practice this drill without a ball.

Inform your partner whether you are using a four- or five-step approach. Partner takes hold of your arm near the wrist. Partner helps move the swing at the right time. If the timing is correct, bowler initiates the movement, and partner will not have to do any work. Partner maintains grip on forearm throughout the approach. Partner helps bowler maintain smooth progress to the foul line while keeping a long, fluid swing. Bowler ends in proper finish position as partner guides the swing all the way through the follow-through.

The bowler who uses a five-step approach will take an extra cheater step before the movement of the ball. Perform 10 repetitions, earning up to 6 points each time, then switch roles.

TO DECREASE DIFFICULTY

- Stop the motion after each step. Partner makes sure the swing moves to the appropriate location for each step of the approach.
- Count aloud the step numbers as the swing moves to each location.
- Say the swing locations aloud (out, down, back, through) with each step.

TO INCREASE DIFFICULTY

- Gradually increase the speed until you are able to move at a normal walking pace.
- Use a ball. Partner walks by your side, holding onto the swing arm just above the wrist as you attempt a complete approach, including the release of the ball.
- Timing and smoothness of the approach should not change when a ball is used. Alternate practicing with and without a ball until you gain confidence.

(continued)

Timing Drill 3 *(continued)*

Success Check

- Partner should feel no resistance. If partner needs to help the swing at any point, you are not in a free swing or not in time with the steps.

Score Your Success

Ball moves down as first step moves forward = 2 points

Partner feels no resistance in the swing = 2 points

Footwork is smooth and continuous = 1 point

You arrive at the foul line as the swing nears completion = 1 point

Your score ___

Timing Drill 4   Continuous Swing Motion

Pendulums gather speed quickly, and you must learn to keep footwork at pace with the swing. This drill helps you understand the pace of the swing. The objective is to let the swing move back and forth with no hesitation, and then, just as a final swing starts, allow the footwork to go with the swing.

From a normal starting position, swing the ball a couple of times without moving the feet. Each time the swing moves to its forward position, tell yourself, "up." On the third upswing, start the footwork. With no hesitation in the swing, complete a full approach with a finish position and release.

Success Check

- Practice this routine at least 10 times until the swing and the steps move together without hesitation.
- If properly executed, the motion will not pause. The step and the swing motions blend seamlessly, and you make a quick, smooth movement to the foul line.
- If you are an inexperienced bowler, have someone else evaluate your success based on the point values noted.

Score Your Success

Practice swings are smooth and continuous = 2 points

As the third swing moves forward, step is made with the throwing-side leg = 2 points

The swing does not hesitate when the steps begin = 1 point

The approach is smooth and continuous without hesitation in footwork or swing = 2 points

Finish position is balanced = 1 point

Your score ___

Timing Drill 5   Assessing the Full Approach, Basic Skills Checklist

Have a skilled observer watch your approach from a short distance.

The observer stands on your throwing side so he or she can see where the swing is in relation to each step of the approach. Start in your normal stance position. Attempt five approaches, complete with follow-through and finish.

TO DECREASE DIFFICULTY

Practice approach without a ball. Assess this approach using the same checklist.

Success Check

- Remember the difference between four- and five-step approaches. Bowlers who use a five-step approach take an extra step (out on two, down on three, and so on).
- The observer evaluates you based on the success scores.

Score You Success

You start from a proper stance = 1 point

Initial step is smooth and short = 1 point

Ball moves into swing when throwing-side leg moves = 2 points

Pushaway moves ball a few inches past the foot after the first step = 1 point

Ball moves down in a smooth arc = 2 points

Arm fully extends as ball reaches bottom of down-drop phase of swing = 1 point

Backswing passes by throwing-side leg before leg moves into third step = 2 points

Swing reaches top of backswing on next-to-last step = 2 points

Downswing moves in a smooth arc from top of backswing until release = 1 point

Foot enters slide as ball approaches bottom of downswing = 1 point

Approach finishes to a stable position just before the release = 1point

Your score ___

SUCCESS SUMMARY

Body position is set in the stance and does not change. The initial swing moves forward and down, and the entire swing traces a smooth arc. When the swing moves, the leg on the throwing side moves with it. There are no pauses, hitches, hesitations, or any other disruptions to the smooth progress of the steps and the swing once the approach starts. The slide foot enters the slide just before the ball reaches the bottom of the downswing. The body reaches a stationary and balanced point just as the ball reaches the bottom of the downswing.

SCORING YOUR SUCCESS

Timing Drills

1. One-Step Swing Away _____ out of 7

2. Discover the Rhythm _____ out of 7

3. Side-by-Side Partner Practice _____ out of 6

4. Continuous Swing Motion _____ out of 8

5. Assessing the Full Approach _____ out of 15

   Total _____ **out of 43**

The next step discusses the release. The release is the end product of a chain of events and is a challenging skill. So much of what happens before the release influences the result. A consistently effective release occurs only if all the movements and positions leading up to it are performed correctly. This is the reason such a significant portion of this book has emphasized the skills that precede the release. When you feel that all the parts are working together, you can roll the ball with confidence.

Perfecting the Release

The release is the culmination of a bowler's efforts. It is the last thing we do to the ball before it leaves our hand. It is the last link in a chain of physical events. Errors in form or mechanics before the release are revealed in the release. For this reason, we work on the basic skills of the game before getting to the details of the release. The goal is to create an effective roll, one that generates sufficient angle and drive through the pins to produce satisfactory pinfall. The ability to control and manipulate the release is a prime ingredient for successful bowling.

Five essential physical factors of the release, three primary and two secondary, influence how the ball comes off the hand. The three primary factors—wrist cup, forearm and shoulder rotation, wrist cock—are related to hand position. The two secondary factors— leg drive into the side, shape of arm swing—are initiated by other physical actions.

HAND POSITION FACTORS

Many bowlers are told to stay behind the ball. But what does that mean? To understand this, we need to see how the hand is positioned behind the ball. We do this by dividing the ball into sections, then determining which section the hand should be positioned in.

Imagine looking from directly behind the ball at the point of release. If we take the bowler's hand out of the way, you will see the thumb hole above the finger holes. The line that passes from the thumb hole to a point between the two fingers is called the *center line,* it divides the ball into a right and left half. Think of the back of the ball as a clock face; the line extends from 12:00 down to 6:00 on the dial (figure 8.1).

Now, imagine a point that is half the distance between the thumb and finger holes. Draw a lateral line through this point across the ball (from 9:00 to 3:00 on our imaginary clock). This is called the *midline*; it divides the ball into upper and lower halves. If this line were to go all the way around the ball so we could see it from the side, we would notice that it is parallel to the ground.

The centerline and midline meet at the back of the ball. Positioning the center of the palm directly behind this point is said to put you *behind the ball*. To keep this baseline hand position, the wrist must be straight and the forearm facing forward. If observing from the side, behind the ball looks like this. First, you see the midline going toward the middle of the palm. The thumb is slightly above the midline and the finger slightly below. The index finger, on the outside of the ball, because it extends another inch or so past the finger holes, appears to be more under the ball (figure 8.2).

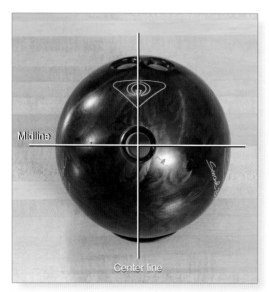

Figure 8.1 The center line divides the ball into left and right halves. The midline divides the ball into upper and lower halves.

Figure 8.2 Hand positioned behind the ball.

Wrist Cup

Wrist cup determines where the fingers are relative to the midline. The more the wrist cups, the farther you can position the fingers under the midline. As the wrist uncups, or flexes back, the fingers move above the midline. Wrist cup influences where the leveraging pressure of the fingers is applied (figure 8.3).

Figure 8.3 Wrist cup: *(a)* flexed back, *(b)* straight, and *(c)* cupped.

Forearm and Shoulder Rotation

Inward rotation of the forearm and upper arm moves the hand outside the centerline. Outward rotation moves the hand to the inside of the centerline (figure 8.4). The inward rotation comes fairly easily. The forearm has a large range of motion in that direction, not to mention what shoulder rotation could add. But, how does one get the hand to turn outward? The forearm rotation (called radial and ulnar deviation) is limited in this direction. For most bowlers, the outward turn is created at the shoulder joint. While inward shoulder rotation at any time during the swing is an error to be avoided, outward shoulder rotation (if properly executed) is beneficial. It helps keep the elbow close to the body, which creates a swing line under the shoulder and a hand position to the inside of the ball.

The hand position relative to the centerline has two effects. It determines the direction from which the force of the swing is applied through the ball. It also influences how much rotation (if any) around the ball the hand makes as the ball releases from the hand.

Figure 8.4   Forearm position: *(a)* outside, *(b)* centered, and *(c)* inside.

Wrist Cock

To imagine what wrist cock look likes, we need to forget about the ball for a minute. Let the arm hang straight down from the shoulder with fingers pointing toward the ground and the palm facing forward. Imagine a line drawn from the center of the forearm to the middle of the wrist. Now imagine another line drawn from the center of the wrist through the middle finger. If there is no offset angle between these two lines (i.e., they make one continual line) the hand is in a neutral position. This line would be directly in line with the ball's centerline if the hand were in the standard behind-the-ball position.

Without moving anything else, try to put your pinky in line with the forearm centerline by uncocking the wrist outward. The palm-to-middle-finger line points away from the leg. Not too easy, huh? That's because most folks have a pretty limited range in that direction. But try going the other way. Cock the wrist inward (to the left for the right-handed bowler) and see how far it will go. For many people, the palm line could be offset 45 degrees or more than the forearm line. Imagine where this puts the fingers relative to the ball's centerline. Without changing anything else, the fingers can be positioned strongly to the inside half of the ball (figure 8.5).

 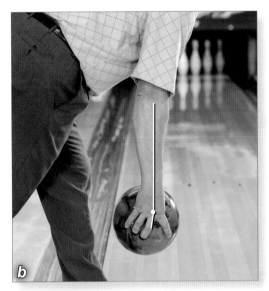

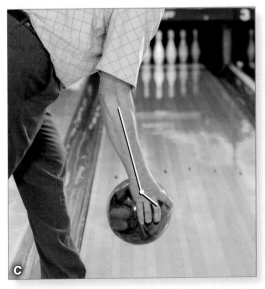

Figure 8.5   Wrist cock: *(a)* cocked, *(b)* neutral, and *(c)* uncocked.

The three major physical factors that influence ball roll are wrist cock, wrist cup, and forearm rotation. As the swing drives the hand through the ball and extends out to the target, the weight of the ball transfers forward to the fingers. Ball motion is a function of the hand position relative to the ball and how that position changes as the wrist uncocks, the wrist uncups, and forearm rotates as the fingers apply their leverage force.

MINOR RELEASE FACTORS

Minor in this case does not mean unimportant. These factors are minor in the sense that they do not directly affect the motion or position of the wrist and hand. Instead, these physical skills, which are discussed in other steps, can be modified to influence important aspects of the release.

If you look at a side view of the swing path, you will see a flat spot in the pendulum. The movement of the body forward during the last step elongates the bottom of the swing. This flat spot helps the bowler get a better feel of the hand working through the ball to the release point. The bowler creates this flat spot in two ways: by changing the shape of the swing and by using a strong leg drive.

Leg Drive

A strong power step helps the bowler more readily feel the hand drive through the ball. The position of the hand is more obviously felt during the flat spot of the swing. If the leg drive is particularly forceful, the acceleration of the body into the slide will press the hand against the back of the ball. The bowler will sense that the swing is being carried along with the body. The feeling of the hand pressing through the back of the ball gives the bowler a sense of power and control through the release point. A feeling of being long and low through the bottom of the swing drives the hand through the ball, helping the bowler maintain ball speed and a strong release. The bowler can temper the release by applying less force with the drive leg. A more passive power step decreases the speed in which the hand moves through the release (tempering the amount of rotation) as well a moderating overall ball speed.

Be careful though. A finish with weak footwork usually produces a ball thrown with insufficient speed. If this happens, do not compensate for the lack of lower-body drive by trying to force the ball through by other means, such as standing up at the finish, throwing the upper body forward, or forcing (pulling) the swing forward. If the release is ineffective because of dropping the ball, evaluate the cause in this order: ball fit, timing, hand position, swing length (momentum), swing line (next to body), and footwork momentum.

Swing Shape

As the swing comes down, you can alter the shape of the swing arc. The shape can be flattened, arced, or redirected upward. How changing the shape of the swing influences the release is discussed in more detail in step 9, Fine-Tuning Your Game.

Creating Ball Motions

Release strength is determined by revolution rate, axis tilt, and axis rotation. The more a ball's axis tilts upward, the smaller the surface of the ball that comes in contact with the lane. The higher the tilt, the easier the ball skids down the lane; a 90-degree tilt is like a spinning top. The lower the axis tilt, the stronger the roll character of the ball and the sooner it will grab the lane and move into its hook phase.

Once a ball starts to hook, axis rotation determines how angular or sharp the hooking motion is. Axis rotation is how much the ball rotates in a direction different from the initial ball path. If the ball's axis rotates 0 degrees from the initial ball path, it rolls end over end. At a 90-degree axis tilt, the ball rotates directly side to side. In this case, the axis point faces directly back at the bowler.

Revolution rate is primarily a function of finger leverage. The longer the fingers stay in the ball after the thumb release, the more the ball weight is influenced by the finger position and hand motion through the ball.

- If you want a stronger rolling motion roll, lower the axis by uncocking the wrist as you feel the ball at its heaviest point at the bottom of the swing.
- To promote greater axis rotation, allow the forearm to rotate the hand around the side of the ball as the swing carries the ball past the bottom of the swing into the extension phase.
- Revolutions are increased by increasing the delay between the thumb release and the finger release. An uncupping motion at the bottom of the swing releases the ball off the thumb quickly so that the ball weight is on the fingers sooner and longer as the swing moves the ball through the extension of the release.

Also, letting the swing extend outward from the shoulder past the slide foot puts the ball at the farthest point on the hand for maximum leverage. In other words, don't hit up on the ball but rather hit through it.

MODERN RELEASE

Breaking back the wrist, as just mentioned, promotes a quicker thumb exit and a more dramatic forward tilt of the ball onto the fingers from which they can apply their leverage pressure. The wrist does not go completely limp and collapse backward. Think of it more like a spring being stretched. The spring is extending to a new position, but there is still tension.

This wrist unloading motion is similar to the spring. The swing weight of the ball extends the wrist, while wrist tension is kept and strong finger pressure is maintained. This layout release position, when combined with a quick hand rotation and firm finger pressure, is a characteristic of many of the strongest, highest-revolution ball motions in the game.

Phases of the Release

The most effective release must time all of these motions and changes in position correctly. If, for instance, the wrist breaks back too early in the swing, the fingers will be above the midline before the release. This is considered a weak leverage position. Another example is if forearm rotation occurs too soon. Now the hand and fingers are on the side of the ball before the fingers have the opportunity to work from behind the ball, which weakens the roll off the fingers. To understand proper release, we need to investigate the phases of the release.

The release is a series of events that allows the ball to come off the hand as the force of the swing sends the ball down the lane. Some bowlers mistakenly think of the swing and the release as two separate elements, as if the bowler first swings and then releases. Nothing is further from the truth. Ideally, the swing flows through the release point.

Of all the identifiable physical elements of the game, the swing and the release are the two most closely integrated. The swing is what applies the force through the hand that allows the hand (based on its position and motion) to create the ball's rolling motion

The five phases of the release during the swing are drive, thumb release, extension, turn, and finger release (leverage).

DRIVE PHASE

The *drive phase* never ceases. It influences the ball until the ball is off the hand. This is the swing's contribution to ball motion. The swing should be a smooth arc. You can modify the direction or shape of the pendulum's arc, but at no time should that movement be hesitant, jerky, or prematurely stopped.

Imagine a bucket full of water. If you swing hard enough, you can swing the bucket in a complete circle over your head and the water will not fall out. The ball has the same effect on the hand. If the swing is continual and the hand is positioned firmly behind and under the ball, the bowler remains in control of the ball. You should feel the ball fall through the downswing. The hand feels as though it is pressing against the back of the ball, and the wrist remains firm. It does not break back (figure 8.6*a*).

THUMB-RELEASE PHASE

The second phase is the *thumb-release phase*. As the ball approaches the bottom of the swing, the thumb starts to slide out of the ball. As the ball passes through the bottom of the swing, the bowler feels the ball's swing weight on the fingers. The thumb controls the ball during the backswing; it does little or no work during the downswing. The pressure of the hand against the ball, plus the grip of the fingers, is all that is needed to swing the ball out onto the lane.

A thumb squeeze that keeps the thumb in the ball too long decreases both accuracy and rotation. Ideally, the thumb is mostly out of the ball before the turn phase begins. Thumb pressure (squeezing) kills revolutions.

If the turn phase starts too early (during the downswing), the thumb will turn downward. This is one of the most common errors in the sport. This forces the bowler to squeeze the ball to prevent it from dropping off the hand. The downward turn of the thumb causes it to act as a pivot point around which the ball turns, creating an ineffective spin release rather than the preferred rolling or hook release. Even if you don't squeeze with the thumb, turning early still causes release problems. Without the thumb squeeze, early forearm rotation points the thumb downward and inward (toward your ankle), and the ball drops off the hand with a weak, ineffective roll.

TURN PHASE

The *turn phase* puts the hand into the desired position for applying torque on the ball. It is used to change the lateral hand position, and thus the application of the swing force through the ball. If the position does not change (the hand stays directly behind the ball), there is no side roll and therefore no hook. Control of hand position (through forearm rotation) is one of the most difficult elements of the game. It is easy to turn the hand too much or too little at the release. Achieving correct hand position without giving up the accuracy of the overall swing line is one of the game's great challenges. A lot is going on at the bottom of the swing, and there is not a lot of margin for error.

EXTENSION PHASE

The *extension phase* is the finish of the swing as it drives the ball down the lane. This part of the swing carries the ball through the bottom of the arc. Many bowlers let go of the ball at this point, allowing the ball to drop onto the lane. These bowlers relax all tension in the hand in the mistaken notion that they must let go of the ball. Dropping the ball creates a weak release. The ball is likely to slip off the hand before the turn and lift phases are completed. There is also the tendency to cut the swing short, sacrificing ball speed and the ability to follow through to the target. With correct fit, hand position, and swing extension, the ball lets go of the bowler!

Ideally, you should feel strongest in the extension phase. As you drive the ball out onto the lane, you want to feel in control. Through the bottom of the swing, feel the weight transfer forward onto the fingers. As described earlier, a slight extension back of the wrist allows this to happen more effectively. Yes, a slight breaking back of the wrist is desirable at this point. The wrist position may soften a little, but the finger pressure remains firm. Now, with the fingers feeling the resistance of the ball's swing weight, the swing continues outward along the target line. This leads to the last phase, and then the ball is on its way (figure 8.6*b*).

MISSTEP

Bad pushaway = bad swing line = bad release. The hand position on the ball varies if the swing does not move in a straight line.

CORRECTION

Make sure the pushaway is straight out from the shoulder. Avoid an excessive looping motion in the swing. Keep the swing along as straight a path as possible.

FINGER-RELEASE PHASE

The *finger-release (leverage) phase* is the final phase of the release. Leverage (often called lift) is the fingers' resistance to gravity's effect on the ball. A smooth release drives the ball down the lane. As the swing passes the bottom of the pendulum arc, it starts to go up. Gravity wants to make the ball drop down. Lift is the pressure on the fingers the bowler feels from these opposing forces. Like a plane landing, the ball glides onto the lane, contacting the surface at a fairly shallow angle.

Just before the ball leaves the hand, only the fingers are in the ball for a fraction of a second. At this point, the fingers' position behind the ball and the amount of finger rotation around the ball determines the type of roll. With a proper release position, the bowler will feel this split-second kick of the fingers just before the ball comes off the hand. Keep in mind, this is not a deliberate, forceful upward movement. The swing's smooth pendulum feel is not radically altered. Instead, a feeling of resistance keeps the ball from dropping weakly off the hand (figure 8.6*c*).

Figure 8.6 (*a*) The drive phase; (*b*) the extension phase; and (*c*) the finger-release phase.

For a strong release, don't relax the fingers. If the mechanics are sound and the fit correct, the ball glides off the hand on its own. Just as important, you should not feel as though you need to open up the hand to let the ball go.

Sometimes fewer revolutions are preferred (e.g., on a dry lane when the ball will hook easily, or when shooting a spare, when your intent is for the ball to follow a straighter path). In these instances, less finger pressure at the release moderates the ball's revolutions.

In that small space of the swing arc after the thumb release, is there extension before the forearm rotation or rotation before the extension? It depends on the bowler and the type of roll desired.

Ideally, the hand would stay behind the ball for as long as possible to give the fingers the best opportunity for leverage. After the ball clears the thumb, will the hand continue to drive and extend through the ball before the start of a turning motion? Or, will the turn be initiated almost immediately after the ball clears the thumb and then continue with the extension and eventual finger release? Bowlers have been successful with both.

If the fingers are strongly positioned under and to the inside half of the ball and the swing continues forward before any turn, the fingers need to rotate to a release position quickly at a point late in the swing arc. These players usually have faster revolution rates. On the other hand, bowlers who start the rotation soon after the thumb start to clear use what is characterized as rolling, stroker release.

HAND POSITIONS FOR DIFFERENT RELEASES

The position of the hand determines how the energy of the swing transfers through the ball. If the hand is directly behind the ball, all the swing's energy goes through the ball. Offsetting the hand will redirect some of the swing's energy around the ball, creating a torque motion. When this happens, two forces influence the ball's movement down the lane. *Translational force* is the initial direction of the ball down the lane. *Rotational force* is the direction of its rolling motion, or the orientation of its axis of rotation. The more a ball's axis of rotation is offset from its translational direction, the more potential hook it has.

Imagine rolling a tire instead of a ball. With the axle of the tire as the axis of rotation, the position and motion of the release become clearer. Using a clock face to picture the hand positions at the release point is a traditional method for describing the release.

There are two basic release positions, one for a straight ball and one for a hook ball. Generally, the straight release is passive; the hand and forearm do not move at the release point. An active release is characterized by movement at the release point; in other words, the bowler changes the position of the hand as the swing passes through the release phases. The action of this release is meant to increase either the number of revolutions or the degree of side roll. Both passive and active releases can create a hook.

A bowler can release the ball in a variety of ways. To make understanding them easier, we will separate them into general categories: straight, passive hook, active hook, and the (undesirable, yet all-too-common) backup ball.

Straight Release Hand Position

The goal of a straight ball release is to create a heavy end-over-end ball roll, which emphasizes accuracy. For a passive straight release, the ball is set in the desired release position at the beginning of the stance and remains there throughout the swing.

In the straight release, the fingers are aligned in a 12:00 and 6:00 hand position (figure 8.7). The thumb and fingers line up directly behind the ball. This position produces little side roll. The direction of ball rotation is the same (or almost the same) as the direction it is thrown.

Figure 8.7 **STRAIGHT RELEASE**

Hand Position

1. Thumb and gripping fingers are in line directly behind the ball.
2. Forearm rotates slightly, enough to line up thumb and fingers with center of forearm.
3. Wrist position is straight or slightly extended back. (No cupping is needed.)
4. For some bowlers, the wrist may break back somewhat when they align the hand position with the forearm; this is acceptable.

Release

1. Near the bottom of the swing, the ball starts to drop off the thumb.
2. Ball rolls forward onto the fingers.
3. As swing extends, ball rolls off the front of finger pads and smoothly onto lane.
4. Fingers apply pressure directly up the back of ball.

Picturing the Straight Ball Setup

Let your bowling arm hang loosely at your sides. For now, pretend a ball is in your throwing hand; the bent fingers are locked into the holes and the thumb is straight. Notice that the elbow is closer to the body than the hand is. This is essential for understanding the position of the swing in relation to the body.

Often, beginning bowlers are told to face the palm toward the target when releasing the ball. But, if the palm faces forward (open position), the thumb points outward. The thumb is not in the middle of the wrist (humans aren't made that way). If the wrist breaks back, the outward turn of the thumb becomes potentially even more dramatic because the weight of the ball will exit off the thumb side. The hand is now in a backup ball position, not a straight ball position.

Let's try something different. With the bowling arm still dangling at the side, imagine an arrow down the center of the forearm that points toward the middle of the palm. Rotate the forearm slightly, just until the thumb lines up with the imaginary arrow. Looking down your arm, you will see the thumb over your gripping fingers. Imagine a clock face on the floor under your hand. Align the thumb toward 12:00 and point the fingers down toward 6:00. This is the 12:00 and 6:00 position for the straight release. Maintain this position throughout the swing.

Using this slightly turned initial position has two benefits. First, it is the first step toward learning the hook release. The hand is not turning past the centerline, and it reinforces the idea of staying behind the ball. Second, it helps prevent the dreaded backup ball (discussed later in this step).

Wrist and Finger Drill 1   Simple Swing Practice for Hand Position

Stand with a ball hanging at your side. Rotate the hand until the thumb lines up with the center of the forearm. Raise the ball to a comfortable level (figure 8.8). Perform five setups and swings.

Score Your Success

Hand is directly under the ball in setup = 1 point

Elbow is next to the hip = 1 point

Practice swings glide smoothly back and forth past the hip = 1 point

Hand stays in position (no twist, no flex) during swing = 2 points

Your score _____

Figure 8.8   Straight release setup.

When using the straight release, try keeping the wrist straight all the way through to the release. (If the wrist breaks back slightly at the release, that's OK. Just be careful not to release with a twist motion or relax so much you drop the ball). Most important, feel the fingers drive through the back of the ball as the swing sends it out onto the lane. The heavy end-over-end roll combined with the stable hand position throughout the swing produce accuracy and consistency.

Because it is the easiest to control, this is the beginning bowler's release. Also, with less hand movement to deal with at the beginning, the bowler can concentrate on other aspects of the game.

From a strategy point of view, a straight ball has a place in all levels of the game. Advanced bowlers must have command of a straight release for several reasons. First, it is excellent for shooting almost any spare. The primary concern (and in some instances, the only concern) during spare shots is accuracy. The absence of side roll minimizes the effect lane conditions have on the ball. Most experienced bowlers intentionally weaken (uncup) the wrist position in addition to the straight release hand position to further reduce any hook potential. Second, difficult lane conditions may be caused by sporadic and unpredictable oil distribution. A straighter path to the pocket might be a better option. Instructors often encounter students who, after learning how to hook the ball, forget how to throw it straight. This lack of versatility must be overcome.

Hook Release

The hook can be accomplished with both an active and a passive release. To create an effective hook, the fingers need to be under the ball and slightly offset from the ball's center. The swing drives the hand through, then up, the side of the ball. The hand does not turn around the ball so much as the ball is turned by the hand. Excessive motion is not necessary for creating an effective hook.

In the basic hook release, the fingers are at a 10:00 and 4:00 hand position at the point of release. The important issue is the ball clearing the thumb. The ball slides off the thumb before the swing reaches the release position.

A *passive hook* release involves presetting the hand position for the hook at the beginning of the swing and keeping it there throughout the swing (figure 8.9). This is the easiest hook release to learn. There is little or no motion at the release. The hand position is set at the beginning, and the bowler merely swings through the position.

Just like before, let the hand hang relaxed at the side. Imagine where the hand needs to be in order to be offset from the center of the ball. Offsetting the hand requires a small rotation of the forearm. The wrist does not change position; it is firm and straight (or perhaps slightly cupped). Imagine looking down the hand toward a clock face lying on the floor. Rotate your forearm until the thumb points toward 10:00 and the fingers are at 4:00. This is the hook release position (figure 8.10). Bend your arm, bringing the hand straight up (keeping it in line with the shoulder); this is the starting position.

Figure 8.9 **PASSIVE HOOK RELEASE**

Hand Position

1. Hand is directly under the ball in the setup position.
2. In the stance position, rotate forearm until palm is facing slightly inward, about a one-eighth turn to the outside of the ball.
3. Palm is not turned completely inward (facing the body), nor does it face the ceiling.
4. Hand position is maintained throughout the swing.

Release

1. The ball slides off the thumb near the bottom of the swing.
2. As the ball passes the drive face of the swing, the fingers maintain their offset position on the ball.
3. As the ball rotates to the inside of the hand, the swing continues toward the target.
4. Imagine the fingers moving in a straight line through the ball; if the fingers are in an offset position, the ball will have side roll.

When it is time to release the ball, it will slide off the thumb smoothly because it is facing slightly down and in toward the ankle at the bottom of the swing, and the fingers swing up the side of the ball. As you drive through the release, be sure the swing stays on line to the target and the fingers remain firm in the ball.

In an *active hook* release, the thumb may point toward 1:00 or 2:00 when the ball clears the thumb. This puts the fingers in a 7:00 and 8:00 position. By cocking the wrist position, as mentioned earlier, the fingers can be offset to the inside of the centerline. As the swing continues and the weight of the ball transfers to the fingers, the turn of the forearm rotates the fingers to 4:00. (They should never rotate past 3:00.) The more the hand rotates around the ball before applying its leverage force, the more axis rotation can be created.

This is the point at which some high-revolution players will allow the wrist to collapse slightly. As described in the modern release section, slightly breaking back the wrist tilts the ball weight onto the finger just

Figure 8.10 Hook release setup: Rotate forearm so fingers point inward and thumb is positioned by the outside of the ball.

before the forearm rotation applies the leverage force of the fingers. For a powerful release, the wrist uncups, uncocks, and rotates slightly.

As the uncocking motion and the forearm rotation turn the thumb inward, the finger will follow in the same direction. Some players try to get the finger to chase the thumb around and up the ball. Bowlers capable of this very strong snap–flip hand action may find that the momentum of the release causes the follow-through to move in front of their face. This is acceptable because the ball was released at the bottom of the swing, when the swing was still on line to the target. The change in the swing line is a consequence of the release forces influencing the follow-through direction after the ball is off the hand.

Rotating the hand to an exaggerated open position provides maximum rotation at the release. Imagine leading with your pinkie in the downswing, then turning from under the ball with the other fingers at the release. Some bowlers try to get into the overrotated position during the stance or very early in the pushaway.

Players who use the overrotated hand position in the setup of the stance should be careful to keep the swing from going where the thumb goes. A thumb pointing outward may cause an outward pushaway. If the pushaway moves away from the body, the backswing ends up behind the bowler. Many wannabe power players give up too much accuracy in order to create a strong release. If overrotating the hand position in the stance, be attentive to the direction of the pushaway. Make sure the throwing-arm elbow swings right next to the throwing-side leg.

Remember, 0 degrees of axis rotation is end-over-end roll; the ball rolls in the direction it is thrown. It will not change direction from its initial path. However, 90 degrees of rotation will cause the axis to point back toward the bowler. The axis of roll is turned 90 degrees from the initial ball path. Although this might create the strongest potential hook, it is the hardest release to control on dry or variable lane conditions. Err on the side of caution—keep the fingers in the 4:00 to 5:00 position as you hit the drive stage of the release if you want the ball to hook in a more controllable manner.

Words of Caution: Too Much Hook

There is such a thing as too much hook. Too many players are so intent on making the ball hook, they lose sight of the far greater importance of keeping the ball in play. Trying to establishing a "wow" factor to intimidate an inexperienced opponent may be useful occasionally, but generally it does not pay off in significantly higher scores.

Hook players must pay attention to what the lanes give them. An old adage admonishes the bowler to only put as much on the ball as needed to carry the pins. Not every release needs to be 100 percent. Yes, you should have 100 percent commitment and 100 percent mental focus on every shot, but not always 100 percent force. Just because you could do more doesn't mean that you should. Keep something in reserve.

All bowlers, as their game develops, will confront the power–accuracy trade-off. If the release is very active, a power–accuracy trade-off is inevitable. A cautious, systematic approach that ties the mechanics of the release to the overall mechanics of the game will give you the right answers. Your answer (what you call *my game*) may be different from another bowler's answer, but it will be one with which you can prosper.

Backup Ball

In a backup ball, the arm rotates to the inside of the ball and the elbow turns into the hip. The palm faces away from the body. The hand is well to the inside of the centerline at the release. If the palm faces outward throughout the release, it is most likely caused by a rotation at the shoulder. The forearm does not naturally allow this motion.

This hand position is often seen in high-revolution players. They get the hand well to the inside of the ball at the release and then drive and turn the hand around the outside. Backup bowlers never change their hand position at the release. The hand works up the inside of the ball. The more active they try to be with this reverse hook position, the more likely they are to rotate at the shoulder. This excessive internal rotation causes problems. Often the backup bowler needs to throw the body out of position to accommodate the inward tuck of the swing. With the body turning off-line, swing tucking in, and the hand (or should we say the whole arm) twisting out, achieving consistency is difficult. Not only are the mechanics faulty, but the amount of reverse hook achieved is also more limited than with more traditional releases. *Correct a backup ball release as soon as possible.*

Some people are more flexible and may be able to hyperextend the elbow. Hyperextension frequently permits an outward rotation of the forearm. People with this flexibility (more often found in women) will have a more natural tendency to throw a backup ball. They may be able to accomplish a passive backup ball release without decreasing swing accuracy. This passive release, however, does limit the ability to create an effective hook. Any attempt to actively increase hook will bring out the inherent problems of throwing a backup ball.

To correct the backup ball release, begin by focusing on the hand position and swing alignment. Practice this using a suitcase, duffel bag, or bowling bag. Grip the handle using only the fingers. The palm of the hand will face the leg. Take a few practice swings with the bag hanging just from the fingers. After a few swings, feel the bag release off the fingers as you try to slide it down the floor. Imagine the bag has wheels on the bottom and is going to glide to a person in front of you. To limit upper-arm rotation, imagine an arrow pointing straight forward from the crook of the swing arm. Keep the arrow pointed toward the target during the swing.

Now, using a ball, practice that same suitcase hand position. Let the ball hang from your arm with the wrist slightly broken back and the thumb pointed toward the thigh. Looking down the arm at the top of the ball as it hangs from the shoulder, the thumb will be at 11:00 and the fingers between 4:00 and 5:00. Without rotating, let the ball roll off the hand after two or three practice swings. Correct the backup ball with the kneeling or one-step practices first. These drills are excellent for isolating swing and release problems. It helps to have an experienced bowler watch. The chosen release position or motion should not affect the smoothness and accuracy of a true pendulum swing.

OTHER ERRORS IN RELEASE MECHANICS

There are a couple other release mechanic errors that beginner bowlers make. They either relax the hand or rotate at the shoulder.

Relaxing the Hand

Many beginning bowlers relax their fingers at the release, opening the hand in order to let go of the ball. No! Firm fingers are needed at the release to kick the ball over into its side roll. If timing and release position are correct and the ball fits properly, the ball will come off the hand on its own. Do not drop the ball; drive it down the lane.

Rotation at the Shoulder

Another common mistake bowlers make is trying to rotate the entire arm around the ball. The elbow moves away from the body as the upper arm rotates in its socket. Instead of working from a strong leverage point that is more behind the ball, the fingers twirl around the ball much too early in the swing arc, which leads to several problems.

First, this type of movement creates a weaker roll. The ball has a tendency to spin rather than roll. Second, the extra movement of the arm sacrifices accuracy. As the arm rotates away from the body, it no longer stays along a straight swing path. Keeping the elbow close to the body is part of an accurate swing.

Wrist Flexion: To Cup or Not to Cup?

Bowlers often have questions concerning this point. If a certain degree of wrist flex (cupping) is important for getting the hand to a strong release position, how much wrist flex is necessary? Can too much flex be bad? Is it acceptable if the wrist is not completely straight?

Of first concern should be finding a comfortable wrist position you feel that you can maintain throughout the swing. If you are strong enough to achieve a degree of wrist flexion during the swing, I suggest being careful about overdoing it. Each joint is strongest at a specific angle. A wrist flexion of 10 to 15 degrees is best. This position is easily maintained and puts the hand in a strong position behind the ball.

- In a typical hook release, the fingers should be below the midline.

- If the fingers are above the midline, the wrist position is weak.

- If the wrist is strongly cupped, the thumb may be down by the midline.

All of these positions have a place in the game. The more dramatic the cup of the wrist, the more leverage from under the ball the fingers can apply to increase revolutions and axis turn. However, there is such a thing as too much cup. If the wrist is so strongly cupped that it starts to straighten out as soon as the pushaway begins, you are cupping the wrist beyond your ability to keep it in place. Rather than starting with a strong cup position just to lose it later, you are better off starting with a more modest wrist angle that will stay in position throughout the swing. Find a wrist position you can comfortably maintain.

If you cannot straighten the wrist at all, and no matter what force you apply, the wrist is still a little broken back, don't worry. As long is the grip is firm and the wrist position does not change during the swing, you can still create an effective and consistent release. In fact, a person typically has three times the grip strength when the wrist is at 40 degrees of extension than it does at 40 degrees of flexion. You will be able to hook the ball with a broken-back position. And although, it might not be a strong hook, it will have enough hook to score well.

Wrist and Finger Drill 2   Wrist Position and Strength Test

This drill tests wrist strength and appropriate ball weight. Stand with your arm bent at about 90 degrees. Hold the ball in the palm of your hand without the thumb or fingers inserted in the holes (figure 8.12*a*). Slowly extend your arm forward until it is almost completely extended (figure 8.12*b*). Do not let the wrist break back. Slowly return to the starting position. Keep a straight wrist position throughout the motion.

If you cannot comfortably complete the movement, the ball is probably too heavy for you. You will have difficulty controlling the wrist position during the swing.

Figure 8.12   (*a*) Hold the ball with the arm at 90 degrees. (*b*) Slowly extend the forearm.

(continued)

Wrist and Finger Drill 2 *(continued)*

Success Check

- During the setup, keep the wrist straight as the ball rests in the palm.
- Extend the arm from the shoulder; return with a slow, smooth motion.
- At no point should you feel discomfort or sense that the ball will roll off the hand.

Score Your Success

Wrist is straight during the setup = 1 point

Arm extends comfortably from the shoulder = 2 points

Ball is returned to starting position without the wrist breaking back = 2 points

Your score ___

Wrist and Finger Drill 3   Locking the Wrist

This drill will help you learn to lock your wrist into position. Let the ball hang freely at your side. Insert your fingers and thumb into the appropriate holes. Relax your wrist, allowing the weight of the ball to pull your thumb down (figure 8.13a). Press up with the fingers in the holes to resist some of the weight. Now press against the surface of the ball, with both your pinkie and index fingers, until the wrist straightens (figure 8.13b).

This technique of locking the wrist into position is useful no matter what the angle of the wrist joint. At times, various wrist positions are needed to create different ball rolls. Practice developing a consistent release using a straight wrist first. From there, experiment with different wrist angles (cupped or bent back) to create release versatility.

Intentionally softening the wrist (breaking it back) puts the hand near the top of the ball at the release. This weakens the release, generally making the ball go straighter; it is a nice option for shooting spares or when bowling on dry lanes. Cupping the wrist keeps the fingers under the ball into the extension phase of the release, creating a stronger roll and potential hook. This skill is useful when lane conditions allow higher scores or when excessive oil takes away ball reaction. Practice this drill 10 times, scoring 7 points each time.

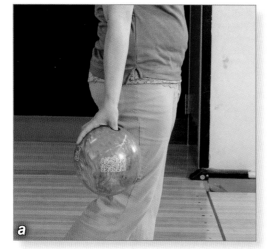 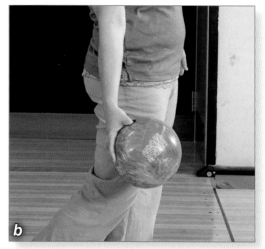

Figure 8.13   (*a*) Relax the wrist, pulling the thumb down. (*b*) Press against the ball until the wrist straightens.

Success Check

- Press index and pinkie fingers against the outside of the ball.
- Apply sufficient pressure to straighten the wrist.
- Maintain wrist position throughout the swing.

Score Your Success

Index and pinkie fingers pressed flat on ball's surface = 1 point

Pressure applied with both fingers = 1 point

Wrist straightens as fingers apply pressure = 2 points

Pressure is applied during full swing = 1 point

Wrist position changes little or not at all during swing = 2 points

Your score ___

Wrist and Finger Drill 4   Finger Pressure Test

With the finger pressure test, you will learn what the lock of the fingers in the holes feels like. You will also learn how the fingers resist the weight of the ball during the swing.

Hold the ball in the palm of your hand. Insert only the fingers in the holes; do not insert the thumb. Allow the wrist to bend back slightly until the ball rolls onto the fingers. Press the fingers against the inside of the finger holes, forcing the ball back onto the palm. Lower the ball until the arm is almost fully extended at the side, cupping the wrist as the ball gets lower. It should feel as if the fingers support the ball's entire weight. Remember to apply pressure with the outriggers (pinkie and index fingers) as well. Practice this drill 10 times, earning up to 9 points each time, to develop a sense of finger resistance to the ball's weight.

TO INCREASE DIFFICULTY

- Try to swing and roll the ball with just the gripping fingers in the hole.

Success Check

- Ball rests in palm with only fingers inserted.
- Flex (cup) wrist as you extend the arm out and down.
- Press back with the fingers to resist the weight of the ball.
- Maintain wrist position as the fingers support the ball's weight.

Score Your Success

Ball is in the palm of the hand, with only fingers inserted = 1 point

As arm extends down to the side, the wrist flexes to keep the hand under the ball = 2 points

Pinkie and index fingers apply pressure on the ball's surface = 1 point

Inserted fingers press back against the ball = 1 point

Finger pressure prevents the ball from rolling forward = 2 points

Wrist position is maintained while bringing the ball back to starting position = 2 points

Your score ___

Wrist and Finger Drill 5   Finger Pressure During Setup

The goal of this drill is to feel the difference between thumb pressure and finger pressure before swinging the ball. Perform this simple task before every throw of the ball.

Pressure situations in particular affect the release and swing. In these situations, you may be more likely to tense up or try to control the ball during the swing. This preparation technique will teach you to feel for the finger pressure and not the thumb squeeze, ensuring a smoother, stronger release.

Assume a normal setup position with a ball, and position hand for the preferred release. Squeeze firmly with both the thumb and the fingers. Relax the hand, letting the ball rest in the palm. Do not soften the wrist position. Again squeeze the ball firmly. Again relax the hand. Now apply slight pressure with just the fingers, not with the thumb. Eventually you will sense the difference between finger pressure and a whole-hand squeeze. When the fingers alone apply just enough pressure to keep the wrist firm, begin the swing.

Success Check

- Squeeze and relax.
- Note the difference between finger pressure and a whole-hand squeeze.

Score Your Success

Setup position is correct = 2 points

Squeeze, relax, squeeze, relax pattern is followed = 2 points

In relax mode, wrist position does not change = 1 point

After second relax, the slight press is with the fingers only = 1 point

Approach and swing are initiated without tension in the upper arm = 2 points

Your score ___

Swing and Release Drill   Evaluating Proper Technique

Have a coach or experienced bowler evaluate your swing and release techniques. Use the following criteria to determine whether your swing and release techniques are sound.

Score Your Success

Swing is a smooth, continuous arc with no excessive bend at the elbow = 2 points

Elbow (swing line) remains close to the hip (swing tucked in) = 2 points

Wrist position is straight throughout the swing = 1 point

For a stronger hook, wrist position is slightly cupped throughout the swing = 2 points

Ball slides off the thumb first as the ball enters the bottom of the swing = 2 points

Hand position behind the ball is stable throughout the swing (passive release) = 2 points

Forearm rotation starts as ball passes bottom of the swing (active release) = 2 points

As the swing passes the ankle, the fingers drive through the ball = 2 points

Swing motion at release is first out (extension), then up = 1 point

After release, the fingers are still in a firm position = 2 points

Your score ___

ENLARGING THE STRIKE POCKET

After this lengthy discussion of the release, a student of the game might be inclined to ask, "Why go through all the trouble? Why not make the release as simple as possible, taking all changes in position or movement out of consideration, and simply make bowling a targeting game—connect point A to point B?" There is merit in this point of view. In fact, I recommend that a beginning bowler adopt this perspective when first taking up the game.

Unfortunately, bowlers soon discover the limitations of a straight release. The accuracy required for a ball entering the pins at a nearly zero angle is so great that few bowlers can achieve success this way. All skilled bowlers create an angle into the pins. You can create angle in two ways.

1. Change position on the lane. Get away from the middle. This should be the first lane strategy all bowlers learn. It is the easiest way to change the ball's entry angle into the strike pocket. You can add almost 1.5 degrees of angle simply by changing your lane position.

2. Create side roll. Learn to hook the ball. Increasing the entry angle greatly improves a bowler's chance to strike. Because the strike pocket enlarges as the amount of hook increases, a bowler can be less accurate and still strike at a high percentage.

Researchers at the testing facility of the United States Bowling Congress use a ramp to determine how much increasing the entry angle (hook) increases the size of the strike pocket. Larger entry angles produce greater pin action. Pins will bounce off the sideboards back onto the lanes, and this side-to-side mixing action increases strike potential. Although it does not guarantee strikes in these ranges, there is no doubt about the potential benefit.

If you were to stay with a straight ball, one that rolls end over end only, you would not achieve more than about 1.5 degrees of angle. The strike pocket is approximately 18 inches (45.7 cm) from the edge of the gutter. Releasing the ball from the very edge of the lane creates an 18-inch displacement (or rise) during a 720-inch (60 ft [18 m]) run. A basic calculation determines the angle. While any angle into the pocket is better than 0 degrees, the strike pocket is still relatively small for entry angles of less than 2 degrees. By combining simple hand-position technique with lane-position strategy, you can create an effective entry angle.

SUCCESS SUMMARY

The release is a precise movement requiring considerable control and feel for how the ball comes off the hand. The release is made up of five phases. In the drive phase, the force of the swing goes through the ball. During the thumb release, the thumb slides off the ball near the bottom of the downswing. At the turn, the hand is positioned (or moves into position) to create the desired ball roll. During the extension phase, the ball passes through the bottom of the swing before leaving the hand. At the finger release, the fingers resist the ball's weight as the swing continues upward into the follow-through.

To ensure a proper release, keep the hand behind the ball during the swing, and maintain a firm wrist throughout the swing. The swing is a straight, relaxed, loose pendulum. Do not change the nature of the swing to accommodate different types of releases.

Review your drill scores. Record your scores in the spaces that follow and total them. Practice each drill until you can earn almost all the point for each one. Then perform each drill once in succession. If you score at least 50 points, you are ready to move onto the next step. If you score fewer than 50 points, review the sections that are giving you trouble, then repeat the drills.

SCORING YOUR SUCCESS

Wrist and Finger Drills

1. Simple Swing Practice for Hand Position	____ out of 5
2. Wrist Position and Strength Test	____ out of 5
3. Locking the Wrist	____ out of 7
4. Finger Pressure Test	____ out of 9
5. Finger Pressure During Setup	____ out of 8

Swing and Release Drill

1. Evaluating Proper Technique	____ out of 18
Total	____ **out of 52**

Not everybody's game fits within a standard performance model, so a cookie-cutter approach does not work when it comes to skill development. The descriptions and practice drills in the previous steps outline the basic skills. Bowlers should strive to perform these movement patterns as closely as possible to the way they were described. Keep in mind that every bowler is unique. No two athletes, even if trained in the same way, are exactly alike. To be successful, athletes must find a way to adjust basic skill techniques to fit their own unique qualities. Some adjustments have been alluded to already. The next step discusses the variations in essential skills that allow bowlers to develop versatility.

Fine-Tuning Your Game

The previous steps introduced the essential physical skills of bowling. Because all athletes require versatility for success, this step explores versatility in three broad areas: the stance, the swing, and the release. As part of that broader range of skill, this step also delves into aspects of the modern release. With each of these adjustments comes opportunities to manipulate your game, either to fit unique physical characteristics or to make strategic adjustments to suit changes in playing conditions.

No successful bowler throws the ball the same way from the same location over the same target every frame of every game. These one-dimensional bowlers might be successful under specific situations, but when taken out of their comfort zone, they tend to struggle terribly. This type of bowler, referred to as *house mouse*, might achieve a high average at a particular bowling center, but be unable to bowl particularly well in other venues. Don't be a house mouse! Strive to be a lion on the lanes everywhere you bowl.

ADJUSTING THE STANCE

A bowler does not stand on the same spot of the approach for every throw. As the position on the lane changes, adjustments in the setup are necessary in order to stay on line to the target. On some occasions, simply turning the whole body to face the target is all that is needed. When squaring up to the target line, neither the stance nor the ball's position in the stance changes. The bowler simply realigns. In some instances, however, changes in the setup of the stance help the mechanics of the approach and swing.

Playing the Outside Line

If the target is closer to the middle of the lane than the ball-side shoulder position, the body must close up. The bowler cannot be expected to walk straight down the approach and then suddenly yank the swing across the body in order to hit the target. Align everything—feet, hips, shoulder, and swing line—in the setup. Beginning bowlers must be convinced to move away from the middle of the lane. The farther they move from the middle, the better angle they will have into the strike pocket (figure 9.1). This is an essential adjustment until they learn how to hook the ball.

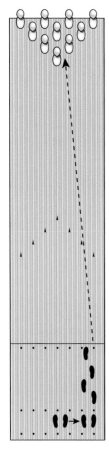

Figure 9.1 Moving away from the middle of the lane will give you a better angle into the strike pocket.

A commonly heard complaint, however, is "every time I move over, I throw the ball toward the gutter!" This indicates that the body was not properly aligned in the stance. The intended attack angle of the ball path was inward (starting closer to the gutter and pointed in toward the strike pocket), but the alignment of the body during the approach or at the finish was not oriented properly for that to happen.

Players who throw hooks need to adjust their position as well. Changes in positioning on the approach that address changes in the visual target frequently require stance adjustments. Under certain conditions, even hook throwers may find that the ball is not hooking. In this case, they need to do one of two things.

One, they need to bring their target inward. Moving the ball path closer to the strike pocket allows the ball to hook into the pocket even if the hook is actually smaller. Bowlers refer to this as moving the *break point* in. The other option is to move the feet out closer to the edge of the lane, like a nonhook thrower would. This creates more angle into the pocket from a positional change. Much like the non-hook-throwing player experiences, a dramatic change in the bowler's position on the lane requires a realignment of the body in the stance.

In all cases, the angle at which the ball is initially sent onto the lane (called the launch angle) is a product of the alignment of the shoulders. Because the swing starts at the shoulder, alignment of the upper body is the first thing to consider when changing the initial ball path. If you have practiced the swing and finish position described in previous steps, your swing and shoulders are working together.

The farther one moves toward the edge of the lane, the more likely it is that the visual target will be to the inside of the swing shoulder. For a right-handed bowler, the target will be to the left of the shoulder. This positioning creates a right-to-left angle on the lane.

For a small adjustment, turning the body may be sufficient. The normal stance characteristics need not change. When setting up, the bowler simply turns everything and faces the target. This means the bowler will not face straight up the lane. The setup (and the subsequent direction of the footwork) will be at an angle to the lane. The bowler need only be concerned with steps and the swing staying on line to the target.

If the adjustment to the side is fairly large, a normal staggered position of the feet may prevent proper lane alignment. Remember, a staggered foot position helps facilitate an open body position. If the target line points inward, some bowlers may be more comfortable adjusting the standard setup position. A simple turn of the body on the approach may not be enough.

So, when playing an outside line and trying to point the ball inward, there are three basic adjustments of the stance:

1. Turn the whole body in the direction you intend the ball to go.

2. Bring the throwing-side foot even or almost even with the opposite foot (figure 9.2). Bringing the foot forward closes the angle of the hips. (For some bowlers the throwing-side foot may actually be in front of the opposite foot.)

3. Position the ball slightly closer to the midline of the body.

4. Make sure the shoulders have the same closed alignment as the hips do. Both the upper and lower body should are similarly aligned to the target.

If there is also a change in ball position, the feel of the swing will be different. The ball will be positioned more toward the middle of the body instead of in front of the shoulder. Although the swing follows a fairly straight path back and forth, the swing plane feels slightly more like it moves out to in. It might feel as though the ball is moving away from the body at the top of the backswing. This sense of an outward movement creates a natural inward feed of the ball onto the lane. Don't fight this feeling. Let the ball swing comfortable along its natural intended line.

Let's not forget about the finish position. You can have the best stance and initial movement in the sport and still run into trouble if you throw yourself out of position at the finish. The shoulders are closed and the balance arm is pulled back slightly. The kick of the back leg is less dramatic. Swing it back to about the 6:30 position.

Figure 9.2   **ADJUSTING TO PLAY THE OUTSIDE LINE**

Starting Position

1. Throwing-side foot is even with opposite foot.
2. Ball is moved slightly inward.
3. Shoulders are closed.
4. Upper and lower body are aligned to target.

If the nonthrowing arm is too far forward or the back leg is kicked around too far, the body will be thrown back into an open position at the finish. The bowler will have a difficult time swinging to the target. The bowler will need to pull the swing across the outward-facing body; this is not recommended.

Playing the Inside Line

Bowlers who throw a substantial hook expect to move across the center of the lane as the lanes dry out. Every time a ball is thrown, lane conditioner is removed from the lane's surface. This depletion of oil increases ball traction. If the bowler has any kind of side roll, the ball will hook sooner and stronger than it did at the beginning of the bowling session.

At this point, an open setup position is required to create a strong enough launch angle across the front of the lane to keep the ball from hooking too soon. It is to be expected that one would make exactly the opposite adjustment as what was made for playing the outside line (see figures 9.3 and 9.5).

The pushaway will still move straight out from the shoulder. But, with an open shoulder angle, it might feel as though it is moving slightly away from the body. Consequently, the backswing may feel slightly behind the back. The actual path of the swing will be in a fairly straight line, but to the bowler it might feel inside to out. Again, the downswing will tuck in next to the hip (inside, close to the body) and then swing out from the shoulder to the target. It will still be close to the ideal 90-degree swing alignment of the shoulder.

For the finish position, the shoulders stay open. The opposite shoulder is forward of the swing-side shoulder. The balance arm may be slightly forward, as well. A strong kick of the back leg will make room for the inward tuck of the swing. Expect the back leg (for a right-handed bowler) to be in the 7:30 or 8:00 position.

When playing an extreme inside line, learn to walk down the edge of the lane or along the length of the ball return. This will feel awkward at first. The approach goes one way, but at the release, the shoulders open to face another direction. Learn to sidestep; allow the feet to turn outward as you walk down the approach. Steps that cross over slightly will keep the feet straight on the approach even though the idea is to play a strong angle across the lane.

Right-handed power players in particular need to learn this technique (figure 9.4). The right side of the lane breaks down faster than the left side. Finding a target left of center is not

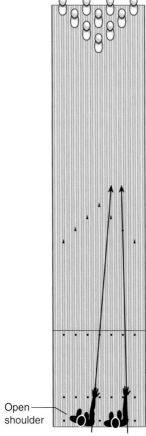

Figure 9.3 A more open setup will create more angle and keep the ball from hooking too soon on lanes that are drying out.

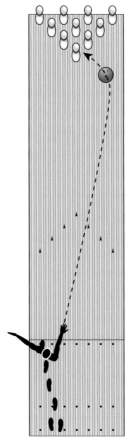

Figure 9.4 Right-handed power players should learn to walk left and throw right.

Figure 9.5 ADJUSTING TO PLAY THE INSIDE LINE

Starting Position

1. Preset the hips by dropping the throwing-side foot a few inches more than normal.
2. Set the hips and shoulders in an open position.
3. Adjust the ball so it aligns with the outside of the shoulder.
4. Drop the throwing-side foot back farther.
5. Align the ball with outside of the shoulder.
6. Open shoulders.

unusual for a right-handed power player. A right-handed bowler (if bowling on an even-numbered lane) can only move so far left on the approach before running into the ball return.

To get around this problem, bowlers adopt a couple of strategies. Some practice a shortened approach. They stand in front of the ball return, then shorten their steps enough to allow a full approach in a very short space. This is not easy, particularly for a tall bowler. Others who start in front of the ball return may choose to take fewer steps. They learn to move the ball into the downswing before they start walking. The first step is imaginary (only the swing is moving), and then they take just three steps. Some people are quite successful with this three-step approach adaptation.

If neither of the previous techniques works, and you just can't get comfortable with the drastic rhythm changes needed to use a very short approach, then consider a third option. Walk one way and throw the other. Adjust the direction of the footwork during the approach. The last step, or two, becomes a dramatic shift off the initial approach line, perhaps finishing in front of the ball return. Your slide may be in line with the left gutter or may even be left of the left gutter. Learning to walk left and throw right is a useful technique for power players to develop.

Footwork Drill 1   Outside Line

Get into setup position using a reverse stagger of the feet. For a right-handed bowler, the right foot will be slightly (1 to 2 inches [2.5-5 cm]) ahead of the left foot. Position the ball to the inside of the swing shoulder. Use an outside-in swing. Note which starting position board you position the slide foot on. Place a marker at the end of the approach, four to six boards to the left of the slide foot's starting position board. Identify the target you are aiming for. The target at the arrows should be four to six boards to the left of the swing-side shoulder's starting position.

Practice this approach line 10 times, earning up to 2 points each time.

Success Check

- Swing follows outside-in pattern.
- Feet are in reverse stagger in setup.

Score Your Success

Approach finishes in front of marker placed at foul line = 1 point

Throw rolls ball over identified target = 1 point

Your score ___

Footwork Drill 2   Straight Down the Lane

Get into setup position using a normal stagger of the feet. For a right-handed bowler, the right foot will be slightly (about 2 inches [5 cm]) behind the left foot. Position the ball directly in front of the swing shoulder. Use a straight swing. Place a marker at the end of the approach, directly in front of the slide foot's starting position board. Identify the target you are aiming for. The target at the arrows should be four to six boards to the right (for a right handed bowler) of the board the slide foot finishes on.

Practice this approach line 10 times, earning up to 2 points each time.

Success Check

- Swing is straight.
- Feet are in normal stagger in setup.

Score Your Success

Approach finishes in front of marker placed at foul line = 1 point

Throw rolls ball over identified target = 1 point

Your score ___

Footwork Drill 3   Inside Line

Get into setup position using a larger stagger of the feet than normal. Throwing-side foot will be 3 to 4 inches (7.6-15 cm) behind the left foot. Turn the toe of the throwing-side foot outward. The offset of the foot opens the hip to a larger degree as the first step starts. Position the ball slightly to the outside of the swing shoulder. Use an inside-out swing. Note which board is between your feet at the start of the approach. Place a marker at the end of the approach, 4-6 boards to the right of the starting position for the feet. Identify the specific target you are aiming for. The target at the arrows should be four to six boards to the right of the swing-side shoulder's starting position.

Practice this approach line 10 times, earning up to 2 points each time.

Success Check

- Swing follows inside-out pattern.
- Feet are in larger stagger than normal in setup.

Score Your Success

Approach finishes in front of marker = 1 point

Throw rolls ball over identified target = 1 point

Your score ___

ADJUSTING THE SWING

Bowlers can adjust the swing from one of two points of view. One is the side view, which allows us to see the shape of the pendulum as it goes back and forth. Adjusting the shape of the swing as it goes toward the release point allows the bowler to redirect the energy of the swing. The other point of view is from above, allowing us to see the lateral movement of the swing. Becoming aware of a swing's side-to-side motion helps us understand how far it may deviate from a truly straight line. It also gives us a sense of how tight the swing line is to the side of the body.

Directing the forward arc of the swing either more upward or outward influences how the bowler applies the leverage force to the ball. The bowler's goal is to adjust the release leverage by making changes to the swing arc's shape without altering the smooth motion of the swing.

The three basic arc shapes are pendulum (half circle), flattened, and V-shaped.

With the advent of the modern, high-tech game, the V-shaped swing is not used as frequently. It is discussed here so that bowlers are aware of its characteristics if they happen to see it being used. When employing the V-shaped swing motion, the force of the swing is quickly redirected upward. This was once a commonly taught technique; one still hears the phrase *hitting up on the ball*. Although redirecting the force of the swing upward may add to the finger leverage, it makes release consistency more difficult.

Today we talk about leverage. Leverage is the finger pressure the bowler feels when the swing is at maximum extension from the shoulder. Even though the ball is being fed onto the lane smoothly, the amount of pressure and direction being applied determines the strength of hook. Various arc motions influence how the force of the swing is applied to the ball. Adjusting the position of the release in tandem with how the swing goes through the ball helps create a variety of ball motions. When adjusting the pendulum shape of the swing, the bowler is really adjusting the direction of the swing's force. Sometimes the direction of the swing is more down the lane in order to reduce the hook and add control to the ball's movement. Other times the energy is directed out and up through the ball, adding more force to the finger pressure of the release.

Half-Circle (or Pendulum) Swing

The half-circle, or pendulum, swing (figure 9.6) is the traditional swing. All players should first learn to bowl with this type of swing, which is modestly aggressive. The most reliable and consistent swing type, it can be used with most release types to create a variety of ball reactions.

The swing is based on a pendulum motion. Once the bowler gets the ball into the swing, the ball will swing along its natural path without effort from the bowler. There is nothing to alter. The inherent consistency and accuracy of the swing makes it an important part of a bowler's development. Because of the muscle-free and reliable movement, it is the easiest for novice bowlers to learn.

Figure 9.6 HALF-CIRCLE (OR PENDULUM) SWING

1. Ball makes a half circle on the way back.
2. Ball makes a half circle on the way through.
3. Swing does not hesitate or accelerate.
4. Hand is behind the ball,
5. Swing flows through the release.

Imagine making a half circle with your swing—trace a half circle on the way back and a half circle on the way through. Relax and allow the swing to complete its full motion without hesitation or acceleration. The arm and the ball fall through the downswing at the same rate as the backswing.

Feel for the hand behind the ball. Do not press forward against the ball as the swing comes down. Applying pressure might cause an acceleration that will disturb the continuity of the swing.

As the swing passes the bottom of its arc, the bowler feels the hand and fingers drive through the leverage position. Just before the ball enters its upswing, the ball will release itself from the fingers. The swing provides the force; the finger leverage position provides the resistance.

Allow the swing to flow through the release. The position and motion of the hand from behind the ball at the release point determines how much side roll the ball has. The swing drives the finger forward and up the side of the ball; gravity makes the ball fall down and in. These opposing forces create the leverage that turns the ball.

You should feel no sense of gripping and throwing the ball out to the target. The swing will carry the ball out onto the lane. A loft of 12 to 18 inches (30.5-45.7 cm) past the slide foot is typical.

Flattened Swing

Imagine stretching out the arc of the swing, creating a long, flat spot at the bottom of the arc. This is a flattened swing (figure 9.7), the least aggressive of the swing types.

Try reaching out to the target rather than bringing the hand up and through the shot. With a flattened swing, it will feel as if the hand is pressing through the back of the ball, as if you were trying to reach through the ball toward the pins. Direct the energy of the swing down the lane.

Figure 9.7 FLATTENED SWING

1. Reach out to the target.
2. Set the ball down softly on the lane.
3. Follow-through tends to be extended and low.
4. Hand feels as if it is pushing through the back of the ball.

The late John Jowdy in his book *Bowling Execution* (Human Kinetics) has described the flattened swing as a drag shot because it feels as if the swing drags the ball along the floor. He also suggests deemphasizing of finger pressure. The hand should feel soft, with just enough pressure to keep the ball in the hand. He particularly espoused a follow-through that was long and low, perhaps not even getting to shoulder high at swing finish. The flattened swing causes little loft. The ball does not drop onto the lane, but is set down softly. For a bowler of average height, the ball will contact the lane 6 to 10 inches (15-25 cm) past the slide foot.

The goal of a flattened swing is to push the ball down the lane. Typically, not a lot of release motion is involved. The whole idea is to promote a straighter, more controllable ball movement. This swing type works best with a softer wrist position. Together, the two provide a nice drive down the lane with minimal hook. The flattened swing is a solid technique to use on dry lanes or to shoot most types of spares when the prime concern is accuracy rather than power.

V-Shaped Swing

The V-shaped swing (figure 9.8) features a sharper angle of descent from the top of the downswing toward the release point, followed by an aggressive upward redirecting of the follow-through. While not recommend for the modern game, many bowlers still try to employ this technique. Some bowlers try to accentuate the kick of the ball off the hand in an effort to create more revolutions. They have the idea that just as the ball rolls forward and down off the fingers, redirecting the swing upward can accelerate the ball's spin. They try to accentuate the forward spin by making the hand kick upward from behind the ball. It may feel as if they are lifting the ball out onto the lane.

The timing window to complete the V-shaped swing and still release the ball off the hand cleanly is small, and it is a relatively easy release to miss. Redirecting the swing upward must work perfectly with the finger release point. Because there is little extension before the finger release, the turn and finger leverage phases of the release are close together. Loft will depend on when in the swing arc the upward redirecting is applied, and the hand motion used at the point of release.

Figure 9.8 V-SHAPED SWING

1. Gently press the swing forward against the back of the ball as it goes into the downswing.
2. Roll the ball forward onto the fingers at the bottom of the downswing.
3. Kick the fingers up from under the ball by redirecting the swing arc just as the ball's weight transfers onto fingers.
4. Press with the fingers only, not the thumb.
5. Move the follow-through upward.

The press of the hand during the downswing is not a quick, jerky motion. It is not like snapping a whip, where you move the hand forward then draw it back rapidly. Imagine pressing against a large spring or squeezing the air out of a bag. The constant pressure smoothly accelerates the downswing.

Depending on how late the release is in the swing, the V-shaped swing may cause greater loft distances than other release types. This is particularly true for bowlers who do not soften the wrist. Bowlers who keep the wrist firm throughout the swing and release rely on the force of the swing and the rotation of the forearm to take the ball off the hand. For bowlers with a firm wrist position and aggressive upward swing at the release point, a loft that goes down the lane as much as 3 to 5 feet (1-1.7 m) is not unusual. Particularly long loft distances, in excess of 6 feet (1.8 m), often indicate excessive thumb-squeeze pressure. Thumb squeeze makes the release less effective and frequently less consistent.

MISSTEP

Your swing sends the ball more than 7 feet (2.1 m) down the lane.

CORRECTION

Make sure that only finger pressure is applied at the release. The thumb does no work.

Caution: The V-swing, in conjunction with a release position in which the hand is strongly offset, generates considerable ball revolutions and a strong axis rotation. Although the entry angle is potentially very large, controlling ball reaction may be challenging. The ball will tend to overskid where there is oil (imagine a car spinning its tires on ice) and overreact (or flip) as soon as it touches a dry part of the lane. As lane conditions deteriorate and become less predictable, this type of swing release and swing mechanics is ill advised.

A truly straight swing is always desired. This swing movement is what you should have been practicing throughout the steps of this book. But, the reality is that almost all bowlers have some degree of lateral swing motion. Sometimes a lateral motion is beneficial, sometimes not. So, let's investigate what is useful and what to avoid. A swing can deviate from a straight line in only two ways: away from the body or into the body (figure 9.9).

Lateral movements away from the body often move the hand to a weaker leverage position on the ball. Lateral movements that draw the swing closer to the body and under the swing-side shoulder frequently enhance the leverage position of the hand at the release.

Subtle changes in the lateral motion of the swing will affect how the ball comes off the hand. Certain styles of play use a swing that does not follow the straight line of a true pendulum motion. Sometimes the movement happens by accident as a result of a bowler's performance characteristics. Sometimes, though, the bowler purposely makes subtle adjustments to the lateral movement to create a different feel for the swing and the resulting release.

Figure 9.9 A swing can deviate (*a*) away from the body or (*b*) into the body.

Loop (or Inside-Out) Swing

The shoulder is a complex joint with a wide range of motion. The goal is to create a swing that accommodates the natural movement of the arm without compromising the accuracy of the swing. A true pendulum is not continuous; it has a stopping point at the top of its arc at which it changes direction. Wouldn't it be nice to have a smooth, powerful swing that uses the natural rolling motion of the arm in the socket but is still dependable and accurate? The loop, or inside-out, swing (figure 9.10) is frequently the power player's swing.

Figure 9.10 **LOOP (OR INSIDE-OUT) SWING**

Pushaway

1. Ball position and initial direction of pushaway is slightly to the inside of the shoulder line.

2. Hand positon is neutral, with thumb pointing slightly inward (11:00).

Backswing

1. As the ball swings back, clearing the hip, bowler feels as if the ball is moving away from the body slightly.
2. The swing will brush past the hip on the way back.
3. At the top of the backswing, the bowler will feel the swing loop back in line with the shoulder.
4. The inside motion is accomplished in two ways. The hand rotates to a slightly open position or the bowler pulls the swing in toward the body or both.
5. At the top of the backswing, the ball is directly behind the shoulder.

Downswing

1. As the back leg kicks out of the way, the swing falls into a slot directly next to the hip. The ball's position is under or slightly to the inside of the shoulder position.
2. Think of the ball filling the space where the back leg has just been.
3. Feel the inside of the arm or the elbow brush past the hip during the downswing.
4. At the bottom of the swing, the ball is directly under the shoulder or slightly inside the shoulder line.
5. The swing drives through the ball and reaches out from the shoulder.

What are the advantages of this type of swing? First, it is a continuous, fluid stroke. The footwork does not pause, so why should the swing? This type of movement keeps the swing moving as smoothly as the footwork. Second, the inward tuck of the swing puts the hand in a better leveraging position behind the ball. Third, many find the mechanics of this swing to be less stressful than a true pendulum motion. The loop swing works well with the natural movement expected from the ball-and-socket structure of the shoulder.

This swing can be as accurate as a true pendulum-type swing. The most important element of swing accuracy is the direction of the swing from the top of the backswing to the release point. If the ball swings forward directly on line with the target line, it doesn't matter too much how it got there on the way back. Yes, while too much lateral movement on the way back makes it difficult to get the ball to the same position at the top of the backswing consistently, a subtle, controlled inside loop can be a practical means of swinging the ball.

Sometimes, the body structure of many bowlers (particularly those whose hips are wider than their shoulders) prevents the development of a true back-and-forth pendulum swing. So why not develop something that works with the body's natural movement?

The benefits of a well-practiced loop swing far outweigh the slight sacrifices in accuracy. By no means does the swing incorporate a large, dramatic loop. The legendary coach Fred Borden often referred to a pro loop of about 4 inches (10 cm). The pro loop deviates from a straight line by no more than 4 inches: 2 inches (5 cm) out, 2 inches in.

The most important aspect to consider is the downswing. The backswing may not be in a perfectly straight line, but the downswing should be. The swing loops back into position at the top of the backswing. From the top of the backswing to the release, the entire downswing will be on line to the target. Bowlers with a more dramatic inward loop (or tuck) at the top of the backswing need to dramatically sweep the back leg out of the way to provide clearance for the downswing.

Outside Loop

A common swing error is an outside (away from the body) loop. While an inside loop is desirable, bowlers should fix an outside loop as soon as they recognize it. Luckily, it is easy to detect. The backswing is usually fairly straight, but then the swing moves away from the body in the downswing, usually because of one of these two factors: pushaway and footwork.

PUSHAWAY

Some bowlers are not comfortable letting the swing pass next to the hip. Others, in an attempt to keep the hand behind the ball, exaggerate the open hand position. In either case, the initial ball movement is away from the hip. If the pushaway goes out, the path of the backswing will end up behind the back. The bowler must then send the downswing back around the hip to provide clearance for the ball.

Sometimes bowlers direct the pushaway too much in front of the body. The swing follows a path that starts inside, moves outside, and then moves farther inside, crossing in front of the bowler quite dramatically. It may be observed that the swing ends up somewhat away from the body at the peak of the backswing. At this point the swing may then loop away even more dramatically, particularly if the bowler tries to force it forward, causing the downswing to swing in front of the bowler. This swing line starts in front of the body and may finish even farther across the body when it is finished.

FOOTWORK

Some bowlers walk in front of the swing, forcing swing realignment. If the initial step with the throwing-side leg is toward the swing line, the bowler is forced to move the ball away from the intended swing line as well in order to make room for the swing to clear the leg on the way back. Remember, the lines of the footwork and the swing do not cross during the approach. The slight crossover step (nonthrowing foot steps in front of other foot) at the beginning of the approach is important; it allows a straight backswing that stays close to the hip and under the shoulder.

Regardless of the cause, an outside loop needs to be corrected immediately. An outside loop is detrimental for several reasons. It diminishes accuracy considerably. The movement of the ball away from the body might pull the bowler off balance. (For most people, the farther a weight gets from the body, the harder it is to hold onto it or control it.) As the arm moves away from the body, it becomes more difficult to keep the hand in position behind the ball for an effective release. Frequently, the hand (and the entire arm) turns around the ball early in the swing. This is known as circling the ball, and it causes a weak release. Release inconsistencies such as dropping the ball are bound to happen.

Make sure the ball is properly aligned with the shoulder during the setup. Position the elbow directly above the hip at the side of the body. The pushaway is straight forward, allowing the swing to pass along the side of the body. Avoid an outward movement during the pushaway that may cause the swing to wrap around behind the body.

Sometimes a slight outside-in motion is useful. The swing follows a straight line, but it starts and finishes slightly in front of the body. This is a swing that helps when playing an outside line. The body may be turned inward (closed) slightly. Although the swing is straight, the bowler will feel the position at the top of the backswing as slightly away from the body. This swing motion helps direct the ball toward the pocket when playing a target line that starts near the edge of the lane and is directed in toward the pins.

Swing Drill 1   Outside-In Swing

This exercise helps you develop a feel for a swing line slightly different from one that goes straight back and forth. Stand in finish position with a practice partner *behind you*. Your partner's hand is slightly to the outside of your shoulder (to the right, if you are right handed). The goal is to swing the ball back so it touches your partner's hand near the top of the backswing.

Set your shoulders in a closed position. Position the throwing-side foot slightly ahead of other foot. Start the pushaway to the inside. Let the ball swing back toward your partner's hand.

The ball should touch your partner's hand at the top of the backswing. If the ball swings back to the wrong location, your partner catches the ball in the backswing and repositions it so you can feel where the correct location is.

Practice 10 outside-in swings, earning up to 1 point per swing.

Success Check

- Feel for the correct location.
- Each swing should be separate, with a distinct pushaway, backswing, and pause.

Score Your Success

Swing touches partner's hand and does not need repositioning = 1 point

Your score ___

Swing Drill 2   Straight Swing

This exercise helps you develop a feel for a swing line that is straight back and forth. Stand in the finish position with a practice partner behind you.

Your partner's hand is directly behind your shoulder. The goal is to swing the ball back so it touches your partner's hand near the top of the backswing.

Start the pushaway straight out from the shoulder and let the ball swing back toward your partner's hand. The ball should touch your partner's hand at the top of the backswing. If the ball swings back to the wrong location, your partner will catch the ball in the backswing and reposition it so you can feel where the correct location is. Practice 10 straight swings, earning up to 1 point per swing.

Success Check

- Feel for the correct location.
- Each swing should be separate, with a distinct pushaway, back-swing, and pause.

Score Your Success

Swing touches partner's hand and does not need repositioning = 1 point

Your score ___

Swing Drill 3   Inside-Out Swing

Follow the same procedure as in the two previous drills. Your partner's hand is slightly to the inside of your shoulder.

Set your shoulders slightly more open than normal. Start pushaway slightly inward. Let the swing loop back toward your partner's hand.

The ball should touch your partner's hand at the top of the backswing. If the ball swings back to the wrong location, your partner will catch the ball in the backswing and reposition it. Practice 10 inside-out swings, earning up to 1 point per swing.

Success Check

- Feel for the correct location.
- Each swing should be separate, with a distinct pushaway, back-swing, and pause.

Score Your Success

Swing touches partner's hand and does not need repositioning = 1 point

Your score ___

ADJUSTING THE RELEASE

Changes in wrist position at the release alter the leveraging position of the fingers. Six basic wrist positions include three positions up and down and three left and right. When discussing these positions, visualize the hand hanging by your side and the palm facing forward.

Up and down describes wrist flexion: cupped, straight, or broken back.

Left and right is the lateral offset, or cock, of the wrist: Fingers point toward the body, toward the floor, or away from the body.

The degree of cup determines how far under the ball the finger are positioned. The lateral position determines how far left or right of center the fingers are positioned. The combination of these two positions (at the release point) determines the leverage strength of the release.

Strong = Cocked inward and wrist cupped

Medium = No wrist cock (finger pointed forward), straight wrist position

Weak = Wrist uncocked (finger pointed out), wrist extended (flexed back)

Some bowlers prefer to set the hand into the desired position in the stance. Others position the hand during the swing.

Weak Release Position

The bent wrist position is the weakest. Use this position when you want very little or no hook. It is a good technique for dry lanes and when shooting spares.

The weakest release position is frequently a motionless release. The hand stays in whatever position it is in as the ball comes down to the release all the way through the release. At the release, the hand is on the top half of the ball and the fingers outside the centerline. The bowler merely swings through the hand position and softly strokes the ball onto the lane.

When setting up in the stance, the bowler prepares for the bent-wrist release by laying the wrist back and turning the fingers to the outside. The wrist remains slightly bent during the swing. With the wrist laid back, the thumb points down and in during the release. This release works well with a relaxed, extended follow-through. An active release can be used with this wrist position. Active means that the bowler may choose to use a slight rotation of the forearm to add a little bit of side roll. Generally, the weak hand position generates a slight hook. Using a slight forearm rotation results in a soft, arcing ball path.

Unfortunately, many bowlers use this release unintentionally. They let the wrist break back excessively and often exert little or no finger pressure. The ball drops off the hand and has a weak rolling motion. This is the main reason beginning bowlers cannot generate an effective hook. Develop a straight wrist position for your typical release before modifying the position to create other types of ball roll.

Medium (or Straight Wrist) Release

The straight wrist position (figure 9.11)—the basic wrist position all bowlers should strive to develop—creates a modest to strong hook, depending on whether the release is active or passive. If the release is somewhat late in the swing, strong extension, firm finger leverage, and aggressive forearm rotation can create an effective hook.

Figure 9.11 Straight wrist position.

To achieve the straight wrist position, imagine a straight line from the elbow to the tip of the index finger. Lock the gripping fingers in place. Feel the pads of the fingers pressing against the inside of the finger holes. Firm pressure against the surface of the ball with the outside fingers locks the wrist in position. This helps maintain wrist position throughout the swing. The palm presses against the back of the ball as the swing enters the release phase. Feel the fingers drive through the back of the ball as the release finishes.

The straight wrist position is the most versatile. You will be free to do just about anything you want to at the release. You can change hand positions (cocking or uncocking the wrist from side to side) and forearm rotation (staying behind the ball or turning around the side) depending on the number of revolutions you want to impart or the amount of side roll you want.

Strong Wrist Position

The combination of motions that takes place during the release characterizes what might be called the modern release. The strong hand position is an active release. (In fact, if you are in a strongly loaded hand position and you don't use active motions at the release, the ball won't come off the hand very well.) The cupped wrist (figure 9.12) is the most difficult wrist position, and it might even cause injury. Not everybody is capable of using a strongly cupped wrist during the release. With the wrist cupped, the ball feels as though it is resting on the heel of the palm. As the flex angle of the wrist increases, turn the hand inward slightly. The fingers will point in (toward 9:00), and the thumb points out (toward 3:00).

Figure 9.12 Cupped wrist position.

Some power players will increase the angle of the wrist as the ball enters the downswing. There is an obvious load–unload motion during the release. The wrist angle increases near the bottom of the swing in a scooping motion. As the swing drives forward toward the release, the momentum of the swing causes the wrist to unflex. The wrist does not relax; the muscles remain tense. The swing weight creates enough force to stretch the hand like a spring under a load. The extension and uncupping movement tilts the ball forward onto the fingers.

MISSTEP

Flexing the wrist straight up. Merely flexing the wrist without an off-setting turn puts considerable stress on the wrist.

CORRECTION

In the stance, point the fingers (from under the ball) toward the wall. Imagine a line from the middle of the wrist to the index finger. This is the line of support positioned under the ball.

So, to maximize the leverage force as the ball comes off the hand and maximize the effect of the strongest hand position, two things happen simultaneously. One, the wrist uncocks. The lateral kick caused by the wrist uncocking accentuates the side roll and provides acceleration of the fingers from under the ball. Two, the wrist uncups. Uncupping the wrist causes the ball to tip forward onto the fingers. For a split second, the fingers take the entire swing weight of the ball. If the finger pressure is firmly maintained, the fingers will kick out from under the ball and then up the side. This finger pressure acts like a loaded spring. The fingers will snap shut as the weight of the ball comes off the hand, and the ball will snap into the strong revolutions it takes to create a strongly hooking ball. As you feel the weight of the ball on your fingers, kick the fingers up from under the ball. Feeling the finger press closed toward the palm maximizes the feel of leverage. Do not press forward (or squeeze) with the thumb, only the fingers. Imagine trying to kick the ball over into a heavy roll (just like you would if you had a small tire in your hand and you were trying to spin your wheels.) Consider how one makes a yo-yo work. The wrist doesn't stay stiff, instead there is an obvious snap-and-recoil motion.

For the power release, the motions must occur late in the swing, and the hand movement is quick. If the release is very late in the swing arc, the ball will come off the hand just as the pendulum of the swing moves upward. Some players are capable of driving the ball down into the lane while accomplishing an aggressive release and follow-through technique. They may be able to impart considerable revolutions of the ball while setting the ball down quickly.

The previous discussion describes the extremes of hand action. Considerable variation exists between these two extremes. What the fingers do at the release has the biggest effect on how a ball rolls. Where they are at the beginning of the release, how they change position on the ball as the ball swings through the release zone, and how much pressure they apply at the release provide numerous ball-motion options that create an arsenal of strategies for the committed athlete.

You should experiment with a variety of release positions. Mastering different releases gives you the ability to adjust the ball reaction to changes in lane conditions. Do not limit the conditions you can succeed in by limiting your release options. Find releases that suit the way you would like to manipulate ball rolls. Also, experiment to understand your body's limitations. Find positions that are comfortable, positions that allow you to repeat a shot and control ball motion on the lane, and do not overly stress your wrist and forearm.

A word of caution: Sometimes a bend at the elbow accentuates the wrist-cupping motion. Excessively flexing the wrist throughout the swing may be accompanied by a bend at the elbow as well. Unconsciously, the bowler is trying to position the hand as far under the ball as possible. Bending the arm puts the hand under the ball in the same way as cupping the wrist. Bending the arm is a compensation movement, increasing the angle of one joint in order to reduce the angle of another. If the bend is slight and there is no alteration of the swing line, this is acceptable. Bending the elbow positions the hand under the ball for a potentially stronger leverage position. It is important, though, that the swing line remain straight. Some bowlers bend the arm while cupping the wrist successfully. Power players using some bend at the elbow usually allow the arm to achieve full extension at the release. The arm rarely stays bent for the entire release. (This technique is particularly noticeable among bowlers who use the thumbless grip. During the thumbless technique, bending the arm is the only way to keep the hand under and behind the ball without dropping it.)

The goal of bowlers whose arm bends during the swing is to allow the arm to reach maximum extension at the release. The swing is like a piston stroke, driving down and through to full extension as the swing reaches the release. Keeping the arm bent the entire time may cause problems.

Ideally, the wrist cup should not be so great that you feel the need to bend the arm. An excessively bent arm sacrifices power—because it is a shorter pendulum—and accuracy. Bending the elbow makes it more difficult to keep the swing in line; the elbow may tend to fly away from the hip. As the elbow moves away from the body, not only is accuracy lost, but the hand also overrotates around the ball too early in the swing, which causes a poor release.

Bending the arm excessively during the swing may cause other problems. The biceps muscles contract when bending the arm, so the bowler is essentially doing a biceps curl while swinging the ball, This creates tension at the shoulder, inhibiting a truly muscle-free swing and increases the chance for injury. Generally speaking, avoid bending the elbow during the swing. Release strength should be a function of the swing and the hand position.

MISSTEP

Chicken winging, or flying-elbow syndrome, is most likely to occur during an aggressive release motion. As the forearm rolls through the release motion, the rest of the arm tends to follow it around the ball.

CORRECTION

Cup the wrist only as much as is comfortable. Keep the arm straight throughout the swing. Feel the arm fully extend at the bottom of the backswing and again at the bottom of the downswing. Keep the swing line next to the hip and on line to the target. Put only as much release motion into the shot as will still allow for consistency and accuracy.

Release Drill 1   Under the Bar

The goal of this exercise is to learn how to get the ball down on the lane sooner. The objective is to minimize the lift and to emphasize swinging down the lane.

While using a normal approach, practice a flattened swing and a longer extension to the target. You may choose to use a weaker wrist position, as well.

If bowling with a partner, use a bar or long handle about 3 feet (1 m) long. Have your partner get in position by the foul line, holding the bar across the lane at a height of about 10 inches (25.4 cm). Your partner should hold the bar far enough out past the foul line that your hand will not hit the bar on the follow-through.

If you are practicing by yourself, support the bar on two boxes placed in the gutter on either side of the lane. The bar must be long enough (45 to 48 inches [114-121 cm]) to reach across the lane. Alternatively, cut a large hole in opposite sides of a large box. The hole should be large enough to allow the ball to pass through. The height of the hole should be no more than 10 inches (25.4 cm).

The objective of this drill is to drive down and through the ball, using a flattened swing and a follow-through that extends down the lane rather than in an upward arc. Try to minimize finger lift and ball loft. Execute 10 consecutive throws, earning up to 4 points per throw.

Success Check

- Swing is flattened.
- Follow-through extends down the lane.
- Finger lift and ball loft is minimal.

Score Your Success

Wrist is in a straight or weak position at the release = 1 point

Ball passes under the bar without touching (or goes through the hole in the box) = 2 points

Ball is not released behind the foul line = 1 point

Your score ___

Release Drill 2   Clear the Towel

This drill is particularly helpful to a bowler who sets the ball down early because of a weak hand position or insufficient swing momentum.

Place a towel on the lane 12 to 15 inches (30.5-38 cm) past the foul line. The objective is to allow the momentum of the swing to send the ball past the towel. Have a partner watch to see where the ball lands. If you are squeezing too hard, the ball will have excessive loft. If there is excessive loft, the partner should hold a bar or hand over the lane to indicate where the ball should land. Getting the ball over the towel but under the bar requires precise release mechanics. Execute 10 consecutive throws, earning up to 7 points per throw.

Success Check

- Swing is smooth and continuous.
- Wrist position is straight or cupped.

Score Your Success

Swing is smooth, with no jerky motion at release = 1 point

Finish position is held; body does not pull up = 1 point

Wrist position is straight or cupped at release = 2 points

Ball is projected past the towel = 2 points

Ball lands smoothly, with no loud thump from excessive loft = 1 point

Your score ___

SUCCESS SUMMARY

This step emphasizes basic ways you can modify the standard set of skills. All bowlers who progress to higher levels of involvement in the game confront a variety of environmental conditions, specifically variations in lane conditions. To maintain the desired scoring level, they must develop adaptive skills.

The variations in the swing, the approach, and the release discussed in this step give you a larger set of tools. Changing the nature of the ball movement (more or less hook), as well as the spot on the lane at which a target line may be established, provides opportunity to adjust to changing lane conditions. You must be confident in your ability to throw the ball in different ways and play all parts of the lane. Once you have firmly established the basic skills (the initial steps of this book), modifying them creates a more complete game.

Review your drill scores. Record your scores in the spaces that follow and total them. If you score at least 170 points, you are ready to move on to the next step. If you score fewer than 170 points, review the sections that are giving you trouble, and then repeat the drills.

SCORING YOUR SUCCESS

Footwork Drills

1. Outside Line   ____ out of 20

2. Straight Down the Lane   ____ out of 20

3. Inside Line   ____ out of 20

Swing Drills

1. Outside-In Swing   ____ out of 10

2. Straight Swing   ____ out of 10

3. Inside-Out Swing   ____ out of 10

Release Drills

1. Under the Bar   ____ out of 40

2. Clear the Towel   ____ out of 70

   Total   **____ out of 200**

This step is the last one to specifically discuss physical skills. As you worked your way through the preceding steps, the complexity of the game should have become apparent. Be confident in your basic skills—footwork, timing, balance, swing line, and release—before attempting any of the more-advanced techniques.

On the other hand, don't be too cautious. As you develop a greater command of basic skills, try new things. Expect to make mistakes. Occasionally, you will be frustrated, but don't be discouraged. Establish reasonable goals, ones that push you to work without seeming insurmountable. Once you reach a goal, determine a new one.

Think through problems. Careful step-by-step analysis reveals issues that are holding back your skill development. Once you identify them, conquer them. Seek advice. Other's observations may lead to insight into your own game. Sometimes the mere notion that another person supports your efforts may be all you need to confidently pursue higher levels of performance. Persevere, nothing worthwhile comes easy. In the words of coaching legend John Wooden, "Nothing works unless you do."

Targeting Strikes

The goal of bowling is to throw strikes, getting the ball to enter the pins at that special spot on either side of the head pin called the strike pocket. This step introduces the basic systems for adjusting the strike line.

Once physical skill grants bowlers the ability to repeat shots and create effective ball roll, three things must follow. One, bowlers must learn strategies that allow them to find quickly a target line to the strike pocket. Two, they must create enough angle and ball drive to actually get strikes when hitting the strike pocket. Lastly, they must develop confidence in their ability to adjust a strike target line as lane conditions change.

Finding a path to the strike pocket is a matter of targeting strategy, but no targeting strategy works if you cannot hit your target. This is where overcoming the challenge of physical skills comes into play. However, understanding lane dimensions helps determine an actual line to the target. Attention to the starting position on the approach, the target on the lane the ball rolls over, and where the ball contacts the pins gives you all the information needed to determine a line to the pocket. The best physical game in the world is useless if you roll the ball on the wrong part of the lane. Additionally, if no adjustment system is in place to deal with miscalculation of the strike line or accommodation for ever-changing lane conditions, there will be little chance of bowling success.

You can adopt two basic strategies for adjusting your target line: a *pivot* system and an *angle-shift* system. Both rely on an understanding of the relationship of distances on the lane. The first system changes the ball's location through simple adjustments to the bowler's starting position on the approach. This is a pivot system. The entire target line rotates around a central point, or pivot, located at the arrows on the lane.

The second system is an angle-shift system. The angle at which the ball enters the pocket is an important factor for effective striking. Increasing or decreasing the attack angle as needed, without changing the ball's contact point, is a necessary adjustment strategy. By maintaining a specific relationship between how much the visual target on the lane is changed compared to how much the starting position on the lane is changed, the entry angle to the pocket can be increased or decreased at will without changing the ball's final location.

All bowling lanes are built to specified dimensions. Bowlers must know three specific lane dimension distances. Knowing the relationship between the distances for each of these lane sections allows you to develop adjustment strategies based on simple ratios.

- The distance from the starting position on the approach to the foul line
- The distance from the foul line to the targeting arrows on the lane
- The distance from the targeting arrows to the pins

For any targeting strategy to pay off, pay attention to every point of the target line. Know exactly where the approach starts and finishes. Know exactly where your intended target is and whether or not the ball rolled over it. If you missed the target, by how much did you miss it? Watch the ball hit the pins. Was the pinfall what you expected?

Pins that remain standing are clues to the quality and accuracy of the shot. Pins stand for a reason. By observing how the pins fall, the knowledgeable bowler can determine whether the problem is physical or strategic. Many bowlers blame bad luck for their lack of pin carry. They get it into their minds that nothing can be done about it. Without analyzing the problem and implementing a revised strategy, they are bound to repeat the same mistake and get the same result.

PRIMARY AND SECONDARY TARGETS

The two primary target points on the lane are the starting position on the approach and the target arrows on the lanes (figure 10.1). These two points define the target line to the pins.

When setting up on the approach, pay attention to the location of your throwing-side shoulder. The ball swings from the shoulder, so aim from the shoulder. The position of the shoulder relative to the position of the visual target determines both the nature of the stance (open or closed) and the direction of the footwork. In many situations, you do not walk straight down the lane; instead, you walk toward the target.

Three sets of dots, usually five or seven dots per set, are evenly spaced across the approach directly in line with the arrows on the lane. One set of dots is 15 feet (4.6 m) from the foul line, another is 12 feet (3.6 m), and the last set of dots is at the end of the approach an inch or two (2.5-5 cm) in front of the foul line.

A line drawn from the dot that the throwing shoulder is positioned over to the arrow identified as the preferred target creates a path on the lane. The direction of this path influences the direction of the footwork. By comparing the starting dot with the dot finished over, you can determine whether or not you walked along the intended path.

Primary Points of the Target Line

The two primary points of the target line are the bowler's starting position on the approach and the visual target on the lane. The arrows, about 15 feet (4.6 m) out on the lanes, are the preferred visual targets for most bowlers. Some bowlers

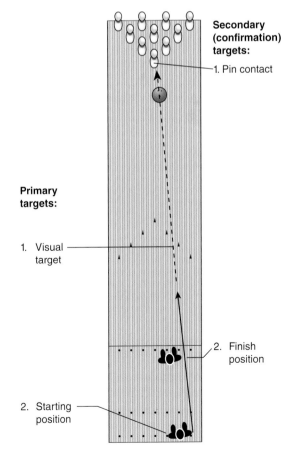

Figure 10.1 Target points.

Secondary (confirmation) targets:
1. Pin contact

Primary targets:
1. Visual target
2. Finish position

2. Starting position

may choose a point between two arrows. In either case, the visual point is closer to the foul line than to the pins.

The pins are not the primary visual target. Learn to be a spot or line bowler, rather than a pin bowler. Pick a spot that is close; it is easier to focus on it and precisely identify the size of an error. Although some bowlers use more than the arrows, the arrows are the obvious targets to start with. Most skilled bowlers do not look at the pins until the ball hits them. If the starting position is correct and the ball rolls over the intended target, the ball's path will be fairly predictable whether the pins are 60 feet (18 m) away or 600.

Why look at the pins at all? Because the pins are a secondary target. Where the ball makes contact and how the pins fall (or don't fall) are clues to how effective the shot was. Always learn from each shot.

Secondary Points of the Target Line

The secondary points of the target line are the finishing point of the approach and the ball's contact point at the pins.

Compare the finishing point on the approach with both the starting point and the visual target on the lane. This indicates whether the footwork was straight toward the target. If the approach is not straight, one of two things happens. Either the bowler will be unable to hit the desired target, or the target will be hit from a different angle than was originally intended. In either case, the ball path will not follow the desired target line.

Develop the habit of looking down at the slide foot after each shot. The final position of the footwork will tell you whether you walked in the intended direction. Frequently, the finish position should split the difference between the start position and the visual target. For instance, if the visual target is 4 inches (10 cm) to the right of the starting position, expect the finishing point on the approach to be 2 inches (5 cm) to the right of the original starting point.

Where the ball contacts the pins is the final point of the target line. Verification of your choice of target line comes from hitting the desired strike pocket. If the ball does not end up where it was supposed to, you need to determine the problem. Either poor technique or an incorrect strategy is to be blamed. Perhaps the ball was rolled improperly or the choice of starting position and target was incorrect.

As your physical performance becomes more consistent, you can begin to eliminate physical factors as a cause for poor results. To be more precise, sensitivity to your physical game will allow you to determine more readily what caused an errant shot. Once you are satisfied that a physical problem is not to blame, you can concentrate your efforts on adjusting targeting strategies.

USING STRIKE ADJUSTMENT SYSTEMS

The two basic strike adjustment strategies (3-1-2 *pivot* and 3-4-5 *angle shift*) rely on the relationships between three reference points—the pins, the arrows, and the starting position on the approach. A third system (the 1-to-2 system) is a variation of the angle-shift system.

The numerical aspect of these systems is based on a relationship of on-lane distances. A bowling lane can be broken down into 15-foot (4.6 m) increments. The 15-foot increments are the distances to the three points that define a ball's target line:

the starting position, the visual target at the arrows, and the ball's contact point at the pins. The ratio of these distances from a fixed point is how the numbers are determined. Adjustments are a matter of bowling math.

3-1-2 Pivot System

With this system, the visual target at the arrows does not change as adjustments are made. The target at the arrows becomes a pivot around which the strike line moves (figure 10.2). When using the pivot system, the bowler needs to determine two things before making an adjustment for an errant strike shot. One, what was the direction of the mistake; did the ball go to the left or to the right of the intended strike pocket? Two, by how much did the ball miss the strike? It is usually easy to see where the ball went, but figuring out exactly how far it missed by takes careful observation (and a little bit of calculation).

ADJUSTING DIRECTION

Consider a seesaw—as one end goes down, the other end goes up. Now, lay the seesaw on its side. As one end moves right, the other end moves left. This is how the *pivot system* works. One end of the seesaw is the starting position. The other end is the ball's contact point at the pins. As the starting position moves right, the ball's location at the pins moves left, and vice versa.

This gives us the most basic adjustment strategy in the game: move in the direction of the mistake. *Mistake* means where the ball ended up at the pins. *Move* means the lateral change of the starting position on the approach.

> **When missing right, move right. If missing left, move left.**

It is 45 feet (13.7 m) (three sets of 15 feet [4.6 m]) from the arrows to the pins and 30 feet (9 m) (two sets of 15 feet) from the arrows to the starting position. This 3-to-2 ratio allows you to change where the ball ends up by making careful changes in the starting position on the lane.

Let's say you move two boards to the right from your initial starting position. (Make sure to turn the body enough to face the original target). If you walk to that target, the approach will end up one board to the right of the original path. (This is the 1 in the 3-1-2 system.) The ball will end up three boards left of the original contact point at the pins.

> **Adjustments are made as multiples of the basic 3:2 ratio: 6:4, 9:6, and so on.**

Keep in mind that the basic adjustment strategies are based on straight lines. If you throw a hook, the numerical relationship of these strategies might change.

Figure 10.2   3-1-2 pivot system.

When using the 3-1-2 system, be aware of a few things. When making very large movements without moving, be sure to realign the body. The realignment may only be a matter of turning the feet in the stance or perhaps changing the amount of foot stagger. These adjustments were described in step 9.

In general, expect to home in on the strike pocket by the second adjustment when using the 3-1-2 system. If the second adjustment of the starting position still does not get the ball near the strike target, it is likely you are missing the intended target. No targeting system will work if you can't hit the target.

DETERMINING THE SIZE OF THE MISS

As mentioned before, knowing the direction of the miss is only one part of the strategy. You also need to determine the size of the miss. If you don't know how much you missed by, you won't know how much to move. Your goal is to remove the guesswork from your adjustments. Determining the amount of the miss is a matter of careful observation. Watch where the ball makes contact at the pins. Compare that to the position of the strike pocket. If you can accurately determine the difference between the two, you will be able to make an exact, immediate change in the stance position as a correction to the errant throw. So what you must learn is how to estimate the distance from the strike pocket to any other contact point on the pin triangle.

STRIKE POCKET

Going down the side of the pin triangle, it is 6 inches (15 cm) from the center of one pin to the center of another. Bowlers need to determine whether the center of the ball made contact directly on one pin or another, or somewhere in between. The space between two pins is called the *pocket*. For strike adjustments, the main concern is the strike pocket—the pocket on either side of the head pin (figure 10.3). A pocket cuts the 6-inch (15 cm) space in half. That means as the ball location moves from pocket to pin or from pin to pocket, it is changing 3 inches (7.6 cm) at a time.

Simply compare where the ball made contact with where the desired strike pocket is. Estimate errors in multiples of 3 inches (7.6 cm). This works very well with the 3-1-2 adjustment system (see figure 10.2). That system allows for 3-inch changes in ball location based on 2-inch (5 cm) adjustments with the feet. The technique for estimating the size of the error coincides nicely with the system for adjusting ball location.

The pivot system is easy to use and easy to remember. But it does have limitations. One of them is limiting the angle to the pocket. For bowlers who throw the ball on a straight path, only one line will go over any given target and still hit the strike pocket. If you find that line and still don't strike, you want to throw a more effective shot, but you can't use the pivot system anymore. The pivot system changes the ball location. If you are hitting the right location and still not striking, you need to find a different strategy. You may ask, "If there is one perfect line

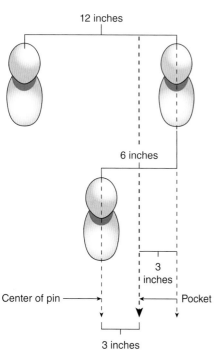

Figure 10.3 It is 3 inches from the strike pocket to the center of the pins on either side of the pocket.

to the strike pocket for any target and if I roll the ball on that line exactly, shouldn't I strike every time?" In theory, the answer is yes. The problem is with us, the bowlers: we are not perfect.

After hitting what looks like the strike pocket and not getting a strike, congratulate yourself on a good throw. Remember that nobody strikes all the time. You may have missed the true strike pocket, but it was by only a small margin. For instance, leaving a 10 pin on a pocket hit usually indicates a miss of about half of an inch (1.25 cm). A 5 pin indicates a miss of only about an inch (2.5 cm). One pin standing is what happens when the ball is thrown well, just not well enough to strike.

If you remember the strike-percentage chart (found in step 8), the larger the attack angle into the pocket, the larger the strike pocket becomes. We all need a larger strike pocket. Nobody hits the perfect spot all the time. We have to give ourselves a chance to miss a little left or right and still strike at a respectable percentage.

If hitting what looks like the strike pocket, a radical change in ball location is not required. The 3-1-2 pivot adjustment changes the ball's final location. If the location looks very close and yet you are not striking, another strategy may be necessary. You could apply the pivot system. There is a good chance that you are not hitting the precise strike area for the target you are using. If you still want to keep that target, adjustments in the starting position need to be precise, perhaps only fractions of an inch. Small misses require small adjustments.

But another system is available. One in which the attack angle into the pocket can be changed without changing the location of the ball impact at the pins. Remember, for an effective strike ball, a bowler needs accuracy, angle, and drive. If the accuracy looks pretty good and you feel as though the ball was released with an effective roll, you need to adjust the other factor.

3-4-5 Angle-Shift System

Figure 10.4 illustrates the 3-4-5 angle-shift system in which the entry angle changes without changing the ball's contact point. When the shots are hitting the strike pocket, only subtle changes in the ball path are needed. You can make very small adjustments of the ball angle into the pocket by moving the starting position and the visual target in the same direction. Moving closer to the middle of the lane reduces the angle. Moving closer to the gutter increases the angle.

It is 45 feet (114 m) from the pins to the target arrows (three increments of 15 feet [4.6 m]), 60 feet (18 m) from the pins to the foul line (four increments of 15 feet), and 75 feet (22.8 m) from the pins to the starting position at the back of the approach (five increments of 15 feet). Be precise! Move the target 3 inches (7.6 cm) at a time with every 5-inch (12.7 cm) change in the starting position. (The approach will finish 4 inches [10 cm]

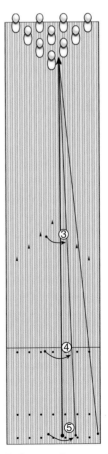

Figure 10.4 3-4-5 angle-shift system.

from the original strike line.) An adjustment in anything other than a 3-to-5 ratio changes the ball's final position.

The 3-4-5 angle shift system works in any multiple. Instead of standing near the middle of the lane and using a target near the middle of the lane, try moving 10 inches (25.4 cm) with the feet and 6 inches (1.8 cm) with the eyes. For even more angle, try moving 15 inches (38 cm) at the start and 9 inches (22.8 cm) at the arrows.

Maximizing the Attack Angle With a Straight Ball

Because a straight ball does not change direction from its initial ball path, the only way you can create a stronger attack angle into the strike pocket is through a position change on the lane. You can use the 3-4-5 system to find a line to the pocket knowing only the location of the strike pocket. You do this by working back from the strike pocket. Multiples of the 3-4-5 ratio get us to the correct visual target, the release point, and the starting position on the lane.

Numerically, the perfect strike pocket is 2.5 inches (6.3 cm) offset from the center. The center of the lane is the middle of the 20th board. Boards are counted from the edge of the gutter (the 1 board) to the center. Because the lane boards are slightly more than 1 inch (2.5 cm) wide, 2.5 inches from the middle of the head pin puts the strike pocket at about the 18th board. Now, by applying the 3-4-5 angle shift strategy (with the 18th board at the pocket as the starting point), you can determine the line to the strike pocket that gives the maximum angle for a straight ball.

The idea is for every 15 feet (4.6 m) you move back from the contact point at the pins, move the line over a specific distance. How far should the line move for each 15-foot increment? You could adjust the line two boards laterally for every 15 feet away from the strike pocket, but the angle into the pocket would be fairly shallow. You could adjust the line four boards for every 15 feet (to create a stronger attack angle), but by the time the line was brought back to the beginning of the approach, the bowler would be out of room; your stance might end up on top of the ball return. (Plus, 18 does not divide by 4 easily.)

So, let's use an increment of a three-board deviation for every 15-foot increment the target line is away from the pins.

- With the strike pocket (60 feet [18 m] from the foul line) on the 18th board, the ball will be on the 15th board at 45 feet (114 m) down the lane. (One set of 15 feet [4.6 m] away from the pins.)

- At 30 feet (9.1 m) down lane (or two sets of 15 feet from the pins), the ball is on the 12th board.

- When 15 feet down the lane, which is at the arrow, (three sets of 15 feet from the pins) the ball is rolling over the 9th board.

Here is where you can see how the 3-4-5 angle adjustment system starts to apply!

- The arrows are three sets of 15 feet (45 feet) away from the pins: 3×3 boards = 9 boards; 18 (strike pocket) − 9 (board shift) = 9. The visual target is the 9 board.

- The foul line is four sets of 15 feet (60 feet) away from the pins: 4×3 boards = 12; 18 (strike pocket) − 12 (board shift) = 6. The release point at the foul line is the 6 board. This means the swing passes over the 6th board as the ball is released.

- The starting position on the approach is five sets of 15 feet (75 feet) away from the pins: $5 \times 3 = 15$; $18 - 15 = 3$. The starting position on the approach puts the swing, or throwing-side shoulder, over the 3 board.

To sum it up: position yourself to start the swing on the 3rd board. Walk in a direction that allows the swing to pass over the 6th board. Maintain a finish position and swing line that rolls the ball over the 9th board. A ball rolling on a straight path ends up at the 18th-board strike pocket.

The 1-to-2 adjustment is a variation of the 3-4-5 system (figure 10.5). For every two boards the starting position is moved, the visual target changes one board in the same direction. The 1-to-2 is a common adjustment for more-experienced bowlers. (Most bowlers refer to the adjustment as the 2 and 1 because they think about the starting position first.)

The adjustment is almost like cutting the 3-to-5 ratio in half. By ignoring the half board, (who wants to think about 1.5 and 2.5?) you get a 1-to-2 adjustment.

Although the 1-to-2 system may not seem to be mathematically exact, it is easy to remember and has practical application. Because it is not in exactly a 3-to-5 ratio, applying the 1-to-2 adjustment does change the ball's final location at the pins. Also, because the feet adjust in a larger increment than the target's adjustment, there is a subtle change in angle.

A simple example: A right-handed bowler's ball hooks too much and hits high on the headpin. The bowler does not want the ball to hit the same spot again. (Remember, any adjustment in a 3-to-5 ratio changes the angle but not the location.) The ball missed the pocket to the left, so the bowler moves left. Consequently, the ball ends up slightly farther right. (A high hit is a miss to the left of the strike pocket for a right-handed bowler. So, miss left, move left.) Additionally, moving the starting position and the target in the same direction (in this case to the left) causes a subtle angle change.

The bowler accomplishes two things when applying the 1-to-2 system. First, he or she changes the ball's final position at the pins using the 1-to-2 ratio in the same way as the basic 3-1-2 adjustment. This is possible because the 1-to-2 system is not an exact equivalent of the 3-to-5 system.

Second, the bowler has made a practical adjustment that allows for a simple angle adjustment in the same manner the 3-4-5 system would. By moving the target as well as the starting position, the ball now rolls along a different part of the lane. This differs from the pivot system, which keeps the target the same. The 1-to-2 system is blend of both of the basic systems. It creates slight changes in the ball's contact at the pins for better strike-pocket location as well as slight changes in angle to adjust how the ball drives into the strike pockets.

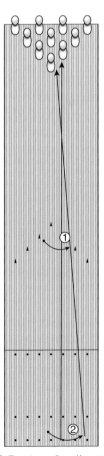

Figure 10.5 1-to-2 adjustment.

The 1-to-2 system allows greater fine-tuning of location than the basic 3-1-2 system.

The 1-to-2 system works well for bowlers throwing a hook. One of the topics discussed in step 12 (about lane conditions) is how the ball removes lane oil. Bowling on the same part of the lane, throw after throw, wears down the oil in that particular area. A ball's hook gets larger as oil on a section of the lane is used up. At some point, changes in lane conditions will become dramatic enough to force the bowler to play another part of the lane. Each time the bowler moves both the stance and the feet in the same direction (like the 1-to-2 system calls for), the ball path moves to a different, fresher part of the lane. The new oil line helps the ball travel down the lane more easily, reducing hook and allowing you to regain control of the ball motion.

The 1-to-2 adjustment also works going the other way. Oil pushed down the lane from ball movement (called *carrydown*) prevents the ball from hooking in time to get back to the strike pocket. Most bowling centers have less oil near the edges of the lanes than they do in the middle. Moving the feet and the target closer to the edge of the lane allows for both an increase in angle and a ball path that is on a drier (and therefore more hooking) part of the lane. Both benefits are useful if the bowler is looking for a stronger angle to the pocket. Because it is easy to remember and has practical application for the way lane conditions change under normal circumstances, experienced bowlers use the 1-to-2 system most often.

Straight bowlers play angles. But, hook bowlers must play the conditions as well.

Special Note for Hook Throwers

All of the diagrams in this step illustrate straight lines to the pocket. The basic adjustment strategies are more easily understood using straight lines. If you throw a hook, these adjustment strategies probably will not work exactly by the numbers as described.

This does not mean the strategies introduced have no place in a hook thrower's game. The direction of the moves either to change location (pivot around a target) or angle (adjusting target and stance at the same time) does apply, just the numbers related to the adjustments are different. The general concept still applies, but the numerical relationship will vary from bowler to bowler.

The more a ball hooks, the more the lane conditions must be taken into account. Pivoting around a target to change the ball's location and moving both target and starting position to create different launch angles are critical adjustment skills.

UNDERSTANDING PINFALL

Many throws appear to hit the strike pocket yet leave pins standing. This is not a matter of bad luck. If a ball strikes on one shot but not on another it is (I am sorry to say) the bowler's fault. As frustrating as this may seem, pins stand because you made a mistake. Pins stand because they are supposed to stand. Bowlers need to learn from the pins. Pins that remain standing tell you something about how the ball hit the pocket. Bowlers only need to understand how strikes happen and why certain pins remain standing. From this knowledge, they can devise a strategy to correct for the less-than-ideal pinfall.

Swallow your pride, take a deep breath, and make an intelligent adjustment. First and foremost, visually estimate the size of the error. From this estimate, follow the adjustment strategy indicated and determine the size of the adjustment. Usually it is obvious if contact was slightly left or right of the ideal strike pocket. Determining the size of the error, and subsequently the size of the appropriate corrective action, takes practice.

For a perfect strike (figure 10.6), the ball hits only four pins. All the other pins fall as a result of pin-to-pin contact. This requires that the ball strike the targeted pins in just the right location to initiate the proper chain of pinfall.

The line from the headpin to the 7 pin is called the accuracy line. You must be able to roll the ball to this location. But, merely rolling the ball to this spot is not enough. The ball must have sufficient drive to push through to the 3 pin after contacting the headpin. The line from the 3 pin to the 10 pin is called the *drive line*. If the ball does not have enough drive (it deflects too much), it will not contact the 3 pin in the correct location. Several factors influence drive: ball weight, ball velocity, traction between ball surface and lane surface, ball location at contact (accuracy), and entry angle.

Light (or Low) Hit

On a light hit, the ball is wide of the strike pocket. For a right-handed bowler, a light hit goes wide to the right of the strike pocket.

The corner pins (the 10 pin for a right-handed bowler and the 7 pin for a left-handed bowler) are the first indicators the ball missed the pocket. If the ball is a little to the right, the headpin pushes the ball to the side. The ball then strikes the 3 pin a little too head on. As the 3 pin cuts straight back, it will slice the 6 pin around the 10 pin.

The error margin for contacting the headpin is larger for heavier balls and sharper entry angles. Shallow entry angles (ball thrown straight down the lane) and lightweight balls are more easily deflected. The perfect contact point for the ball is 2.5 inches (6.3 cm) offset from center. To throw a strike, a bowler with an average hook has about a

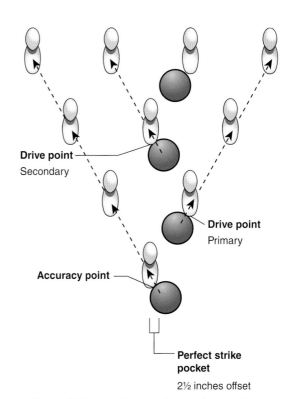

Drive point
Secondary

Drive point
Primary

Accuracy point

Perfect strike
pocket

2½ inches offset

Figure 10.6 Ball path of a perfect strike.

2-inch (5 cm) range of contact (error margin) at the pins—from 1.5 to 3.5 inches (3.8-8.9 cm) offset. The error margin drops to about 1 inch (2.5 cm) for a throw with no entry angle.

The 5 pin indicates an obvious light hit. Leaving the 5 pin is a blatant error. The expression "no drive, no five" applies to this situation. Using a ball that is too light or that enters at an entry angle that is too shallow frequently results in a 5 pin that remains standing.

A right-handed bowler who throws a light hit usually leaves one of these pin combinations:

- Single pins: 10, 5, 7, 2, 8 (the 8 pin is somewhat rare)
- Two-pin combinations: 5-7, 5-10, 5-8, 2-8, 2-10, 8-10, 7-10 (also known as the swishing 7-10)
- Other multipin combinations: 2-8-10, 2-4-5-8 (bucket), 1-2-10 (washout), 1-2-4-10 (washout)

If your shot consistently comes up light, first make the most obvious adjustment: move your feet and change the ball's contact point. Remember, miss right, move right. If that still doesn't pay off, then apply other adjustment strategies.

Experienced bowlers try to change the roll of the ball. This can be done in a variety of ways:

- Move the visual target closer to the foul line. Looking closer on the lane creates a slight forward tilt of the upper body. Changing upper-body tilt makes the incline of the downswing into the lane sharper. This results in releasing the ball onto the lane sooner, creating earlier roll and a hook motion.

- Move back on the approach. If you have room, move the starting position back. Moving back a couple of inches at the start allows the ball to hook a couple of inches sooner on the lane.

- Try to create a stronger hook. Adjust your hand position by using a stronger wrist cup, or position your hand more on the side of the ball at the release to increase the axis tilt and create a sharper entry angle into the pocket.

- Change ball speed. Slowing the ball's speed gives the ball a chance to grab the lanes, decreasing skid and increasing potential hook. Lower the ball position in the stance, or slow your feet.

Heavy (or High) Hit

A ball that hits more toward the middle of the headpin is said to be high. For a right-handed bowler, this is a miss to the left of the strike pocket. Adjust the location, or reduce the entry angle. For a right-handed bowler, the 4 pin gives the first indication the ball is too high; for a left-handed bowler, it's the 6 pin.

A right-handed bowler who throws a high hit usually leaves one of the following combinations:

- Single pins: 4, 6, 9 (the 9 pin is more common for bowlers with a strong hook)
- Two-pin combinations: 3-6, 6-10, 3-10 (baby split), many types of splits including 4-9, 4-10, 7-10
- Other multipin combinations: 4-6-7-10 (big four), 4-6-7-9-10 (Greek church), 4-6-7-8-10 (Greek church)

Again, the basic adjustment is to move in the direction of the mistake. If you miss left, move left. If the ball is only a little high—you are hitting the pocket but not striking—use the 3-4-5 method (moving both the feet and the target closer to the middle) to reduce entry angle.

Other adjustments are exactly the opposite of those for light hits.

- Increase ball speed to reduce hook or delay when the ball starts hooking.
- Move the visual target farther down the lane to help accentuate a longer and flatter swing. This creates more of a drive down, which also delays or reduces the hook.
- Use a softer release. Weaken the wrist position; get the fingers on top of the ball.
- Keep the hand more behind the ball throughout the release to create end-over-end roll and less side roll. Avoid a dramatic change in the hand position (forearm rotation) at the release.

MAKING OTHER ADJUSTMENTS

For bowlers who throw a hook, simply changing the angle on the lane will not always be enough. Hook throwers play lane conditions, not just angles. The game becomes more complex as the interaction between the ball and the ever-changing lane surface becomes more dramatic. It is important to develop the proper adjustment tools. Ideally, the strategy for surmounting challenges should be in place before the challenges present themselves. (Adjusting to lane conditions is discussed in more detail in step 12.)

Too many bowlers get comfortable with only a certain area of the lane. This limits opportunities to create a scoring advantage when lane conditions change. Many bowlers start the day scoring well, but as lane conditions change, their scoring pace declines. As oil patterns shift, the bowler needs to adjust position on the lane as well as adjust technique.

Purdue Target Practice

During one Purdue University team practice, I used targeting tape to lay out a line on the lane. After a few unsuccessful attempts to hit the tape, let alone the pocket, one team member turned to me and said, "This isn't my line." My response was, "You only have one?" That bowler did not bowl for Purdue the following year. If you are willing to play only one line to the pocket, you will not be successful at more competitive levels.

Avoid a feast-or-famine approach, one in which you score well in only one condition and struggle in others. Instead, become a hunter. Seek out the areas of the lanes giving the best scoring advantage, no matter where they are located. Learn to play all parts of the lane. Finding the areas that present a playable line and an advantageous attack angle to the pocket allows you to feast while others around you starve.

Parallel Move

In the angle adjustment strategies discussed earlier, the ball is projected at an angle in relation to the lane. The ball path will cross boards. When moving toward the middle, for instance, the ball will end up closer to the gutter as it gets farther down the lane. If the ball is hooking too much, sending it out wider on the lane gives it more room to hook. If the size of the hook and the accompanying adjustment are both judged accurately, the ball will hook into the pocket instead of in front of it.

In some bowling centers, the outside parts of the lanes have considerably less oil than the middle. As a result, the wider you send the ball, the more it hooks. You will not get anywhere with standard adjustments. In some situations, the dry part of the lane is so dry that the ball loses energy. The ball will roll out (hook early and abruptly) and then quit hooking altogether. The outside part of the lane appears unplayable. Now is the time for a *parallel move*.

In a parallel move, the feet and the target are moved the same amount in the same direction. Now, you are playing a new part of the lane. Both up front as well as down lane, the ball travels on a new part of the lane. The entire line has been moved.

Use a parallel adjustment to find a playable part of the lane (controllable ball reaction), then use one of the two basic systems to fine-tune the line to the strike pocket.

Adjust Distance of Visual Focus

As mentioned earlier, one way to change when the ball starts to hook, without needing to change lane target, is to move the visual focus spot up or down the lane. Most bowlers are comfortable with moving the target left or right, but it takes practice to learn how to look closer or farther down the lane. The targeting arrows may the obvious visual attention getter. Yet, you can imagine a line (ball path) that passes through the target. Now simply change the point of focus up or down the imagined path. Because many bowling centers have synthetic lanes with no distinguishing characteristics, this takes practice. The inconsistencies of natural wood's coloration can be helpful when targeting is based on something other than the arrows.

Many manufacturers of synthetic lanes imprint alternating light and dark boards. They might alternate light-dark-light-dark across the lane surface. Other lanes may use groups of boards of varying darkness, creating sections of lane that are darker than other sections. One manufacturer (Brunswick) puts 3-feet-long (1 m) areas of dark coloration on board 10 and board 15 very far down the lane. Look for visually distinctive characteristics at different points down the lane to help determine a target line.

Looking down the lane means to move the visual focus down the lane. It is a means of delaying the hook. This technique tends to change upper-body position. The farther the target is down the lane, the more upright the body tends to be at the finish. This may cause an increase in the ball's loft. (Be careful not to create excessive loft.) *Loft* is the distance the ball travels in the air after the release. The longer the ball is in the air, the less time it spends on the lane. Therefore, it will not grab the lane as soon. Also, bowlers who look farther down the lane tend to accentuate the follow-through. Swinging long through the ball, with an exaggerated extension, drives the ball to a later break point.

This technique is useful when the lanes begin to dry out. If you do not want to abandon your current line entirely, but the ball is not holding that line as well as it was, a slight adjustment to delay in the hook may be just enough to keep the ball in the pocket.

Looking short on the lane, moving the visual target in front of the arrows, has the opposite effect. You will tend to lay the ball down early. If the ball is on the lane longer, it will have more time to get into a roll. Oily lanes cause the ball to stay in a skid longer; therefore, the sooner the ball gets into a roll, the sooner it can enter into the hook phase to counteract the hook-delaying effect of the extra oil. Looking short causes a slight increase in the forward tilt of the upper body. It feels as if you are swinging down into the lane rather than swinging along it. In addition, you tend to throw where you are looking. If the target is close, you will throw down into the lane. The release motion starts when you try to drive the hand down through the ball. Overall, the release is quicker and the loft minimal.

DEVELOPING ACCURACY

Table 10.1 lists performance characteristics of bowlers at different skill levels based on a range of average scores. At higher levels of scoring potential, there are also subsequent improvements of other performance characteristics such as accuracy, velocity, speed consistency, and revolutions.

Table 10.1   Performance Based on Skill Level

Average	Initial velocity (mph)	Velocity variance (mph)	Target range (inches)	Entry angle (degrees)	Initial rotation (rpm)
139 and lower	15.5	1.10	6.8	1.4	77
140 to 149	15.5	0.85	5.9	2.2	118
150 to 159	17.3	0.97	4.8	2.3	133
160 to 169	17.0	0.79	4.6	2.6	156
170 to 179	16.9	0.77	4.1	3.1	177
180 to 189	17.2	0.76	3.9	3.7	210
190 to 199	17.7	0.75	3.5	3.6	235
200 to 209	18.1	0.71	3.5	4.2	272
210 to 219	18.2	0.58	2.5	4.4	285
220 and higher	18.5	0.60	2.1	5.2	374
Professional	18.9	0.47	1.7	5.9	385

To convert measurements to metric, visit www.worldwidemetric.com/measurements.html.

The information in this table represents data collected from participants in the Computer Aided Tracking System (CATS) program. The CATS program is a setup of sensors and cameras installed on the lanes to measure characteristics of both the bowler and the ball. The ITRC (bowling's International Training & Research Center) in Arlington, Texas, has a permanent installation. The goal of the program is to guide the development of an athlete's abilities based on empirical data, comparing the characteristics in the bowler's current game with the skill level he or she would like to achieve. Bowlers do not develop individual skills at the same rate. Certain elements of bowling may come easily for a bowler even as he or she struggles with other elements.

Initial velocity is the ball's speed at release, an indicator of swing efficiency and footwork. Velocity variance is the variation in ball speed from shot to shot. Target-range accuracy is determined by noting the left and right error margin (at the arrows, 15 feet [4.6 cm] from the foul line) where 95 percent of the shots were thrown. This is the most important characteristic. Accuracy is affected by footwork, swing line, timing, and body alignment.

To track the initial rotation, tracer tape is put on the ball. Videotaping the release reveals just how far the tape moves for each frame on the video. This rotational velocity (angular movement per amount of time) is converted into revolutions per minute (rpm).

Skill improvement varies from one level to the next. For example, initial velocity jumps from 15.5 in the average range of 140 to 149 and to 17.3 in the range of 150 to 159. These thresholds come at different times for different characteristics, which is typical of skill development. Early in the learning process, you establish consistency in footwork and rhythm. This naturally leads to ball velocity increases and speed consistency. Later on, the more difficult elements—body-position control and release efficiency—begin to fall into place.

Using Targeting Tape

Whenever possible, use additional targeting aids on the lane. These attention getters will confirm your accuracy and help you improve.

Often where you think you see the ball going is not where the ball actually goes. Eye dominance plays a role when determining the target the ball is rolling over. For instance, a right-handed bowler with left-eye dominance will appear to miss the target more than a right-handed bowler who is also right-eye dominant. The eyes are watching from an angle that differs from the angle of the throw. When your brain processes the visual information, you see the ball roll over the target. In reality, you are not.

There are two ways around this problem. One, position a helper directly behind your swing to tell you where the ball rolls. Second, place targets on the lane that give both visual and auditory feedback.

Coaches: Before placing targets on the lane ask permission from the bowling center manager or proprietor. If you are not a coach or instructor, do not expect to be able to put targets on the lanes. Not just anybody is allowed to stroll down the lane, dry off an area of oil, and place a target on the lane. Generally, only employees of the bowling center are allowed past the foul line. Ask permission before modifying the lane surface. (Do not be surprised if permission is denied because of liability issues.)

Simple Targeting Device

A popular tool for targeting practice is one that can easily be made out of PVC pipe. A 50-inch (127 cm) length of 1.5-inch (3.8 cm) pipe with support legs only requires short lengths of pipe hanging down. The spacing between the hanging pipes provides the challenge. The smaller the space, the greater the accuracy demands.

To make these for my classes, I drilled holes 1 inch (2.5 cm) apart along the length of the pipe. The target pipes are attached to eyebolts passed through the holes in the pipe. Unscrewing a nut from the bolt is all it takes to change the spacing of the target.

This device is easily moved up or down the lane to alter the challenge or train the bowler to target at a different point on the lane. Multiple devices on the same lane provide great training for playing a line rather than simply throwing through a point. Many lines may go through one point, but only one line will connect two points.

As an instructor, I have had great success using medical tape. Be sure to use thick, waterproof medical tape. This durable tape will not break down from the oil on the lane and stays in position despite balls rolling over it repeatedly. **Do not** use masking tape, clear adhesive tape, or cloth medical tape; these types of tape leave a sticky residue on the lane.

The thickness of the medical tape makes quick removal and replacement easy. More important, the ball will make an audible "tha-dumb" sound as it rolls over the tape. This sound confirms that the ball has gone over the intended spot. If you don't hear it, you didn't hit it!

Less-experienced bowlers may have trouble distinguishing the sound of the ball rolling over the tape from the background noises in a typical bowling center. Using a double thickness of tape makes the sound more distinct. When doubling the tape, do not put one piece directly over the other. Instead, stagger the placement to create a miniramp over which the ball passes (figure 10.7). Pay attention to where you place the tape; the glare from lights or reflection on the lanes from colorful masking units may obscure the marker.

When you are trying to focus on a particular spot on the lane, one extra target is usually enough. Remember, the arrows on the lane are permanent targets. The temporary target can be placed either in front of or past the target arrow. The placement of the extra target will influence the nature of the swing and the approach.

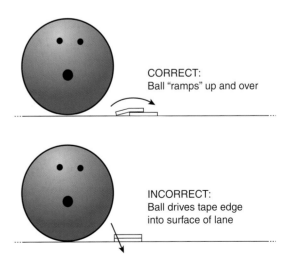

CORRECT:
Ball "ramps" up and over

INCORRECT:
Ball drives tape edge into surface of lane

Figure 10.7 Staggering tape on the lanes to create a miniramp.

You might find yourself thinking, "Hey, I hit my target! Why can't I get good results?" Slight changes in the approach or the swing change the angle to the target. If you are hitting the target from a slightly different angle each time, the ball makes contact with the pins at a different location each time.

Two points define a line. As soon as possible, try to visualize target lines rather than just a target spot. Two targets on the lane allow for the line of the approach to match the target line down the lane. The first target usually is near the arrows; the second is farther down the lane. When setting up on the approach, your body alignment should be toward the first target. As you start into the motion, your focus should move up the line to the second target. This *spotting down the lane* reinforces a vision of the target line and contributes to a relaxed, free swing that extends out from the shoulder to the target.

A variety of games and drills can challenge you to develop targeting skills or learn to play different parts of the lane. Pull your attention away from the actual score on the score sheet; be concerned only with the task.

Accuracy Drill 1   Wiedman's Target Game

This game is a test of accuracy. Place two pieces of tape on the lane. The length of each piece of tape and the spacing between them vary depending on skill level. For beginners, each piece of tape should be 1.5 inches (3.8 cm) long, and the pieces should be placed 3 inches (7.6 cm) apart. This gives an overall error margin of 6 inches (15 cm). Intermediate bowlers should place two 1-inch (2.5 cm) pieces of tape 2 inches (5 cm) apart for a 4-inch (10 cm) error margin. Skilled bowlers use two .75-inch (2 cm) pieces of tape set 1.5 inches (3.8 cm) apart for a 3-inch (7.6 cm) error margin.

Roll the ball between the pieces of tape. For the most basic variation, pinfall or lane conditions are not a concern. Your main objective is to establish concentration and targeting skills. Do not worry about shooting spares; with every throw of the ball, the primary goal is to throw between the pieces of tape. This drill focuses on the first 15 or 20 feet (4.6 or 6 m) of the lane.

Variation

The game consists of 10 consecutive throws. If the ball rolls between the tape pieces (you do not hear it hit tape), score the throw as a strike. If the ball hits one of the pieces of tape, meaning a slight error, score the throw as a 9 and a spare. If the throw completely misses the range of the tape, score the throw as an 8 and a miss.

Record your scores on the scorecard shown in figure 10.8. Give yourself a bonus—add 3 pins to your final score—if you hit the target and throw a real strike.

Once you are consistently scoring "excellent" or "very good," position the tape pieces closer together or make the tape pieces themselves smaller.

Be creative, and always pursue a challenge. As certain tasks become easy with increased skill, find ways to push yourself to a new level.

1	2	3	4	5	6	7	8	9	10

Figure 10.8 Scorecard for Wiedman's target game.

TO INCREASE DIFFICULTY

- As skill improves, make the size and spacing between of the targets more challenging. Two .5-inch (1.27 cm) pieces of tape separated by 1.5 (3.8 cm) inches yield an error margin of only 3 inches (7.6 cm). Aim small; miss small.

- Skilled bowlers can change the location of the tape as well. Putting the tape at different places on the lanes lets bowlers practice lane play as well as develop accuracy.

- Try moving your starting position on the lane without moving the tape. This helps you practice different angles on the lane.

- Once you are hitting the space consistently, pay attention to where the ball hits the pins. Try to adapt to lane conditions. Find a line to the strike pocket while still trying to throw through the predetermined spot.

Success Check

- Properly align setup to the target.
- Focus on the space between the tape pieces.
- Watch the ball roll through the space.
- Listen for the sound of the ball rolling over the tape. This indicates inaccuracy.

Score Your Success

Version 1

Excellent = 210 or more

Very good = 180 to 209

Good= 150 to 179

Average= 120 to 149

Keep trying= 120 or less

Your score ___

Accuracy Drill 2   Targeting Effectiveness

Count pinfall during this drill. All throws are first balls at a full set of pins. Use a piece of tape 3 to 5 inches (7.6-12.7 cm) across or an equivalent spacing if using a targeting device. (A ball is about 8.6 inches (21.8 cm) wide, so the space between the hanging targets needs to be 12 to 14 inches (30.5-35.6 cm). This drill will create an effectiveness index, a number that is the relationship between the bowler's ability to hit a target while using a strategy that maximizes pin count.

Throw 10 strike shots, and record only the pinfall of shots that went over the target area. Scoring: Calculate average pinfall of only shots on target. Calculate percent of shots on target. Multiply those two figures together.

Example: Bowler hit target 7 out of 10 times = 70% or .7

Average pinfall of those 7 shots = 6.4

(first-ball average) × (target percent) = targeting effectiveness index

6.4 × .7 = 4.48 TEI

First ball average is the average pinfall of the first ball of each frame (figure 10.9).

	1	2	3	4	5	6	7	8	9	10	Total pins	÷	10	=	Average pincount	X	Target percentage	=	T.E.I.
Pincount																			

Figure 10.9   Target effectiveness index scoresheet.

TO INCREASE DIFFICULTY

If you consistently score in the very good or excellent range, you are not challenging yourself. Make the target spacing smaller.

Score Your Success

Excellent: 9 × .9 = 8.1 TEI

Very good: 8 × .8 = 6.4 TEI

Average: 7 × .7 = 4.9 TEI

Needs work: 6 × .6 = 3.6 TEI

Keep trying: 5 × .5 = 2.5 TEI

Accuracy Drill 3 Pincount Multiplier Game

For this game you will need two target areas: a smaller, high-accuracy area, and a larger, general-accuracy area. When using a targeting device, leave a 5- to 6-inch (12.7-15 cm) error margin between the target pipes and a 1- to 1.5- inch (2.5-3.8 cm) piece of tape centered under the target area. If using tape only, use two 2- to 2.5-inch (5-6.3 cm) pieces of tape separated by 1.5 inches.

For a round of ten throws at a full set of pins, a "perfect game" would be a 300. This score could only be achieved by rolling the ball over the smallest target area every time and striking (knocking down all ten pins) every time. This would give you 10 frames of 30 points (multiplier of 3 x 10 pins).

If you are consistently scoring over 200 with this scoring system, you may not be challenging yourself enough. Make the target areas smaller!

Pincount		Multiplier		Frame Total
	X		=	
	X		=	
	X		=	
	X		=	
	X		=	
	X		=	
	X		=	
	X		=	
	X		=	
	X		=	
Final Total				

Figure 10.10 Pincount multiplier game.

Score Your Success

Scoring: All throws are at a full set of pins only, and every throw counts in the score.

Hit small target area: (pincount) × 3

Hit larger target area: (pincount) × 2

Miss target area: (pincount) × 1

Accuracy Drill 4   *Four-Arrow Challenge*

In this simple drill, you practice on all parts of the lane. The oil on a lane is not evenly distributed, so each part of the lane gives a different ball reaction. The goal of the drill is to learn which combination of release, speed, and ball selection keeps the ball in the pocket no matter what line is played on the lane.

Line up using the first arrow. Attempt 10 throws, making small adjustments on the approach or with the release until you hit the pocket. Keep playing only the first arrow for all 10 throws. After 10 throws, line up over the second arrow. Repeat the drill. Continue moving to a new arrow every 10 throws.

After 10 throws over the fourth arrow, go back to the first arrow and start again. Keep track of your first-ball average, recording your scores on the scorecard shown in figure 10.10. To calculate your first-ball average on each arrow, divide the total number of pins for that arrow by 10. The following are good first-ball averages: beginner 6.25, intermediate player 7.5, and skilled player 8.75. Go back and practice over the arrow where you scored your lowest first-ball average.

Five-Dot Challenge: Mark Roth Variation

I attribute this variation to professional bowler Mark Roth, one of bowling's all-time greats. He was one of the dominant players on the tour during the late 1970s and early 1980s. In a bowling article, he indicated that this was his favorite practice drill.

Instead of moving from arrow to arrow, move your starting position on the approach one dot. Start the drill with your swing over the first dot. Don't change your starting position until you have met a personal goal. Once you meet the challenge, move to the next dot. Repeat for dots three through five. Then go back to first dot and start the challenge series again.

TO INCREASE DIFFICULTY

- Set a particular criterion for moving from one arrow to the next. For example, do not move to the next arrow until you hit the pocket four times in a row.
- If you have more than one ball, do not change balls. Instead, find the correct combination of speed and release that allows the ball to work from any line.

Success Check

- Focus on the target.
- Watch the ball roll over the target.
- Pay attention to body position and footwork direction each time you adjust for a new target line.

Score Your Success

For each arrow played, rate your skill.

Excellent: first-ball average of 8.5 or higher

Very good: first-ball average of 7.75 to 8.49

Good: first-ball average of 7.0 to 7.74

Average: first-ball average of 6.25 to 6.99

Below average: first-ball average of 5.5 to 6.24

Needs work: first-ball average lower than 5.5

Your score ___

Throw	First arrow	Second arrow	Third arrow	Fourth arrow
1				
2				
3				
4				
5				
6				
7				
8				
9				
10				
Total				
	÷ 10	÷ 10	÷ 10	÷ 10
Average				

Figure 10.11   Four-arrow challenge worksheet.

Accuracy Drill 5   Swedish National Team Drill

The Swedish national team has enjoyed considerable success in international competition. Because lane maintenance varies so much around the world, international competition presents a unique challenge for the experienced bowler. Even within the same city, you can find considerable variation in lane conditions from one bowling center to the next.

This drill emphasizes keeping the ball in play. The goal is to make quality shots. Lucky strikes are just that—luck! And luck eventually runs out. On the other hand, a quality shot is something you can depend on. It is only a matter of time before quality shots pay off. Strikes are nice but useless if open frames follow them.

This game does not reward lucky strikes. Strikes can happen in all sorts of unusual ways. Just because somebody is scoring well does not mean they are bowling well. This scorekeeping system helps discern, to a certain extent, the quality of the performance.

As a coach, I would rather use a player who is keeping the ball close, even if his score is not very high. This player may be only one small adjustment away from a great game. The player who has as many minus frames as plus frames is unreliable and as likely to throw splits as strikes.

(continued)

Accuracy Drill 5 *(continued)*

TO INCREASE DIFFICULTY

- Missing a single-pin spare is considered inexcusable at higher levels of the game.
- To increase the penalty, subtract 3 points for a missed single-pin spare.
- Play a 10-frame game.

TO DECREASE DIFFICULTY

- For each consecutive pocket strike after three, make the point value equal to the number of strikes.
- The third consecutive pocket strike is worth 3 points.
- The fourth consecutive pocket strike is worth 4 points, and so on. In this system, the maximum possible points for 12 consecutive pocket strikes is $2 + 2 + 3 + 4 + 5 + 6 + 7 + 8 + 9 + 10 + 11 + 12 = 79$.

Success Check

- Use a relaxed and smooth swing.
- Maintain unwavering focus on the target.
- Adjust for changing lane conditions.
- Use practical spare-shooting strategy.

Score Your Success

Hit strike pocket and strike = 2 points

Hit the strike pocket and spare = 1 point

Miss strike pocket and get a strike or spare = 0 points

Open frame = –1 point

Miss single-pin spare = –2 points

Perfect = 20 points

Excellent = 13 to 19 points

Good = 6 to 12 points

Average = 0 to 5 points

Needs work = –1 to –6 points

Practice spare shooting = –6 or lower

Your score ___

SUCCESS SUMMARY

Successful strike targeting requires the following:

- Focus: See the target; hit the target.
- Assessment: Did you achieve your goals? If not, what was missing?
- Strategy: What adjustments are needed to make the next shot better?
- Implementation: Trust yourself to do what needs to be done.

The important element for finding a strike line is shot consistency—you must have a reliable physical game. The inability to throw the ball the same way over an identified target makes adjustments less reliable and judging changes in lane conditions more difficult. You'll be less likely to determine whether the problem is the chosen line to the pocket (which requires strategic changes) or technique (which requires identifying and correcting performance errors). As you develop a more consistent physical game and reliably throw the ball the way you want and where you want, the targeting systems start to pay off.

This step described two basic systems: the 3-1-2 pivot system and the 3-4-5 angle-shift system. The 3-1-2 system allows the bowler to change the location of the ball at the pins. By pivoting around a target, the bowler redirect the ball's final location at the pins through carefully determined adjustment in the bowler's starting position on the approach. For the system to work best the bowler needs to accurately assess the size of the error (amount the ball missed the strike pocket) before making adjustments to the starting position.

The 3-4-5 system allows the bowler to change the angle at which the ball enters the strike pocket. This is an important fine-tuning element. With this system, adjust the visual target and the starting position in the same direction.

The 1-to-2 system, a simple variation of the 3-4-5 system, is a rough approximation of the 3 and 5 portions of the angle-shift system. This easy-to-remember system allows for precise adjustments and can also be applied to adjust for changing lane conditions.

Review your drill scores. Record them in the spaces that follow.

SCORING YOUR SUCCESS

Accuracy Drills

1. Wiedman's Target Game   _____ points

2. Targeting Effectiveness   _____ TEI

3. Pincount Multiplier Game   _____ points

4. Four-Arrow Challenge   _____ points

5. Five-Dot Challenge: Mark Roth's Variation   _____ points

6. Swedish National Team Drill   _____ out of 20

It would be nice to strike every time you throw the ball, but nobody is perfect. Spare shooting is a critical part of consistently high scores. When asked, most elite professional bowlers confess that they did not reach their level of success until they developed reliable spare-shooting strategies. We all want to roll high scores; spare shooting is a critical part of consistently scoring well. Strategies for shooting spares are the topic of the next step.

Picking Up Spares

et's face it, strikes are tough. Nobody strikes all the time. Even at the professional level, almost half of all frames include spare chances. For average and beginning bowlers, strikes account for only 10 to 30 percent of all frames. Because relatively few frames have strikes, spares become important for a bowler's success.

Put another way, open frames negate the positive effects of strikes. For every open frame in the middle of a game, the bowler needs to throw two strikes in a row (a double) twice or three strikes once to have a chance of shooting a score of 200. Once three or four open frames occur, there is little chance of rolling a respectable score.

On the other hand, a decent score is achievable from nothing but spare shooting. An all-spares game can be as high as 190. A score of 190 is considerably above what the typical bowler scores. For many of the simpler spares—single pins or two pins next to each other—the error margin is much greater than for a strike ball. If you recall the strike-percentage chart from step 8, you know the error margin at the pins for strikes (i.e., *the strike pocket*) is 1.5 to 3.5 inches (3.8- 8.9 cm) for the typical entry angle. For any single-pin spare that is not a corner pin, the error margin is over 13 inches (33 cm). For corner pins, the 7 pin and the 10 pin, the error margin is still over 9 inches (23 cm).

THE UNIVERSAL SPARE SHOOTING GUIDE

Tables 11.1 and 11.2 give the bowler a mathematically determined line for every commonly used target for each of the keys pins. The math is quite simple: It is 15 feet from the back set of dots to the foul line, and 15 feet from the foul line to the targeting arrows. If you know the exact location of the pins and arrows, you should be able to bring a line back from any pin, through any arrow, all the way back to the beginning of the lane and calculate two things: Where the line intersects the foul line (ball's release point), and where the line starts at the beginning of the approach (position of the ball in the bowler's stance).

First, you should start with what you know already:

- The exact location of each key pin (measured in boards from the edge of the lane)
- The exact location of each target arrow (also measured in boards from the lane's edge)

- The distance from the pins back to the target arrows (45 feet)
- The distance from the arrows back to the foul line (15 feet)

Then keep the following things in mind as you bowl:

- Bowling's "unit of measure" is the board. A lane is 39 boards across.
- A lane must be from 41-42 inches wide; therefore a board is slightly more than 1 inch wide.
- Right-hand bowlers count boards and arrows from the right edge of the lane. Left-hand bowlers count boards and arrows from the left edge of the lane.
- The seven dots at the start of approach line up with the seven dots at the foul line. All of these dots line up with seven target arrow 15 feet beyond the foul line.
- The dots and the arrows do not directly line up with the seven key pin location. Except for the middle dots and arrow (these are in line with the center of the head pin [pin #1])

However, this guide is not mathematically perfect. For convenience's sake, some things were assumed to make the calculations easier:

1. **All targeting arrows are 15 feet from the foul line.** Not all of the target arrows are exactly 15 feet from the foul line: simple observation reveals that the arrows angle inward. So, the arrow nearest the gutter (1st) is slightly less than 15 feet from the foul line, while the center arrow (4th arrow) is somewhat more.

2. **All key pin locations are 60 feet from the foul line (75 feet away from the bowler's stance position).** In reality, it is about 31 inches from the center of the head pin to the center of the pins in the back row. This roughly 31 inches of extra distance is less than 3.5% of the entire 75 foot target path. Where the ball is calculated to be as it passes the headpin's location (based on the guide) is only fractionally off from where it will actually be when the ball path crosses the back row at 62 feet, 7 inches.

3. **All starting positions (ball's location in the stance) are 15 feet from the foul line.** Obviously, many bowlers start their approach nearer to the foul line than 15 feet. Starting a little closer to the foul line (e.g., 8, 10, or 12 feet back), instead of all the way at the back of the approach, makes only a slight change in the ball's final location by the time it reaches the pins.

4. **A pin's width is about 4.77 inches, the ball's diameter is about 8.6 inches.** The error margin for most pins is about 13.3 inches. Given reasonable accuracy (i.e., ability to roll the ball over a predetermined target area), none of the three previous generalizations make a significant change in the ball's final location as determined by the guide. Make adjustments in the stance and/ or target area to fine-tune the guide for your game. Figure 11.1 breaks down the spare error margin.

When a negative number appears, it means the ball path is to the left of the left-hand gutter. On an even-numbered lane, with the ball return to your left, you may not have enough room. For a right-handed bowler, it is to the right of the right-hand gutter and the odd-numbered lane may have insufficient room.

What about the other side? For the average bowler, the outside (or nonball side) hip is about 10-15 inches (9-14 boards) from the ball's position in the stance. The outside hip may run into the ball return if using an arrow near, or in, the center of the lane. The outside hip may end up positioned somewhere between boards 38-49,

Table 11.1   Universal (Straight Line) Spare Shooting Guide (Right Handed)

	Key Pin Number							
	7	4	2	1	3	6	10	
Location	36.2	30.6	25.1	19.5	13.9	8.35	2.78	**Pin location (Boards from right gutter)**
Between 1st and 2nd	7	7	7	7	7	7	7	**Target location (at arrows)**
	-2.74	-.88	0.98	2.83	4.69	6.55	8.41	**Release point (at foul line)**
	-12.5	-8.76	-5.04	-1.34	2.38	6.1	9.82	**Starting position (of swing in stance)**
2nd Arrow	9.5	9.5	9.5	9.5	9.5	9.5	9.5	**Target location (at arrows)**
	0.59	2.45	4.31	6.17	8.02	9.88	11.7	**Release point (at foul line)**
	-8.32	-4.6	-0.88	2.84	6.54	10.3	14	**Starting position (of swing in stance)**
Between 2nd and 3rd	12	12	12	12	12	12	12	**Target location (at arrows)**
	3.94	5.79	7.64	9.5	11.4	13.2	15.1	**Release point (at foul line)**
	-4.12	-0.42	3.28	7	10.7	14.4	18.1	**Starting position (of swing in stance)**
3rd Arrow	14.5	14.5	14.5	14.5	14.5	14.5	14.5	**Target location (at arrows)**
	7.27	9.12	11	12.8	14.7	16.6	18.4	**Release point (at foul line)**
	0.04	3.74	7.46	11.2	14.9	18.6	22.3	**Starting position (of swing in stance)**
Between 3rd and 4th	17	17	17	17	17	17	17	**Target location (at arrows)**
	10.6	12.5	14.3	16.2	18	19.9	21.7	**Release point (at foul line)**
	4.18	7.9	11.6	15.3	19	22.8	26.5	**Starting position (of swing in stance)**
4th Arrow	19.5	19.5	19.5	19.5	19.5	19.5	19.5	**Target location (at arrows)**
	13.9	15.8	17.6	19.5	21.4	23.2	25.1	**Release point (at foul line)**
	8.24	12.1	15.8	19.5	23.2	26.9	30.6	**Starting position (of swing in stance)**
Between 4th and 5th	22	22	22	22	22	22	22	**Target location (at arrows)**
	17.3	19.1	21	22.8	24.7	26.6	28.4	**Release point (at foul line)**
	12.5	16.2	20	23.7	27.4	31.1	34.8	**Starting position (of swing in stance)**

Table 11.2 Universal (Straight Line) Spare Shooting Guide (Left-Handed)

				Key Pin Number				
	7	4	2	1	3	6	10	
Location	2.78	8.35	13.9	19.5	25.1	30.6	36.2	Pin location (Boards from right gutter)
Between 1st and 2nd	7	7	7	7	7	7	7	Target location (at arrows)
	8.41	6.55	4.69	2.83	0.98	-.88	-2.74	Release point (at foul line)
	9.82	6.1	2.38	-1.34	-5.04	-8.76	-12.5	Starting position (of swing in stance)
2nd Arrow	9.5	9.5	9.5	9.5	9.5	9.5	9.5	Target location (at arrows)
	11.7	9.88	8.02	6.17	4.31	2.45	0.59	Release point (at foul line)
	14	10.3	6.54	2.84	-0.88	-4.6	-8.32	Starting position (of swing in stance)
Between 2nd and 3rd	12	12	12	12	12	12	12	Target location (at arrows)
	15.1	13.2	11.4	9.5	7.64	5.79	3.94	Release point (at foul line)
	18.1	14.4	10.7	7	3.28	-0.42	-4.12	Starting position (of swing in stance)
3rd Arrow	14.5	14.5	14.5	14.5	14.5	14.5	14.5	Target location (at arrows)
	18.4	16.6	14.7	12.8	11	9.12	7.27	Release point (at foul line)
	22.3	18.6	14.9	11.2	7.46	3.74	0.04	Starting position (of swing in stance)
Between 3rd and 4th	17	17	17	17	17	17	17	Target location (at arrows)
	21.7	19.9	18	16.2	14.3	12.5	10.6	Release point (at foul line)
	26.5	22.8	19	15.3	11.6	7.9	4.18	Starting position (of swing in stance)
4th Arrow	19.5	19.5	19.5	19.5	19.5	19.5	19.5	Target location (at arrows)
	25.1	23.2	21.4	19.5	17.6	15.8	13.9	Release point (at foul line)
	30.6	26.9	23.2	19.5	15.8	12.1	8.24	Starting position (of swing in stance)
Between 4th and 5th	22	22	22	22	22	22	22	Target location (at arrows)
	28.4	26.6	24.7	22.8	21	19.1	17.3	Release point (at foul line)
	34.8	31.1	27.4	23.7	20	16.2	12.5	Starting position (of swing in stance)

depending on target and body type. The lane is only 39 boards wide. The left-hander may find the ball return (to their right) getting in the way for some left-side spare attempts. Likewise, right-handed bowlers may find a ball return to their left (when bowling on an even numbered lane) getting in the way of their right-side spare attempts.

An accommodation some bowlers make is to walk along, or around, the ball return to get a strong cross-lane angle. They don't walk straight towards their target. They may even walk right to throw left or vice versa. They may not start in the correct position for the target line (based on the guide); but, by the time they get to the foul line, the ball will be at the correct release point.

Examples of these exceptions are:

- A left-handed bowler aims at 7-pin by targeting at 4th arrow. He or she starts the ball on board 25 in the stance, walks straight down the lane, and releases at board 25. As long as the bowler gets the body position to direct the swing line (also called the launch angle) from board 25 towards the 4th arrow, he or she will make the 7-pin.

- A right-handed bowler aims at 10-pin by targeting at 4th arrow, and then follows the same procedure as the lefty in order to make the 10-pin.

Generally, spares are easy, and strikes are tough. It makes sense to put a lot of practice time into what's easy. It is rewarding and more likely to have an immediate positive impact on your game. How much time, you may ask? Consider average bowlers who strike about 30 percent of the time. In the first 10 frames they average three strikes and therefore have seven other frames for spare attempts. This makes a total of 17 rolls of the ball—10 first balls for strike attempts and 7 others for spare attempts—and 7 out of 17 is slightly over 40 percent. If 40 percent of a bowler's throws during the game are at spares, it makes sense they should spend at least 40 percent of their practice time on spare shooting.

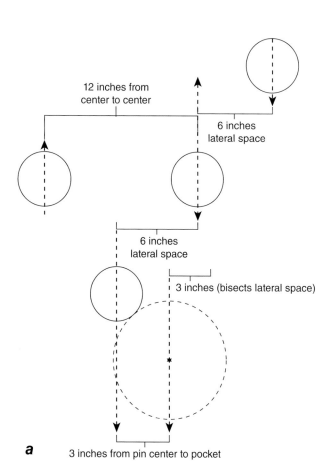

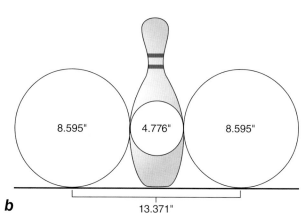

Figure 11.1 Spare error margin.

Fortunately, the basic spare strategies are simply variations of strike strategies. On every shot, strike or spare, we need two things: a starting position and a target, which if determined correctly, will send the ball in the desired direction. Whether the direction is toward the strike pocket on the first ball or some other location for a spare attempt, it is still basic targeting.

Remember the pivot system? It allows the bowler to make adjustments to the strike line by systematically changing the ball's location at the pins. This is what spare shooting is as well. But, instead of aiming for the strike pocket, we are trying to miss it! We are trying to adjust the ball path away from the original strike line as much as necessary to direct the ball towards the spare setup.

The basic spare-shooting system is simply an expansion of the pivot strike-adjustment system. For strikes, we use the pivot system to correct an errant shot and realign toward the strike pocket. For spare shooting, we start with an established strike line and adjust away from it to steer the ball one direction or another toward the remaining pins.

Other spare-shooting systems that appear in this step (for example, sectioning the triangle) apply to bowlers who might have a nonstandard strike starting position. Some bowlers' normal strike position is very far left or right on the approach. Adjusting from the strike starting position as a means of shooting spares may not be practical. Also, bowlers with a very strong hook need to modify the ball's roll for spare shooting; some spares are almost impossible to make if throwing a large hook. Because their release technique for spare attempts is different than that for their strike shots, these athletes may need to create spare-shooting strategies that are independent of their strike line as well. In any case, their strategies are modifications of the pivot system.

As with all targeting systems, it is critical to know exactly where the footwork starts. When adjusting the starting position, movements must be precise. Counting boards is as important for shooting spares as it is for throwing strikes. The basic system applies to most players in a majority of playing situations. However, it is only a starting point. You may very well develop your own unique system. As you become more involved with the game and bowl on a variety of lane conditions, you may find it necessary to alter the basic systems to fit your needs. Do not be afraid to tweak these strategies.

KEY-PIN SPARE-SHOOTING STRATEGY

The basic spare strategy is the key-pin strategy. There are seven key pins. When looking straight at a full set of pins, you will see seven pins spread across the lane.

If you have a strategy for rolling the ball to each of the seven locations, you will be able to make almost any spare encountered. One of these pins will either stand alone or, in a set of pins that remain standing, will be the pin closet to you. For almost all spares, you will need to make initial contact with one of these pins in order to make the spare.

All spares, no matter how unusual looking, can be reduce to a single-pin spare attempt. Now, you don't have to fear a split or a washout. You merely need to identify the one pin of the setup you need to hit and apply a strategy that will put the ball in that location.

3-6-9 AND 4-8-12 PIVOT SYSTEMS

The nice thing about a pivot system is that the bowler's lane target has little need to change. For the most part, the target used for the strike ball can be the pivot point around which the spare target lines are adjusted. The spare-shooting system is a rough approximation of the 3-1-2 strike adjustment system.

Another, benefit of the pivot system is that the gutters never come into play. The pivot system is also called the cross-lane spare-shooting system. The target line will always cross the lane through a target that is nowhere near the edge of the lane. I have never met a decent bowler who consistently rolls the ball down the right edge of the lane for right-side spares and the left edge for left-side spares. Although there may be a rare circumstance when this is done for a particularly unusual spare attempt, as a consistently applied strategy it has a very high failure rate.

To make the process of developing a spare strategy easier, we are going to eliminate calculations. With the strike system, you had to visually determine by how far the ball's contact point at the pins missed the strike pocket. Then, once you had a reasonable estimate, you adjusted the starting position using the 3-to-2 ratio.

Because of the more generous error margin for most spares, you want something that is easier to remember and can be applied quickly and reliably. The 3-6-9 and 4-8-12 systems accomplish just that.

Once you establish a line to the strike pocket, adjustments from the strike line (figure 11.2) allow you to shoot any spare. The six basic adjustments include three to the right for left-side spares (figure 11.3) and three to the left for right-side spares (figure 11.4). For spares in the center, there is no adjustment. For a right-handed bowler, here are the seven basic spare positions:

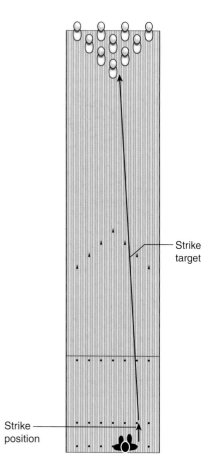

- Left corner, 7 pin (9-board adjustment to the right)
- Left, 4 pin (6-board adjustment to the right)
- Left center, 2 pin and 8 pin (3-board adjustment to the right)
- Center, 1 pin and 5 pin (no adjustment; use strike line)
- Right center, 3 pin and 9 pin (4-board adjustment to the left)
- Right, 6 pin (8-board adjustment to the left)
- Right corner, 10 pin (12-board adjustment to the left)

Strike target

Strike position

Figure 11.2 Strike line for a right-handed bowler. Spare adjustments will be made based on this strike line and the strike target.

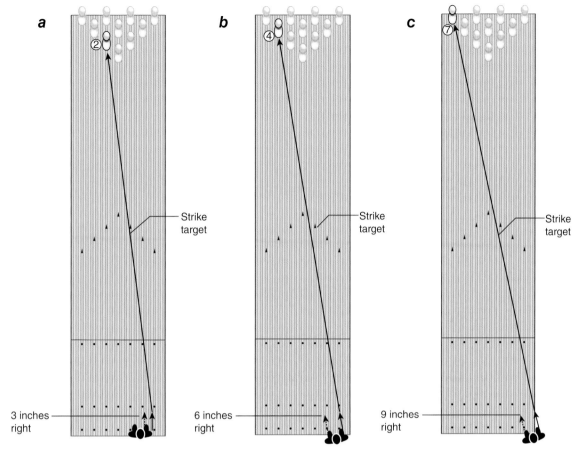

Figure 11.3 Left-side spares for a right-handed bowler: *(a)* 2-pin spare, 3-board adjustment to the right; *(b)* 4-pin spare, 6-board adjustment to the right; *(c)* 7-pin spare, 9-board adjustment to the right.

a — Strike target — 3 inches right

b — Strike target — 6 inches right

c — Strike target — 9 inches right

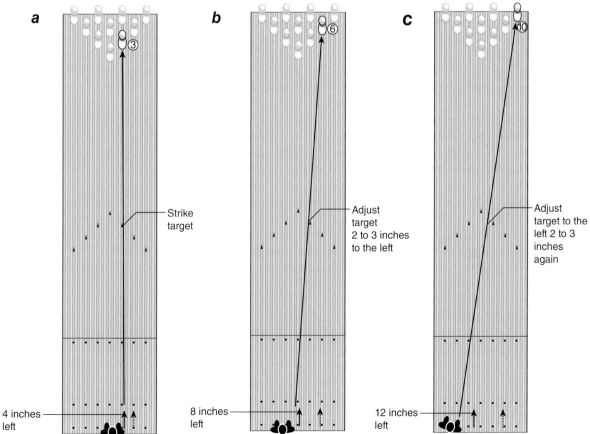

Figure 11.4 Right-side spares for a right-handed bowler: *(a)* 3-pin spare, 4-board adjustment to the left; *(b)* 6-pin spare, 8-board adjustment to the left; *(c)* 10-pin spare, 12-board adjustment to the left.

a — Strike target — 4 inches left

b — Adjust target 2 to 3 inches to the left — 8 inches left

c — Adjust target to the left 2 to 3 inches again — 12 inches left

Focus on one pin only. For a group of pins, identify the key pin, usually the one in front, and adjust for that pin. Remember, always walk toward the target. After setting up on the approach, turn the body—not just the shoulders—and face the target. The line of the approach should be oriented toward the target, not straight in relation to the lane.

Why move only three boards when adjusting to the right but four boards when going left? This is a practical "err on the side of caution" adjustment. This system attempts to accommodate bowlers who roll the ball fairly straight as well as those with a slight hook. The right-handed bowler has already established an angle from right to left because of the hook of the ball or the starting position on the lane. Right-handed bowlers could make larger incremental moves to create more angle, but if they had any kind of hook (or if they missed slightly left of target) the left gutter could come onto play. The 3-6-9 system creates enough angle for the straight bowler to direct the ball to each proper location while still leaving enough room for bowlers with a modest hook.

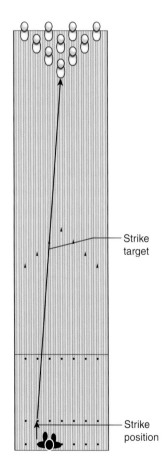

Figure 11.5

Strike line for a left-handed bowler. Spare adjustments will be made based on this strike line and the strike target.

For most bowlers throwing with their natural angle, moving in three-board increments should be enough. When throwing against their natural angle, four-board moves are needed.

The illustrations shown in figures 11.2, 11.3, and 11.4 are from a right-handed bowler's perspective. Left-handed bowlers must reverse the numbers. You still move left for a right-side spare, just not as far. You still move right for a left-side spare, but more than a right-handed bowler would. Figure 11.5 shows the left-handed bowler's strike line and target.

A left-handed bowler can also make six basic adjustments, three to the left for right-side spares (figure 11.6) and three to the right for left-side spares (figure 11.7). For spares in the center, no adjustment is needed. Here are the seven basic spare positions for a left-handed bowler.

- Right corner, 10 pin (9-board adjustment to the left)
- Right, 6 pin (6-board adjustment to the left)
- Right center, 3 pin and 9 pin (3-board adjustment to the left)
- Center, 1 pin and 5 pin (no adjustment; use strike line)
- Left center, 2 pin and 8 pin (4-board adjustment to the right)
- Left, 4 pin (8-board adjustment to the right)
- Left corner, 7 pin (12-board adjustment to the right)

This system will work well for bowlers who use a standard strike target. The 3-6-9 and 4-8-12 adjustments from a previously established strike line work best if the bowler's strike target is between the second arrow on the left and the second arrow on the right (the middle 20 boards). In this case, there is enough room to move the starting position without the ball return getting in the way.

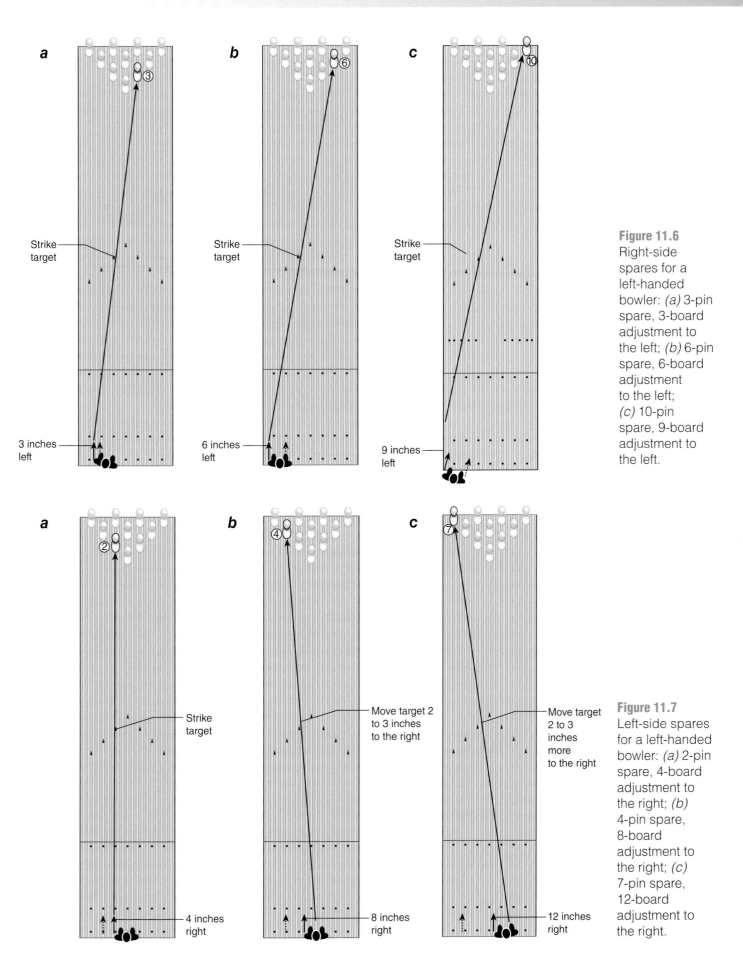

Figure 11.6
Right-side spares for a left-handed bowler: *(a)* 3-pin spare, 3-board adjustment to the left; *(b)* 6-pin spare, 6-board adjustment to the left; *(c)* 10-pin spare, 9-board adjustment to the left.

Figure 11.7
Left-side spares for a left-handed bowler: *(a)* 2-pin spare, 4-board adjustment to the right; *(b)* 4-pin spare, 8-board adjustment to the right; *(c)* 7-pin spare, 12-board adjustment to the right.

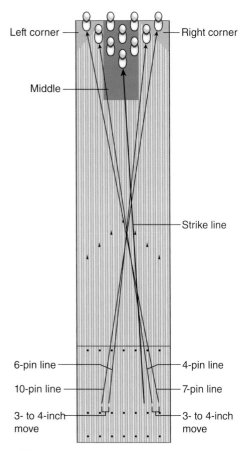

Left corner

Right corner

Middle

Strike line

6-pin line

4-pin line

10-pin line

7-pin line

3- to 4-inch
move

3- to 4-inch
move

Figure 11.8 Right-corner, left-corner,
and middle spare lines.
The spare lines for left-
and right-corner spares
are independent of the
strike line.

SECTIONING THE TRIANGLE

Like in any basic system, there are exceptions. For players who use less-common strike targets (such as first or fourth arrows), the basic spare system may not always work. If you find the ball return consistently getting in the way when making the standard adjustment for spares, you may need to adopt a spare-shooting system independent of your strike line.

One spare-shooting system that works independently of the strike line is to section the pin setup. With this system, the pin triangle is broken into three sections—right corner, left corner, and middle. The left-corner and right-corner spare lines have nothing to do with the strike line (figure 11.8).

For a right-corner spare, find a line to the 10 pin. Play as much angle across the lane as you comfortably can. Take lane conditions out of the equation by letting the ball cross through the area with the heaviest oil. Use a straight ball release. (Learn one if you don't have one.) Anticipate targeting somewhere near the fourth (middle) arrow. Adjust four boards to the right from the 10-pin starting position to shoot for the 6 pin.

For a left-corner spare, find a line to the 7 pin. Once again, throw much less hook than normal, and keep the ball on the oil. Adjust four boards to the right from the 7-pin starting position to shoot for the 4 pin.

For a middle-of-the-lane spare, use the already established strike target. Unless you have a very strong hooking ball, use a normal release. Adjust four boards to the right from the strike starting position to shoot the 2 pin. Adjust four boards to the left from the strike starting position to shoot the 3 pin.

Avoid Hooking the Ball at Spares

Be particularly careful about back-row spares. Because the pins are farther away, the ball rolls farther down the lane before making contact with the pins. For example, the 8 pin is almost 21 inches (53 cm) farther away than the 2 pin. A ball that hooks into the 2 pin is likely to hook past the 8 pin. For most spare-shooting scenarios, a straighter ball is the best choice. Learn to tone down a strongly hooking ball.

FOCUSING ON A KEY PIN

For all spares, you must throw the ball to a particular place in order to convert the spare. If you focus on a particular pin—the key pin—you can reduce almost all spare setups to one of seven basic positions. Using the seven key pins limits confusion. Simply think of where you want the ball to end up, determine which key pin is closest to that position, and then make your spare-shooting adjustment for that pin.

This is particularly useful when facing difficult spares or splits. In these situations, it is unlikely you will be able to make the ball hit all the pins. You need to put the ball where it will deflect one pin into another. Chances are, that place is close to one of the key pins.

Now you don't have to panic—you have a strategy for making almost all spares. Think of a split as a variation of a single pin. You know the strategy for any single pin; therefore, you have a strategy for every spare.

Figures 11.9 and 11.10 illustrate examples of using certain key pins for making spares. Do not be too concerned if you do not make these spares all the time. Many of the difficult spare attempts—splits and washouts—have error margins of less than half an inch (1.3 cm). The more extreme splits, such as the 6-7 or 4-10, have error margins of about a quarter of an inch (.63 cm). The placement of the ball must be precise. Focusing on a key pin gives you an idea of where the ball needs to go. You will not be able to throw the ball exactly where you need to every time. The key-pin strategy will get you close, though. Be confident. Every once in a while, you will make a difficult spare and it will become the highlight of your day.

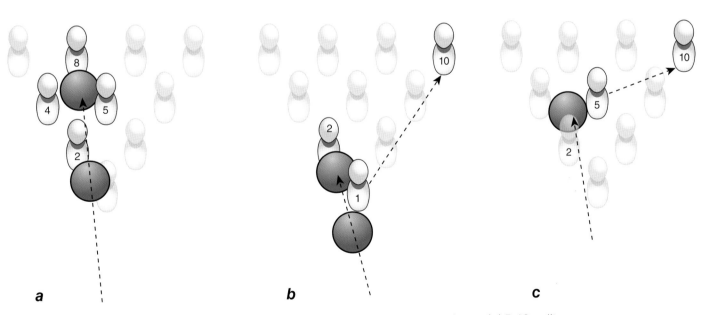

Figure 11.9 Variations on the 2 pin as key: *(a)* 2-4-5-8 bucket, *(b)* 1-2-10 washout, *(c)* 5-10 split.

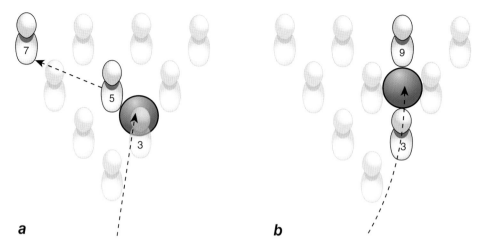

Figure 11.10 Variations on the 3 pin as key: *(a)* 5-7 split, *(b)* 3-9 double wood.

Do not let the disappointment of an errant first shot keep you from focusing on your second one. Every spare is makeable. Put the last shot out of your head. Focus only on the task at hand:

- Determine where you want to put the ball.
- Identify the key pin closest to that location.
- Relax; take a deep breath.
- Make your adjustment based on your spare-shooting strategy.

SHOOTING SPLITS

When shooting at a split, you may need to roll the ball at an imaginary spot. The key pin you want to throw at may not be one of the pins standing. The location of the ball is what is important.

First, determine where you want the ball to go. For most splits, you need to hit the outside of the pin in order to slide it over into the other pin. Once you know where you want the ball to end up, determine which key pin is closest. Make your adjustments on the approach as if you were throwing at that pin, whether or not it is actually standing.

Some splits are almost impossible to make; the standing pins are directly across the lane from each other, and a considerable distance separates them (figure 11.11). The 7-10 and the 4-6 splits come to mind. With these splits, make sure you knock down at least one pin. This is called *saving count*. In some nearly impossible splits, such as the 4-6-7-10 (called the big four) and the 4-6-7-9-10 (called the Greek church), several pins remain standing. Unless you are in a do-or-die situation, get as many of the remaining pins as possible.

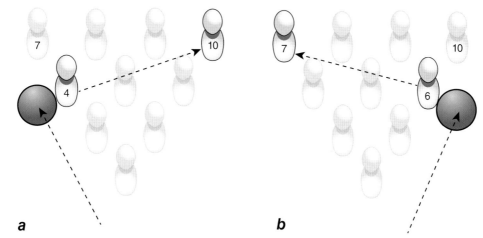

Figure 11.11 On nearly impossible splits, practice the corner pins: *(a)* 4-10 split and *(b)* 6-7 split.

It is amazing how many needless pins of count are thrown away because of inane attempts at nearly impossible spares. The bowler ends up getting no pins at all, which is particularly hurtful after a strike. Experienced bowlers know that "one is two" after a strike. This means after a strike, the pins on the spare attempt count twice. The pins count in the frame they are knocked down in as well as back in the frame with the strike. In this situation, every pin missed on the spare attempt is two pins lost from the final score.

Unless you are near the end of the game and making the spare is absolutely critical for determining the outcome of the match, you are better off being conservative in your spare attempts. Far more matches are lost because of needless loss of pin count during the game than are won by someone converting an almost impossible split.

SPECIAL SPARE-SHOOTING CIRCUMSTANCES

For the most part, cross-lane angles work for most spares. When confronting multiple pins, not only is the correct location important, but so is an appropriate angle. Spares are best made when the ball has a chance to contact as many of the pins as possible.

For instance, the 1-2-4 spare can be made by hitting the right side of the head pin. The head pin hits the 2 pin, and then the 2 pin drives into the 4 pin, much like the pinfall for a right-pocket strike. But, that spare could more easily be made if the initial contact were left of the head pin. One simply makes the adjustment for the 2 pin as the key pin: a move to the right of about four boards. Not only would this put the ball in the right location, but the move would also create a right-to-left attack angle, which helps the ball deflect down the line.

This is also true of the *baby split* (3-10). The move to the left puts the ball in the 6-pin location (splitting the difference between the 3 pin and 10 pin). Additionally,

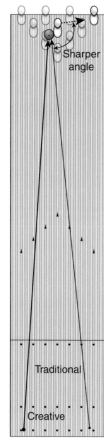

Figure 11.12 Nontraditional spare shooting diagram.

the large move left (eight boards for the right-handed bowler) creates a strong angle that facilitates the ball's deflection off the 3 pin into the 10 pin.

When you are left with a spare attempt such as the 1-2-10 (washout), standard spare-shooting practice dictates a move to the right. Aiming for the 2 pin would cause slight contact with the head pin. The glancing hit would send the head pin to the right in the direction of the 10 pin. But, moving to the right makes for a sharper deflection angle between the path of the ball and the deflection line of the head pin. In this case, the important aspect of making this spare is the line from the 1 pin to the 10 pin. The error margin would be larger if the ball path came from the left side of the head pin.

Now wait a second. Wouldn't this require a move to the left for a left-side spare attempt? Yes indeed. This is also true for spares such as the 5-10, 5-7, 2-10, and 3-7. The move creates a better look at the angle, a cut that is less sharp (to use a billiards phrase). See figure 11.12.

At times, standard spare-shooting practices are not the best option. Like the situations mentioned earlier, a left-side movement for left-side spare attempt (and right-side movements for right-side spares) is a better option. It is important to practice those situations. Intentionally moving left to hit the left strike pocket (or even the 2-4 pocket) as a right-handed bowler may go against what is familiar, but is an essential tool if you want a versatile game.

Many experienced bowlers play on a variety of lane conditions. Cross-lane spare shooting also requires crossing the lane condition patterns. Sometimes crossing the pattern makes standard spare-shooting practices unreliable, particularly, if the bowler has any hook in the spares at all. When on variable or confusing lane conditions, some bowlers prefer a more parallel spare-shooting strategy. While there will be a slight right-to-left angle for the left corner (7 pin and 4 pin) and likewise a slight left-to-right angle at the right corner (6-pin and 10-pin), it will in no way resemble a strong cross-lane attempt.

When to use cross-lane spare-shooting practices instead of other spare-shooting strategies depends on the skill of the bowler, the demands of the lane conditions, and the nature of the spare being attempted. To be fully prepared, one needs a spare-shooting guide for every possible target line. The following composite spare shooting diagrams (figure 11.13) give you target lines (starting position, target at the arrows, and key pin) for different cross-lane spares.

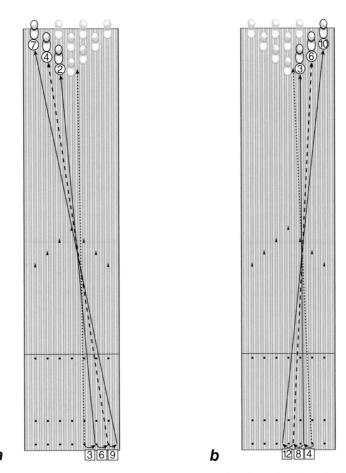

Figure 11.13 Composite spare shooting diagrams showing *(a)* the 3, 6, and 9 board adjustments for left-side spares and *(b)* the 12, 8, and 4 board adjustments for right-side spares.

A Word of Caution

How challenging is it to pick a corner pin out of a full rack of pins? There is only about a 2.5-inch (6.3 cm) margin between the gutter and the next pin over. This is about the size of the strike pocket. It takes considerable discipline and concentration to achieve this consistently.

Spare-Shooting Drill 1   Corner-Pin (Low Ball) Game

This is a classic game of targeting and concentration. The basic premise of the game is to bowl the lowest possible score without throwing the ball in the gutter.

The goal is to pick off just the 7 pin and the 10 pin out of the entire set of pins. Try for the lowest possible pinfall on each throw. Gutter throws are assessed a penalty. Some versions of the game assign a particular pin count to gutter balls, such as 10 pins for a gutter ball on any first throw, and 5 pins for missing all of the remaining pins on any second throw. Other versions of the game score marks for any gutter ball: a strike if the first ball is in the gutter, a spare if the second throw gets no pin count.

(continued)

Spare-Shooting Drill 1 *(continued)*

The version of this game you play may be influenced by whether you keep score by hand or use the automatic (computer) scoring system found at most bowling centers. Some automatic scoring systems are preprogrammed with a version of the low-ball game.

Low Ball for Automatic Scoring: Wiedman Variation

Bowl a 10-frame game. Throw twice in each frame. The first can be at whichever corner you choose. The goal of the second shot is to hit at least one of the remaining pins, but as few of the remaining pins as possible. You don't want to make a real spare. With most automatic scoring systems, a dash shows up on the screen anytime someone misses all of the pins. This can be from a gutter on the first ball or missing all the remaining pins on the second attempt.

For each dash on the screen during the game, add 10 pins to the final score. All other aspects of scoring are taken care of by the automatic scorers. Automatic scoring will take care of adding strikes and spares; don't worry about penalties for these.

The lowest total after penalties wins. Example: You get a 7 on the first ball then miss the remaining three pins on the next ball. That frame is worth 17 points (7 pins plus a 10-point penalty). The scoring system would record the 7 as usual; you have to remember to add 10 to the final total at the end of the game.

TO DECREASE DIFFICULTY

A gutter on the first ball is a much worse result than a mere miss of all the pins on the second ball. Consider a penalty of only 5 points for a second throw that misses all the remaining pins.

Success Check

- Apply corner-pin spare-shooting strategies.
- Make sure the adjustments are large enough to get the ball to each corner.
- Be conservative. Keep the ball on the lanes.

Score Your Success

Perfect game: 20

Excellent = 21 to 59

Very good= 60 to 89

Good= 90 to 119

Average= 120 to 149

Keep working at it! =150 or more

Your score ___

Spare-Shooting Drill 2   Ball Placement Points Game

Sometimes pins roll around and knock over other pins, giving you a higher score in a low-ball game than is otherwise deserved. In this version of a spare strategy game in which we practice spares with all pins standing, pinfall is not considered at all. The bowler need only recognize which pin is contacted first. Simply assign a point value for each of the key pins. As the pins get farther away from the center, the value of the pins increases.

To make left-side attempts worth the same as right-side attempts, consider assigning the same value for both sides. This is what I do when playing the game in my classes. The head pin is worth 1 point and each subsequent pin is valued at 3 points, 6 points, and 7 points as you progress down each side of the triangle.

We don't put a higher value on the corner pins because picking off the very last pin out of a full set of pins is not only difficult, it also has no value in actual game situations. If there is no reason to intentionally pick off corner pins, there is no sense in giving them a substantially higher value. Practice in a manner that is useful in a real game situation.

Every first throw of a frame is a corner-pin practice. To make the practice more like a real game, be sure to alternate left-side and right-side attempts each frame. Make sure there is a full line of pins (all four pins that make up a side of the pin triangle) standing on the side you are throwing at when attempting your second ball. Strikes and spares are not recorded. If you throw a strike on the first throw, a second throw in the frame must be taken anyway.

A practical strategy for this game is to play for the 4 pin and the 6 pin. Hitting close to each corner yet staying well away from the gutters gives you 12 points for each frame. After 10 frames of 12, your score would be 120, an excellent score.

From a practical point of view, throwing a ball that hits the 6 pin first would also take out the 10 pin in a normal game situation. The same is true for the 4 pin and 7 pin on the other side.

Success Check

- Know your strike line.
- Make adjustments based on one of the spare-shooting systems.
- If you're not getting to the corners consistently, modify your starting position or adjust your target on the lane.

Score Your Success

Perfect score = 140

Outstanding = 120 to 139

Excellent = 100 to 119

Good = 80 to 99

Practice, practice, practice = 79 or less

Your score ___

Spare-Shooting Drill 3   Two-Pocket Practice

It is not always easy to practice other types of spares in a nongame situation. Yet, if you only practice them in a real game situation, you may not be fully prepared. Essentially, you are taking the test before the lesson. For example, learning how to intentionally throw at the other strike pocket is a useful skill. For a right-handed bowler, this would be the 1-2 pocket. Learning to put the ball in this area is good practice for shooting the 2-8 spare, the 2-4-5 spare, and the 2-4-5-8 bucket spare as well as washouts such as the 1-2-10.

A good practice regimen is to work on both right-side and left-side strategies in every frame. It makes the practice more efficient (every throw serves a purpose) and more challenging (you don't always know what you'll be left with).

One simple practice drill is to throw the first ball at the 3-6 pocket. If you are successful, you will leave the 1-2 or the 1-2-4 standing. Your second throw is at these remaining pins.

(continued)

Spare-Shooting Drill 3 *(continued)*

If you miss the 3-6 pocket on the first ball, the best you can do is break even for the frame. You must knock over all the remaining pins (make the real spare) for the frame to be worth 0. With any other result (pins remain standing) points are subtracted.

Score Your Success

Bowl 10 frames. Keep track of your score on a sheet of paper.

Hit the 3-6 pocket on the first ball = +5 points

Hit the 1-2 pocket on the second ball = +3 points

Hit 3-6 pocket on first ball, but miss 1-2 pocket on second = –1 point per pin left standing

Miss 3-6 pocket, make actual remaining spare = 0 point

Miss 3-6 pocket, don't make remaining spare = –2 points per pin left standing

Perfect: 80

Excellent= 70 to 79

Very good= 50 to 69

Average= 30 to 49

Below average= 0 to 29

Be patient and keep trying: 0 or less

Your score ___

Spare-Shooting Drill 4   Modern-Day Kingpin: Head Pin Game

Many years ago, the most common form of bowling was ninepins. The pins were set in a diamond shape. In one version of this game, the objective was to knock down all the pins except the one in the middle—the kingpin. (The 5 pin in today's game has the same location and name. This term is also the origin of the title of a Woody Harrelson movie.)

This spare-shooting drill uses the modern triangular pin setup. For the purposes of this game, we put the headpin in the role of the kingpin. The goal is to leave just the headpin standing. This requires knowing where to aim in order to hit the 3-6 pocket and the 2-4 pocket. Bowl a 10-frame game, keeping track of the points earned in each frame.

Score Your Success

Just the headpin is standing after two throws = +10 points

After two throws, headpin and other pins remain standing = –2 per extra pin (i.e., all pins other than the headpin)

Headpin is hit on the first throw = –5 points

Saving throw: Make remaining spare = +5 points (i.e., If you make the remaining spare, you break even for the frame.)

Headpin is missed by first throw, but hit on the second throw = –3 points

Throw a real strike on first ball = –5 points

Kingpin perfection = 100

Spare-shooting royalty = 70 to 99

Well-done = 40 to 69

Average = 10 to 39

Below Average = -19 to 9

Keeping Practicing = -20 or lower

Your score ___

Remember, after hitting the headpin on the first throw, there is still a chance for a saving throw. To save the frame, you must knock down all the remaining pins. A real spare gets you back to even for the frame. If you strike on the first throw, there are no pins standing and no chance for a saving throw.

TO DECREASE DIFFICULTY

- If you don't want to keep score, set a certain standard for the practice.
- How many frames does it take you to leave the headpin by itself five times?
- How many times can you leave the headpin by itself in a specific number of frames?

TO INCREASE DIFFICULTY

- Make it a team challenge! Have a race! See who can leave the head pin by itself 5 times in the least number of frames.

Scoring Special Circumstances

What should you do if you miss the head pin on the first throw and still get a strike? While it is rare to strike without contacting the headpin, it does happen. Technically, the bowler achieved the practice objective on the initial throw, but pure luck produced a real strike. In this case, consider allowing a do-over. A player shouldn't be punished for luck, but neither should they get credit for a frame that has no second throw.

Spare-Shooting Drill 5   Beggar Thy Neighbor

Spare practice can involve more than one bowler. In this game, no bowler shoots his or her own strike shot. Instead, the initial throw is an attempt to leave as difficult a spare as possible for the opponent. The goal is to force your opponent to score lower than you did.

Each person bowls the first throw of his or her opponent's frame. The first bowler attempts to leave the most difficult spare possible. The opponent takes the second throw of the frame in an attempt to pick up the remaining pins. The goal of the game is to leave enough difficult spares that the opponent's score remains low.

Gutter balls are not allowed. If the leadoff throw goes into the gutter, change the score to a strike. Yes, your gutter ball becomes your opponent's strike!

Switch leadoff bowlers every frame. Remember, you throw your opponent's first ball, and your opponent throws your first ball. This game is best played on a pair of lanes. Each player throws the initial shot on adjacent lanes. Then, each bowler

(continued)

Spare-Shooting Drill 5 *(continued)*

switches lanes for the spare attempt that counts for their own score. The winner is the one with the highest score.

A leadoff bowler who is especially daring could try to take out just the 7 pin or 10 pin. This leaves as many pins as possible and also limits the pin count added back if the opponent had a successful spare attempt in the previous frame.

On the other hand, the leadoff bowler could try to hit the headpin head-on, leaving a nearly impossible split for the opponent. This tactic may backfire, though. Hitting the headpin could result in a strike. If the leadoff bowler inadvertently throws a strike, it is awarded to the opponent; the opponent has no spare to shoot. Hitting the headpin might also result in a high pin count for the opposing bowler.

Score Your Success

Your success will depend on the skill of your opponent; therefore consider your wins and losses against this factor to determine how you are progressing.

Spare Shooting Drill 6   2-3, 4-6, 7-10 Game

I was first introduced, along with other coaches, to this drill by Gary Sparks at the first Indiana High School Bowling Summer Camp. If played in its most demanding format, it is one of most challenging of all the ball-placement games.

In this rotation game, the bowler alternates between left- and right-side attempts. The difficulty increases as the throws must be directed increasingly closer to the corner pins.

Round 1

Ball must make initial contact with the 3 pin. Next throw makes initial contact with the 2 pin. Repeat. (If a player chooses to start with the 2 pin, the next shot must be at the 3 pin.) Bowler may only move on to the next round if he or she successfully made alternating contact with the 2 pin and 3 pin four throws in a row (two on each side). As soon as the bowler misses the object pin, the bowler starts the round over.

Round 2

Use the same format as round 1, but the object pins are the 4 pin and the 6 pin. Again, success for the round is four consecutive, alternating contacts with the object pins. Miss even once and the round starts over.

Round 3

Use the same format as in previous rounds, but the object pins are the 7 pin and the 10 pin. Yes, you must hit just the 7 pin and just the 10 pin (out of a full rack of pins) on four alternating shots, two on the 7 side and two on the 10 side.

TO DECREASE DIFFICULTY

- As described earlier, each round has its own challenge level. Once bowlers have completed one level, they move on to the next. If they miss in a particular level, they only restart at the beginning of the challenge level they are currently at.

- Make four successful throws at the level being played. They don't have to be consecutive. For example, as soon as the 2 pin and 3 pin are initially contacted twice, round 1 is finished. Errant throws between successful attempts don't require a restart of the round.

- Only require two consecutive successful attempts (one on each side) to advance to the next level. The game could be finished in as few as eight precisely placed rolls of the ball.

TO INCREASE DIFFICULTY

- As soon as the bowler misses in any round, he or she must go back to the start of round 1.

- In this format, the bowler must make 12 consecutive successful contacts (three sets of four throws) at the proper object pins without missing in order to win. I suggest setting a time limit, or the game may never end. (Some bowlers might not ever get to the round of 7s and the 10s, but they will get lots of practice on their 2s and 3s.)

Score Your Success

Although there are too many ways to modify the game to fit all skill levels here, commit yourself to keeping track of how far you get. With each game, work to decrease the number of frames it takes to finish a game and thus increase your skill level.

SUCCESS SUMMARY

For the beginning bowler, spare-shooting is the best way to improve scores. It is also an essential ingredient to success for bowlers of all skill levels. Strikes are difficult. The size of the strike pocket is a few inches at best. On the other hand, most single-pin spares have better than a 13-inch (33 cm) error margin—the width of the ball (8.59 inches [21.8 cm]) plus the width of a pin (4.77 inches [12.11 cm]).

Although the gutter takes away a few inches, the error margin for corner-pin spares is still more than 9 inches (22.8 cm). It makes sense to spend practice time on an aspect of the game that has an immediate positive impact on scoring.

Without a doubt, as your strike ball becomes more accurate, the spares you leave will become easier. You will have more one- and two-pin combinations as opposed to the nearly endless variety of the more difficult spares. Although strike practice is always a prime concern, it should not be undertaken to the exclusion of developing sound spare-shooting strategies through regimented spare practice sessions.

Most spares can be made by adjusting from an already established strike line. Start with what you are comfortable with. Most spare attempts are based on six adjustments of the approach position—three to the left for the three right-side key pin locations (the 3, 6, and 10 pins) and three to the right for the left-side key pins (the 2, 4, and 7 pins).

Review your drill scores. Record your scores in the spaces that follow and total them. Never stop practicing spares. Each of the practices (or challenges) described are ways of practicing a variety of spare shooting strategies. If there are certain types of spares (corner pins for instance) that you struggle with, then by all means consistently work at the challenges that emphasize those types of spares. Be sure to keep track of your score for each of the challenges to get an idea as to how well your skills are developing.

Skilled bowlers should score consistently in the above-average or excellent categories for the first four practice games described.

If you are scoring consistently below average, don't be discouraged. Trust that your time and effort will pay off. As you become more capable at these drills, you will see their benefits in your actual game scores. Keeping the correct mind-set and focusing on the task at hand (literally being concerned with only one shot at a time, the one you are about to make) will allow the strategies you develop in practice to carry over into real game situations.

SCORING YOUR SUCCESS

Spare-Shooting Practice Games

1. Corner-Pin (Low Ball) Game   ____ lowest score possible: 20

2. Ball Placement Points Game   ____ out of 140

3. Two-Pocket Practice   ____ out of 80

4. Modern-Day Kingpin   ____ out of 100

5. Beggar Thy Neighbor   ____ won or lost

6. 2-3, 4-6, 7-10 Game   ____ number of frames to finish round 1

____ number of frames to finish round 2

____ number of frames to finish round 3

The last two steps have discussed spare-shooting and strike-throwing strategies. These basic strategies are applicable to many situations. Now it is time to apply your skills and strategies to the ever-changing environment you find on the lanes.

Every throw of the ball changes the lane conditions. The best bowlers can modify their basic strategies to accommodate the wide variety of lane conditions the sport presents.

You cannot overlook versatility in physical performance. That is why a large portion of this book concerns itself with physical skill development. It is the combination of physical skills, versatility, and strategy that creates a successful performance.

Your ability to recognize the lane conditions and the changes they undergo—and then modify your skills to adjust to those changes—defines you as a bowler. The variety of conditions you must learn to recognize and the means to adapt to those conditions is the topic of the next step.

Understanding Lane Conditions

In this step, we discuss three factors in the performance environment:

1. Lane patterns. What types of oil patterns are typically found in bowling centers?
2. Lane changes. How does the oil move? What does the bowler need to do to adjust to these changes?
3. Ball motion. How does the ball perform as it rolls? What can be done physically and technologically to manipulate the ball's performance?

LANE CONDITIONS

Lane condition refers to the distribution of oil on the lane. The main purpose of this thin layer of oil is to protect the lane surface against the impact and friction created by rolling a ball. But, from a bowler's perspective, the way the oil is distributed on the lane influences the scoring environment. Manipulating the distribution of lane conditioner (also called the *oil pattern*) is intentional.

In recreational bowling situations, commonly encountered during league play, the pattern enhances the scoring pace. In other situations (collegiate bowling, professional bowling events, and other special competitive events), the conditioning pattern creates a specific challenge that tests the skills and strategies of the competitors.

Other factors (many of them outside the control of the bowler) influence how quickly the initial lane condition changes. The following are some of these factors.

- The number of games bowled in each round of the event before the lanes are reconditioned affect lane condition. The more games bowled on a lane, the more dramatic the changes in the lane condition become. Oil picked up by the ball (and wiped off by the bowler) is oil removed from the lane.

- How bowlers throw the ball and where they choose to play the lane affects lane conditions. The lane-play strategies of each bowler determine which areas of the lane are bowled on the most. Those areas used most change the fastest. The rate at which the changes occur influences each bowler's adjustment strategy to accommodate an ever-changing playing environment.

- Temperature and humidity affect how quickly the conditioner moves on the lane and how quickly it dissipates from the lane surface.

- Some types of bowling ball coverstocks (the surface material of the ball), such as polyester, act like snowplows and push the oil around. Other types of ball materials (e.g., reactive resin), act like oil sponges and wick the oil off the lanes entirely.

- A player's skill has an immediate impact on how lane conditions change. Skilled players are able to wear away (called *breaking down*) the conditioner on a specific area of the lane. Skilled players working together can make challenging lane conditions easier to play. Inexperienced players tend to push the lane conditioner in various directions and break down the conditioner in a variety of areas. When shots are "sprayed" (i.e., when unskilled bowlers miss in a variety of different directions) the changes in the lane condition become less predictable; potentially this unpredictability will have a dampening effect on the scoring pace over a period of time.

Every bowling center conditions its lanes differently; so every bowling center presents a unique performance environment. The great challenge in bowling is to recognize these variations and devise a strategy to overcome them. Few standards have been established to dictate the amount and distribution of oil. Bowlers are not allowed to reach out and touch the lanes to test how much oil is out there. So you will use trial and error to determine how to play the lanes if information is lacking. The more consistently you throw the ball, the more reliable the information you gather about each section of the lane. How far the ball skids down the lane, how quickly the ball transitions into its roll phase, and how dramatically the ball changes direction are all pieces of information around which you can devise a strategy.

The following are three general parameters for evaluating lane condition.

> *Volume*—the amount of conditioner (in milliliters) applied to the conditioned surface
>
> *Length*—the distance down the lane (measured in feet from foul line) conditioner is applied
>
> *Ratio*—a crosswise (gutter-to-gutter) comparison in the depth of the oil on the part of the lane with the thickest application compared to the area with the thinnest

Let's discuss examples. There is obviously a difference between a few ounces of oil spread on a 44-foot (13.4 m) pattern, which is relatively long, and a 28-foot (8.5 m) pattern, which is pretty short. If you only consider the 44-foot length, you would assume lots of skid and much less ball reaction. But if most of the oil was applied in the first 15 feet (54.6 m) and only a thin layer remained to the end of the pattern, a strongly rolling ball might grab the lane earlier than on the 28-foot pattern with oil more evenly applied for the entire length.

This leads us to another consideration: the tapering of the oil from front to back. When lanes are inspected, measurements are taken in at least two places: by the arrows (about 15 feet past the foul line) and 3 feet (1 m) before the end of the pattern. If a lane condition pattern has a short taper zone (it goes from heavy oil to no oil in a short distance) just before pattern's end, a hooking ball will change direction abruptly. On the other hand, if the transition zone is long, featuring a more gradual decrease in oil, a hooking ball will make a smoother arcing motion into its hook phase.

To understand oil patterns, one must consider the oil distribution from left to right as well. There is no requirement that the oil be applied evenly from gutter to gutter. In fact, in only the rarest of instances is the oil placed in an even layer across the lane. If two lane condition patterns had the same length and volume, they would play considerably different if one had a 10:1 ratio and the other had a 2:1 ratio. To achieve a 10:1 ratio would require considerable amounts of the available oil to be stacked near the middle of the lane. These would leave only a very thin layer for the sections of the lane at the edges.

The bowler's goal is to negotiate the terrain and find the best path to the pocket. There are a variety of patterns used on the lanes at the Purdue Memorial Union for example. The almost flat (approximately 1:1 ratio) patterns used some years ago are different from the much more scorable pattern (about a 7:1 pattern) currently programmed into our lane machine. In general, the more evenly the oil is distributed, the more difficult the lane conditions. If the lane has a very large amount of oil in the middle of the lane compared with a relatively shallow depth of oil near the edges, the lane conditions play easier.

Why does a sharper contrast in oil volume help increase scores? Because the pattern has a steering effect on the ball. If there is a large volume of oil in the middle, the bowler can miss in and the ball will hold the line to the strike pocket; it is less likely to hook through the headpin. If the outside edge of the lane is very dry, the bowler can miss wide and the ball will recover back to the strike pocket. The extra friction creates extra hook. So, under the most favorable situations, the bowler can miss considerably in or out and still hit the strike pocket.

Some bowling centers and tournaments allow bowlers to look at the graph of the lane conditions before competition starts. Athletes and coaches try to get as much information as possible so they can make informed decisions. With this knowledge, decisions about lane play, equipment selection, and team lineup enhance the strategic aspects of the sport of bowling.

Similar to a golfer with a yardage book and knowledge of green speeds, a lane graph helps the bowler map out the best path to the pocket while avoiding hazards. In fact, some bowling tournaments make their conditions known to the public through printouts of the lane graph, uploading the graphs on a website, or by using one of the many lane condition patterns found in the Kegel Bowling Co. lane condition pattern library. With the proper lane conditioning machine, another bowling proprietor would then have an opportunity to replicate that tournament conditions in their own center.

Another aspect of understanding lane conditions is *oil migration*. The oil on the lane is not stationary. As the ball moves across the lane surface, it picks up oil. Some of the oil rubs off farther down the lane, but much of it stays on the ball. The skidding and rolling actions of the ball dry out the oilier areas of the lane and (sometimes) move oil to the dry parts. Let's discuss how lanes change.

LANE CHANGES

With every throw of the ball, the lanes undergo subtle changes. Eventually, the cumulative effect is enough to alter ball movement. The ball moves through three phases on its way down the lane: skid, hook, and roll. As the oil distribution changes on each section of the lane, the motion of the ball changes on each section. The skid may be more or less, the hook may become sharper or flatter, and the roll may begin sooner or later. The bowler's perception of how the ball moves down the lane and drives through the pins may alert the bowler to the need for an alternative lane-play strategy. Equipment selection, position on the approach, ball path on the lane, release variations, and ball speed are all strategy elements a bowler must be comfortable adjusting in order to adapt to the lane conditions. One of bowling's great challenges is recognizing these changes and making the correct adjustments. Adapting to varying lane conditions, not just from bowling center to bowling center, but also from shot to shot, is what separates the average bowler from the skilled bowler.

Lanes go through three basic phases: fresh shot, carrydown, and breakdown. The fresh-shot lane condition (figure 12.1) occurs just after the lane machine finishes conditioning the lanes. When the ball comes off the oil and enters the dry area of the lane, the ball reaction is usually obvious and consistent.

The *fresh shot* phase does not last long. As mentioned at the beginning of the step, several factors influence the rate of change into the other phases. Particularly, the area of the lane the bowlers are using influences the lane change. If many bowlers are using the same line to the pocket, that area of the lane will change quickly. Initially, the adjustments are small but are done quickly. It is not difficult to find the ball reaction area (some call it *the burn*) and move when it starts to expand. If a group of bowlers is playing all over the lane, the transition will be sporadic and less predictable. As you adjust your line to accommodate lane changes, you may end up running into somebody else's line. Small adjustments on the lane are often followed by large adjustment jumps.

One can get a good idea of what the initial lane condition is by following a simple practice regimen. Throw one shot directly up the lane over each arrow, starting from the first arrow and moving in. Go straight up the 5th board, the 10th board, and the 15th board. Then, throw one shot across the lane at the 10 pin using a normal release and strike ball followed by an across-lane attempt at the 7 pin, again using normal release and strike ball.

> *Remember, you are not trying to throw strikes in practice. You are trying to figure out how the oil is distributed so that you throw strikes when they count.*

As you move across they lane, pay attention to the area where the ball experiences a sudden decrease in the length of the initial skid. If it hooks off of one arrow and skids over another, the oil dry line is somewhere between those two arrows. If the 10-pin shot has a longer skid phase, there might be higher oil volume in the middle. If the 7-pin shot hooks early, there may not be much oil on the edge of the lane. If you notice these two things together, the pattern may have a high left-to-right ratio.

What if the shape of the shot is the same over all the arrows? Then one can assume the oil is distributed evenly across the lane. Decisions on lane play will not be made on left-to-right preference alone. On a flat pattern, you have to be attentive to how the ball reacts at the end of the pattern—how soon and how strong. So, instead of angling the ball's launch left or right to find the hook on a dry spot or the hold on an oil line, you might make parallel moves (feet and target) to fit the shape of your shot to the breakpoint off the end of the pattern, a shape that actually gets the ball into the pocket.

The first transition from the fresh-shot phase is *carrydown* (figure 12.2). Oil picked up from the head of the lane is deposited farther down. Ball reaction becomes weaker. A line that once reached the strike pocket now comes up light. Carrydown starts to occur during warm-up. From the very first practice ball, the lanes begin to change. Within the first few frames of the first game, you may need to adjust your line to the pocket.

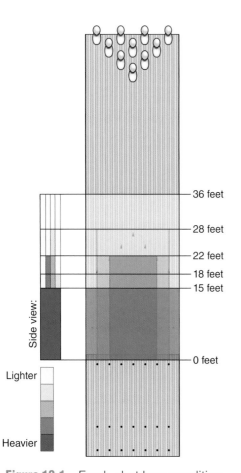

Figure 12.1 Fresh-shot lane condition.

The easiest adjustment is made with the feet. Move in the direction of your mistake. If the ball comes up light—wide of the headpin—move the starting position on the approach wider. Remember: *miss right, move right*. In many bowling centers, the amount of oil decreases near the edges of the lane. Moving the starting position wider changes the angle on the lane, and you may also find an area of increased traction.

Choosing a different ball is another option. A more textured ball surface will create traction on the oil. A dynamic drilling layout causes the ball to move into the hook sooner (called *turning over*). This allows the ball to set up its attack angle sooner and drive through the carrydown.

As the game progresses, the oil depletes: this is called *breakdown* (figure 12.3). In the long run (or not-so-long run with high-tech coverstocks), balls remove oil from the surface. Once the oil on the lane starts to break down, it will continue to do so for the remainder of the session. To stay near the strike pocket, you must make quick decisions about ball selection and target line on the lane.

Balls with high-friction surfaces and dynamic drilling layouts cause the breakdown effect much more rapidly than other types of ball. To adjust to this breakdown, first, chase the oil line. As the oil on a certain area of the lane is used up, an oil line develops. Right next to the section of dry lane, you will find an oily section. Move your starting position (and sometimes your target as well) in order to catch a part of that oil line. (Remember the 1-to-2 adjustment system from step 10.)

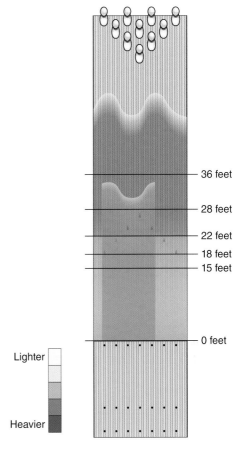

36 feet
28 feet
22 feet
18 feet
15 feet
0 feet

Lighter

Heavier

Figure 12.2 Carrydown lane condition.

Carrydown Controversy

Some experts in the field claim there is no such thing as carrydown. Under certain conditions, I agree with this. In circumstance where skilled players using high-tech equipment and implementing similar lane-play strategies, carrydown is not a factor. The depletion of lane conditioner in the high-traffic areas of the lane is almost immediate.

However, many of you reading this book do not bowl under these circumstances. For inexperienced bowlers using entry-level equipment and applying a variety of targeting strategies (if any reliable strategies at all), carrydown is a real phenomenon. One only needs to look at the streaks of oil past the end of the pattern (some going all the way to the pin deck) after a typical league session. Even in more serious events, not every roll is made with a high-tech ball. Most bowlers have at least one low-end ball (e.g., polyester) for shooting spares, which could cause carrydown with each throw.

Once you find the optimal area for a controllable ball reaction, stop moving. After playing a line for a while, the oil will deplete there also. Now you must move your feet and target again. Again, the 2-to-1 adjustment works well under these circumstances. The 2-to-1 adjustment dictates a two-board move of the feet for every one-board adjustment of the target at the arrows.

Ball choice is critical in lane breakdown conditions. A ball with a low-friction surface will clear the heads (the front part of the lane) cleanly. A smooth, controllable arc is preferred when the lane gets squirrelly. Stable drilling patterns, which generally create less angle to the pocket, produce more predictable movement on unstable lane conditions. When the lanes get tough, a smart bowler chooses a ball that is easy to keep in play.

Good bowlers anticipate the changes and make slight preemptive moves. They do this not just to keep throwing strikes, although it is nice when that happens, but also to avoid bad frames. Do not wait until a bad frame before moving. Good bowlers adjust after strikes or spares, learning from their successes. Average bowlers adjust after open frames, learning only from their mistakes.

BALL MOTION

Visualize the lane in three sections: heads, midlane, and back end (figure 12.4). The *head* is the front part of the lane where the heaviest oil is found. How heavy that oil is—its

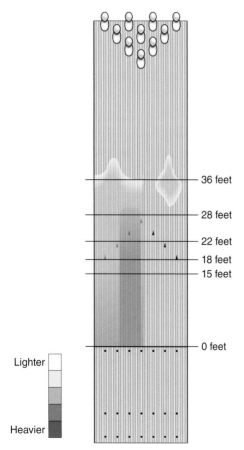

Figure 12.3　Breakdown lane condition.

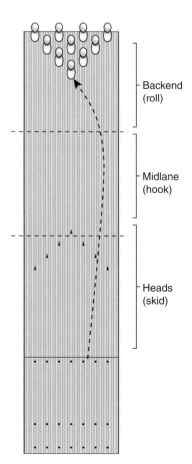

Figure 12.4　The lane can be divided into three sections: head, midlane, and back end.

depth—will determine how soon the ball makes the transition to a midlane motion. As the oil tapers out, the ball starts to hit the midlane.

In the *midlane*, the ball stops skidding and starts moving in the direction of the side roll. This is not an abrupt change. The ball skids less and less as it starts to move more strongly in the direction of the side roll, giving the ball a smooth arcing (hook) motion on the lane. Ideally, the ball stops skidding entirely in the back end. It is now in a full end-over-end roll. If oil is excessive or if the ball was thrown too hard, the ball might still be skidding at this point. If the ball is in a skid, it will tend to deflect when it hits the pins. When the ball is in a true roll, it maximizes the traction effect between the lane surface and the ball surface. The friction between the two surfaces minimizes deflection off the pins. It will drive (hold line) through the pins better.

As the ball passes through each section, it moves smoothly through the three phases: skid, hook, and roll. With the advent of newer ball technology, three distinct elements can be used to manipulate these movement phases: surface, construction, and balance. Although the surface of the ball is always in contact with the lane, and thus always influences the nature of the ball's movement, it is easier to consider each technological element as influencing just one part of the ball's motion.

Skid Phase

The amount of oil on the lane and the velocity of the ball largely dictate the length of the skid phase: more oil = less traction = more skid. If the ball is thrown very fast, it will tend to hydroplane on the oil (similar to driving too fast on wet roads), and there won't be enough time for the ball surface to grab the lane: speed = skid.

The technological element that influences the skid is ball surface. If there is too much skid, a higher-friction surface helps the ball move into the hook phase soon enough to bring the ball back to the pocket. If there is too little skid, the early transition into the hook and roll phases may make controlling ball reaction difficult.

When confronted with too much skid, you have several options:

1. Move away from the center. During the setup, move toward the edges of the lane. Releasing the ball from a wider position will compensate for the angle lost from reduced hook.

2. Move the target in. If the excessive skid keeps the ball from hooking, bringing the ball path closer to the strike pocket compensates for the lack of lateral movement the ball would normally make.

3. Decrease ball speed. Skid is like being stuck on ice. Revving the engine only spins the tires in place. Give the ball time to dig into the lane and establish traction.

4. Use a ball with higher surface friction. Get rid of those racing slicks and find some studded tires. In other words, try using a ball with a rough surface. Talk to your pro-shop expert about balls with a high coefficient of friction. Try one. It will grab the lanes better.

5. Change your release and reduce loft. Get the ball down onto the lane sooner. Use a heavy roll release. Strong axis rotation, axis tilt, and revolution rate all exaggerate the skidding effect.

Some bowling centers don't put much oil on the front part of the lane. Sometimes the oil in the front may dissipate very rapidly by the bowlers themselves. Using aggressive equipment—balls with dull or textured surfaces—with a high degree of friction will also cause the lane to change more rapidly. Sometimes the bowlers are their own worst enemy when it comes to how fast and dramatically lane conditions change. Oil depletion is noticeable when the ball moves into its hook and roll phases much sooner than expected. A dry lane head may cause the ball to lose so much energy before it gets to the pins, that pinfall is negatively affected. Drying out the head is a natural phenomenon of the game. In particular, if many bowlers roll the ball over the same area, they will wear out the oil on that part of the lane.

A key element of adjustment strategy is to pay attention to where other bowlers are playing. Expect changes on those parts of the lane soonest.

If there is too little skid, use the opposite strategies:

1. Move the setup position more toward the center of the lane. The center of the lane frequently has more oil. Additionally, moving toward the middle increases the launch angle to the target, sending the ball wider before it starts to hook.

2. Aim the ball path wider; give the ball more room to make a potentially larger lateral motion.

3. Increase speed or loft. Letting the ball travel through the air longer preserves ball energy. The less time the ball is on the lane, the less opportunity it has to create friction.

4. Switch to a ball with a smoother surface.

5. Use a drive release. Keep the release motion passive. Reduce hand action. Or, try to spin the ball more. The higher a ball's axis tilt, the less traction is has.

Hook Phase

As the ball comes off the oily part of the lane, it starts to generate friction and slow down. As it slows, it will start to move in the direction of its side roll. The stronger the side roll (or axis rotation), the sharper and more abrupt the change of direction is likely to be. In addition, a distinct transition from the oily part of the lane to the dry part of the lane enhances the change of direction. Some centers have a defined line between where the oil stops and the dry part of the lanes begins. For certain types of bowlers, this radical change of direction makes it difficult to control the ball's movement. Other bowling centers allow the oil to taper off gradually (called the *buff zone*); this allows a smoother transition from skid to hook.

Adjust ball speed to alter the hook point. Increasing or decreasing ball velocity has an important effect on how soon the ball starts to hook. Greater speed drives the ball farther down the lane, delaying the hook. Slower speed allows an earlier transition into the hook.

Promoting an earlier transition through reduced speed or heavier end-over-end roll helps the ball create an angle to the pins when oily lanes minimize ball reaction. A strong side roll (axis rotation angle) allows a longer initial skid followed by a stronger hook motion farther down the lane. A sharp late hook, although somewhat unpredictable for less-skilled bowlers, offers benefits. The longer a ball skids, the more energy it retains (less frictional energy loss). Balls that move into the roll phase very late have more of the ball's energy to put to use at the pins. A late-hooking ball has the potential to come in at a sharper angle. As discussed in Step 8, Perfecting the Release, the more entry angle a ball has going into the pins, the larger the error margin at the strike pocket.

Ball construction also affects the hook point. Bowling balls have two basic types of internal construction. If the center of mass is positioned away from the geometric center of the ball, the ball is said to be surface heavy (figure 12.5a). The center of mass makes large, slow circles, which allows the ball to retain energy. This is an excellent ball to switch to as the lanes dry out. Balls with their center of mass concentrated in the middle are said to be center heavy (figure 12.5b). Instead of big, slow circles, the center of mass makes small,

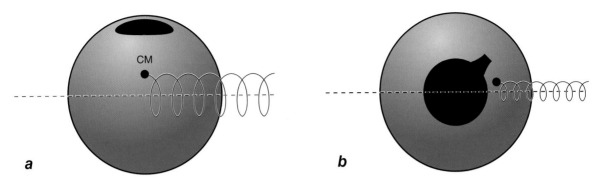

Figure 12.5 *(a)* A surface-heavy ball's center of mass (CM) makes big, slow circles and is a good choice for a dry lane. *(b)* A center-heavy ball's CM makes small, fast circles and is a good choice if the lane is preventing the ball from hooking.

quick ones. These types of balls rev up. They are an excellent choice for lanes on which the ball hesitates to hook.

Roll Phase

Ideally, the ball should be in a roll just before it hits the pins, soon enough to maximize drive but not so soon it loses energy to friction. When the ball makes contact with the pins, you want maximum surface-to-lane contact with all of the ball energy directed forward. If the ball is still hooking when it hits the pins, then it is still skidding and is more likely to deflect on pin contact.

If the ball starts rolling too soon, friction will cause it to bleed energy. Watch the ball's movement to ensure it enters this final transition at the correct place. If it appears there are too many end-over-end rolls, you know the ball is bleeding off energy from friction. You will see the ball lose speed and its arcing motion well before it gets to the pins. For many bowlers, this will cause greater deflection after initial contact, reducing strike potential.

Some bowlers are successful when using a lot of roll at the back end. Bowlers with a strong axis rotation, under the proper lanes conditions, may establish an entry angle relatively early in the ball path. The ball hooks so much in the midlane, it stops hooking altogether at the back end. This is described as a hook-set ball motion. If the angle into the pocket is fairly strong, the ball can get into its roll phase relatively soon and still strike often. In fact, the strike pocket may get larger. The roll motion gives the ball enough deflection to avoid the high-pocket splits, yet the entry angle would still be strong enough to carry light-pocket strikes.

The balance of the ball influences how soon the hook turns into a roll. Both dynamic and stable drilling layouts are available. Dynamic drillings (figure 12.6) are imbalanced. The core of the ball wobbles, and the ball's effort to find a stable rotation point creates a stronger ball reaction. These balls read the midlane sooner, and the transition into the hook and roll happens sooner. Dynamic balls are great on medium-dry to medium-oily lanes. The ball's reaction and subsequent angle to the pocket are strong and predictable.

Stable drillings eliminate core wobble. They are designed to create a smooth arcing motion. When dry lanes make hooking more uncontrollable (or when the lane

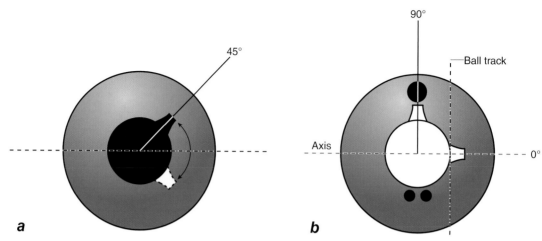

Figure 12.6 *(a)* A ball with dynamic drillings is a good choice on a medium-dry to medium-oily lane. *(b)* A ball with stable drillings is a good choice on a lane that is either extremely dry (surface-heavy ball) or extremely oily (center-heavy ball).

conditions are spotty and less predictable) you want a ball that behaves itself. A stable drilling helps restore control.

Stable drillings are also a good option on extreme lane conditions. A surface-heavy ball with stable drilling is useful for very dry lanes, especially dry back ends when the bowler needs to get the ball down the lane and still have a controllable hook. A center-heavy ball with stable drilling performs well on an oily or spotty lane when the bowler wants a strong, predictable arc to the pocket.

LANE PATTERNS

With the current generation of lane machines, the conditioning patterns are almost infinite. Your goal is to determine the general lane pattern and then fine-tune your line, using sound adjustment strategies based on that unique lane condition.

Bowlers are always seeking a dry area or ball reaction zone, what I'll refer to as *the wall*. The wall is the dry area of the lane just outside your intended target (figure 12.7). Ideally, you will also find an oil line just to the inside of the intended target. Playing this line creates an error margin. If you miss in a little, the ball will hold the line; if you miss out a little, the ball will recover. Sometimes the wall is hard, and the ball will react as soon as it touches it. Other times it is soft; when the ball touches the drier area, its recovery is moderate.

MISSTEP
The ball reacts too much.

CORRECTION
Too much reaction is a result of hitting the dry part of the lane too soon. Reduce the side roll of the ball, or move your feet to change the ball's point of contact with the wall.

MISSTEP

The ball doesn't react enough.

CORRECTION

Not enough reaction results when the ball hits the wall too late or hits it at the wrong angle to recover to the pins. Increase the revolutions on the side roll, or move your feet closer to the wall to create earlier recovery into the pins.

The launch angle is the trajectory of the ball across the lane after the release. It dictates when the ball will hit the wall. Bowlers who use little hook or are bowling on oily lanes should use an out-to-in launch angle. Bowlers with a modest hook want a launch angle that goes straight down the boards. An in-to-out launch angle is used by power players or when the lanes are drying out. The launch angle in combination with the release strength determines how strongly the ball rebounds off the wall.

Bowlers with weak releases need to contact the wall sooner. The ball will need the extra time on the dry zone to make it to the pocket. A bowler with a stronger release needs to just barely touch the wall or to contact the wall farther down the lane in order to keep the ball from hooking too soon. If the wall is soft—the dry part of the lane does not radically differ from the oily part—bowlers of all types will need to get the ball into the dry part sooner and keep it there longer to generate enough friction for the ball to make the corner (i.e., hook enough to bring the ball back to the strike pocket).

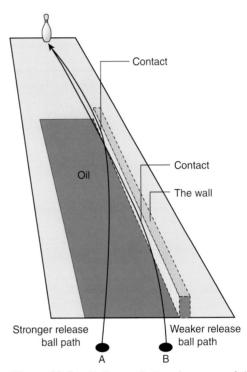

Figure 12.7 At the wall, the dry area of the lane just outside the target, ball reaction is stronger.

The three basic types of lane patterns are crown, block, and reverse. Though there are almost an infinite number of possible lane condition patterns, any given pattern will fall into one these three broad categories. Some patterns create a high-scoring environment and others have a dampening effect on the scoring pace. Certain patterns may favor certain styles of bowlers; for example, some favor those who hook the ball a lot while others provide an advantage to the straighter-throwing player.

Crown

The crown condition (figure 12.8) is characterized by more oil near the middle of the lane and a gradual tapering off toward the edges. Ideally, this condition allows players of any style to be successful. A player with modest or little hook can move

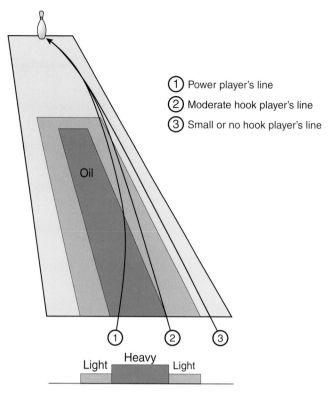

① Power player's line
② Moderate hook player's line
③ Small or no hook player's line

Figure 12.8 A crown lane condition. More oil is in the middle of the lane.

out and find drier boards from which to create ball reaction. Moving away from the center will create a better angle, while the drier boards will generate a stronger roll. Power players step inside and use the oil to get the ball down the lane or control ball reaction. They need to touch only enough of the drier boards to make the ball hook back to the pocket.

MISSTEP

You overreact to the crown lane condition by playing too close to the dry area for your type of release. Or you underreact by playing too far away from the dry area.

CORRECTION

For either error, adjust your feet, your target, or both until you find the ideal strike line.

Block

With block, or walled-up, lanes, it is as if a large block of oil has been placed in the middle of the lane (figure 12.9). Any part of the lane outside or past the block is very dry. The block condition is like the crown condition on steroids. The middle is bulked up, and the outsides are trimmed down. Once upon a time, blocking the lanes was considered unethical and unworthy of the sporting ideals of the game. Now, it is the standard of play.

The block lane condition is common to most league and recreational bowling situations. Centers modify the crown condition to create a favorable scoring environment. If the bowler misses to the inside, the oily part of the lane keeps it from hooking. The ball will hold the line all the way to the pins. If the bowler misses outside, the dry area of the lane guarantees a hook back toward the pocket. The error margin is ludicrously large. The best strategy for a blocked lane is to play along the oil line, reduce the ball's side roll, and control the arc off the dry part of the lane.

Although this lane condition favors many bowlers, unfortunately, it also puts bowlers of some styles at a particular disadvantage. If you do not throw a hook, you cannot take advantage of the recovery area. A straight ball does just that—it goes straight, on dry lanes just as well as on oily lanes. A move out toward the edge of the lane cre-

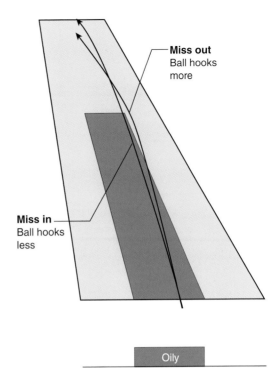

Figure 12.9 A block lane condition. The middle of the lane has a large block of oil, while the outside edges are dry.

ates an angle, but the increase in angle will not be large enough to create an enhanced scoring environment. It is not that the bowler who throws a straight ball will score any lower than normal, but that the average hook bowlers score much higher than their skills would dictate. The disparity is not created by a difference in skill but primarily by the discrimination characteristics of the block lane condition.

Power players who hook the ball a lot also may struggle on a blocked lane as mentioned in figure 12.10. The ball will tend to jump as soon as it touches the dry area, but a move into the oil provides too much skid. This condition often gives a power bowler an overreaction or underreaction from the ball. The term *over/under* refers to significantly different reactions between two balls rolled over two different areas of the lane. If thrown to the outside, the ball overreacts on the dry area and misses high on the headpin. If thrown inside, the ball skids on the heavy oil and misses light of the headpin. For this style of bowling, very small adjustments on the lane create large variations in where the ball ends up. It may be frustrating for the power players bowlers to find just the right line to the strike pocket. These bowlers are better off using a more conservative approach. Tone down the number of ball revolutions or the side roll or both. If the lanes already have an obvious hook zone, why try so hard to make the ball hook even more?

Reverse

The reverse (or reverse block) lane condition is bowling's version of a cruel joke. The middle of the lane has less oil than the outside (figure 12.10). If bowlers throw

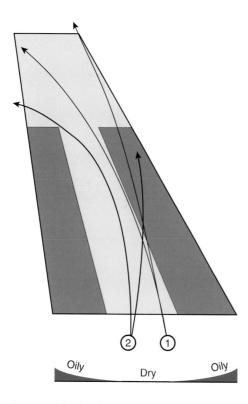

Figure 12.10 A reverse block lane condition. The middle of the lane is dry while there are increasing amounts of oil near the edges.

their normal line, the ball may hook too much. When they moves in to adjust for the extra hook, the ball hooks even more. If they play an outside line, the ball doesn't hook enough. If they move farther out to adjust for the loss of angle, the ball hooks even less. None of the standard adjustments seem to work.

It is like bowling on top of a wall. Stray just a little to one side or the other, and the ball falls off the edge. Bowl a little too wide, and the ball ends up way wide of the strike pocket. Bowl just a little too in, and it hooks way inside of the headpin. All but the most highly skilled bowlers will be frustrated on these conditions.

The only satisfaction a bowler can gain from this condition is that everybody is competing under the same circumstances. When confronted with a seemingly impossible lane condition, keep your head. Play for a relatively straight line to the pocket. Straighter is greater; nothing fancy! Try to leave yourself easy spares. A good spare-shooting strategy uses straight lines that mostly take lane conditions out of the equation. A good spare-shooting game that minimizes open frames will allow you to average 170 to 180 even if you are not striking much.

Reverse block patterns are rarely put on the lanes intentionally, but they might occur as a consequence of normal play. If the lane condition is fairly flat initially—the oil is evenly distributed from gutter to gutter—a reverse block may develop as a result of the collective lane play strategies of the bowlers. Most bowlers are comfortable using the common track area (around the second arrow) right from the start. This part of the lane often develops a dry area pretty quickly. As more and more players move their lines in to avoid the dry track, the track area expands. After enough games, little oil remains in the middle. Nobody has bowled on the outsides, so the oil remains relatively heavy there.

Two common strategies are used to get around this difficult situation (figure 12.11). First, try moving way outside and pointing the ball through the oil into the pocket. It is a touchy line to play. Point the ball off the corner, and throw a relatively straight ball—very little hook. You may want a little hook action for carry, but it will be small and entirely off the back end of the pattern. Playing the outside line requires accuracy and precise speed control.

The other option is to try moving way inside and driving the ball through the dry area of the lane. The goal is to generate enough ball speed to allow the ball to hold the line. Chances are the angle will be weak, so lower your expectations of striking often.

A power player might try to use the oil on the opposite side. Because there are fewer left-handed bowlers than right-handed, the left side of the lane doesn't change

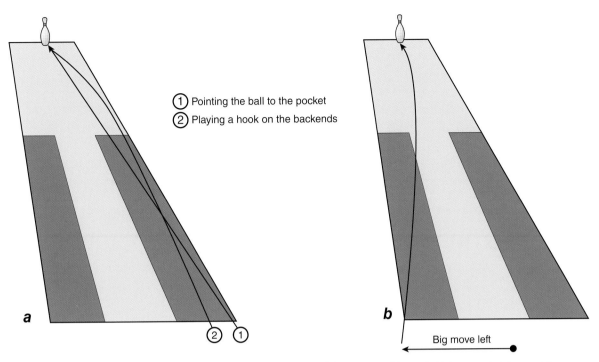

① Pointing the ball to the pocket
② Playing a hook on the backends

Big move left

Figure 12.11 Strategies for playing a reverse block lane condition: *(a)* Move outside and try to force the ball through the oil into the strike pocket. *(b)* A right-handed power player might try moving to the left side of the lane to use the oil on that side, keeping the ball away from the dry area for as long as possible.

as dramatically as the right side. A right-handed bowler might be able to play for a very late hook. Adjusting very deep inside allows opportunity to keep the ball in the oil for as long as possible.

Some power players in this situation use excessive loft (distance the ball travels in the air before landing on the lane), as much as 15 feet (4.6 m) down the lane. (Some players use even more.) After all, a ball can't hook in the air. The more distance covered in the air, the less chance a ball has to hook on the lane. The combination of a dramatic move with excessive loft, while effective, is a difficult technique to master.

SPORT BOWLING

The United States Bowling Congress (USBC) established a series of lane conditions specifically designed to challenge bowlers. Specific lane condition standards, called *sport bowling*, include a separate certification level for participants. For an additional fee, bowlers compete and establish an average on one of the approved sport conditions. The idea is to give bowlers the option of bowling on the more recreational conditions found in most bowling centers or stepping up to the challenge of the more difficult sport shots.

Sport conditions require a more even distribution of oil. A variety of sport patterns are available. Most sport bowling patterns feature oil distribution pattern ratios of 3.5-to-1 or less. One of the toughest challenges bowlers face is patterns describes as U.S. Open. The U.S. Open, being one of the premier bowling events in the world, demands the most out of its competitors. U.S. Open–type lane conditions feature a

1:1 oil distribution. In other words, the lane conditioner is applied in a perfectly even layer from gutter to gutter.

Under the most challenging sport condition, there is no obvious line to play. Small areas of the lane allow ball reaction, but they are bounded by areas that are more difficult. Finesse and accuracy are at a premium on these shots. Most bowlers find that speed control is the critical factor for success. Variations in speed cause the bowler to overthrow or underthrow the line, creating a large variation in ball reaction.

If the center you bowl at has a sport-sanctioned league, ask to see the graph. Currently, all bowling centers conducting sport-sanctioned competition are required to take a lane reading before each day of competition and forward the data to the USBC. This ensures that the sport standard of the competitive condition is maintained for every day of the competition.

SUCCESS SUMMARY

This step is largely informative. There are no specific drills for lane conditions other than the drills you have already seen in previous steps. The best advice is to bowl in as many bowling centers as possible.

Challenge yourself to master all lane conditions. If you have only one bowling center in your area, try to bowl at different times. Bowling early on a Sunday when there has been very little play will differ considerably from bowling late at night after the last league shift is finished. Bowl with different levels of competitors. A friendly couple's league, which may not have very many serious bowlers, may present a different challenge than a serious scratch league.

Keep notes every day you bowl. Keep track of days when you scored poorly because you were not bowling well and days when the lane conditions had you baffled. Recognize the difference between bowling well and scoring well. Develop confidence in altering a ball's motion by changing its velocity, number of revolutions, and the amount of side roll. You must also get comfortable moving the starting position and using different visual targets.

Variations in lane conditions are what make bowling such a unique challenge. It is one of the few indoor sports where you do not know exactly what to expect on any given day. Every subtle change of the ball's movement from one throw to the next gives clues to the observant bowler about the lane conditions on that day. Watch other bowlers. Ask yourself: What part of the lanes are they playing? How are they throwing the ball? What is their style? What type of ball are they using? Learn from them.

Once you have developed some skill at the game, you may want to involve yourself in the more competitive aspects of the sport. The competition does not have to be serious. Bowling is a great social activity. But, besides the social aspects, competition gives you the opportunity to demonstrate your skills. If you have reached some the goals you have set for yourself, you have every right to be pleased with yourself. But don't stop there! As you get better and you feel a greater sense of satisfaction in your game, it becomes time to put your skills to the test. The next step discusses the variety of bowling competitions and what to expect if you choose to take your game to that level.

Competing in the Sport

The social aspect of a sport like bowling cannot be overstated. Particularly when bowling with a group of people and there is considerable downtime between shots. Similar to golf, where one can share a cart with your partner or stroll down the fairway with a foursome, bowling provides ample opportunity for social interaction. For many, the sole reason for participating is the simple pleasure of sharing a common activity with a group of friends or family.

Socializing, relieving stress, developing physical fitness, creating that sense of self-satisfaction that comes from participating in an activity and achieving personal goals: all of these offer positive mental and physical health benefits. None of them have anything to do with a competitive environment, but they have a lot to do with one's quality-of-life choices.

Competition can take many forms, from the friendly competition of a social gathering to the intensity of professional match play. Leagues are the most common form of organized bowling competition. Not everybody aspires to a competitive status; some people pursue an activity solely for the satisfaction of achieving personal goals.

For many athletes, though, it's a natural progression of sport involvement to eventually compare their skills with another person's skills. Sometimes this happens in an informal manner, what might be called a pickup game. At other times, this challenge of skills might take place in a specific venue, with rules and regulations outlining the format of the competition and the conduct of the competitors. For bowlers who cannot resist the urge to match their skills against those of another athlete, who constantly ask themselves, "Am I better than they are?" a variety of competitive formats are available.

LEAGUE BOWLING

Leagues are by far the most common form of competitive bowling. A league is a group of teams, usually made up of two to five players, that compete at regularly scheduled times. A schedule is posted in a conspicuous place or distributed to the team captains so that all players know when, where, and against whom they are bowling.

Leagues come in two basic types: certified and uncertified. A certified league is one in which the participants are all dues-paying members of the national governing body. In the United States, that would be the United States Bowling Congress (USBC). Most leagues, whether certified or not, have a formal organizational structure with someone in charge of scheduling, collecting fees, establishing rules, and settling disputes.

All USBC-certified leagues are required to have elected officers—president, vice president, secretary, treasurer—and a board of directors. The board of directors usually consists of league officers and all team captains. A written set of league rules, or bylaws, outlines organizational and financial responsibilities. Certified leagues must have access to copies of the official USBC rule book. This brief manual covers almost all of the organizational and competitive concerns of the sport. If a hard copy is not immediately available, an online version can be found at bowl.com, the official website of the USBC.

Individual leagues are free to create their own rules to cover special circumstances. All leagues must establish policies for collecting fees, the format of competition, how to handle absent bowlers, the use of substitute bowlers, team or league sponsorship, length of the season, and other matters. All leagues should have an organizational meeting a few weeks or more before the start of the season to iron out disputes or confusion concerning the membership and organization of the league.

Qualification for league membership varies. Some leagues are purely social in nature, organized around the number and gender of team members. They could be all male, all female, mixed, or couples. Other leagues base membership on affiliation with specific groups such as civic organizations, churches, or businesses. If interested in joining a league, talk to the bowling center's league coordinator or manager. He or she will describe the leagues available and provide contact information for the leagues you are interested in.

The league format determines certain aspects of competition: most important, how a winner is determined. Most leagues award a certain number of points for each game a team wins. Some also grant additional points to the team with the highest cumulative total.

Some leagues incorporate individual match-play points. In match play, the individual score not only contributes to the team total, but is also matched one to one against an individual on another team. Usually, the leadoff bowler of one team tries to outscore the leadoff player on the other team, number two in the lineup bowls against the other team's number two, and so on down the line. Frequently, these individual points are part of the total points a team accumulates during the competition. If you are considering joining a league, please consider the following rules of etiquette and protocol before taking the plunge.

Leagues Are Formal Organizations

No person's behavior has the right to take away from others' enjoyment of the sport. It is expected that each member act in a manner that is respectful to both the sport of bowling and other members of the league.

Personal Commitment

Make time for regular attendance. It is disruptive to team unity (and competitive success) if poor attendance is a consistent issue. If it is unavoidable to miss an occasional league session, be sure to inform the team captain. The USBC rule book outlines the responsibilities of a team captain. One basic responsibility is ensuring that a full team is present on the day of competition. Both you and your team captain are responsible for finding a replacement. All leagues have strict guidelines dictating the use of substitutes; know the rules for your particular league.

Consider Team Chemistry

Avoid personality conflict. The friendly and patient person you know in one setting may display completely different personality traits in a competitive environment. When organizing a team, make sure all the players are committed to bowling in that league. Select people who get along. Be sure the players are tolerant of and helpful to teammates who have less skill.

Financial Obligation

Each team is responsible for each league session's fees. A portion of league fees goes to the center to pay for the bowling (called *lineage*). The remainder goes toward league expenses such as secretary fees, the prize fund, awards, end-of-season banquet, and so on. If an individual does not pay, the whole team is held accountable. Every member is required to pay the league fee at every bowling session.

The fee each league pays to the center for lineage is a contractual obligation. All members of the league are legally bound to uphold the contract. A bowler who falls behind in league-fee payment (who is *in arrears*) is subject to several penalties: the most basic is not being allowed to bowl until fees are caught up.

Leagues may set certain requirements or conditions for participation. For example, a league might dictate the combination of male and female participants. Or leagues might limit participation based on average. This is called an *average cap*. The sum of the individual averages cannot exceed the cap. If it does, the members are not allowed to bowl together. The team must find a combination of bowlers whose combined averages fit under the cap. The purpose of an average cap is to prevent the best bowlers from bowling on the same team. An equitable cap spreads out the skill levels of the participants.

TOURNAMENT PLAY

Tournaments are another popular form of competition. They are not held as frequently as league play and are usually on a larger scale. Tournaments can follow a variety of formats. Many require membership in a governing body. Sometimes they require your membership card when checking in.

In the United States, the basic rules of the game, as described in the USBC rules book, are always followed in bowling tournaments (whether they are certified or not). But, each tournament may place certain restrictions or conditions on its format. Be sure to read all entry forms carefully. If you are not an experienced bowler, talk with somebody who is to make sure you know what is going on. If you are still uncertain of an aspect of the event, talk to the tournament director. After all, it is in his or her best interest to run as successful a tournament as possible. Don't let a misunderstanding or miscommunication get in the way of a satisfying bowling experience.

The tournament fee is based on the type of tournament and the structure. Some tournaments offer multiple events, such as singles, doubles, and team, which may require separate fees. Some keep a separate prize fund for handicap and actual (scratch) events. Many tournaments expect you to have a certified average from the current or previous year or both. If you do not have a certified average, you may be assigned one.

Most inexperienced bowlers get their feet wet by bowling in local tournaments. This is a good place to start your tournament career. The competition is usually more relaxed, and there is a better chance of crossing lanes with people you know.

The following are the most common types of tournament play. Choose one to suit your playing and personal style.

Round Robin

In this particular match-play format, each bowler or team bowls against every other bowler or team. If enough games are available in the tournament format, following a full round-robin schedule will allow each team to bowl every other team the same number of times. Some tournament formats (such as many Professional Bowlers Association events) award bonus pins for each match won. Often, when a round-robin cycle of games is finished, an additional round may be scheduled. The additional round is often a position round. In a position round, the team with the best win–loss record will bowl the team with the second-best record; third will bowl against fourth, fifth against sixth, and so on.

Bracket

This is an elimination match-play format, with teams being seeded. Sometimes the seeding is based on performance from a previous round of competition (called the qualifying round), and sometimes the seeding is purely random.

Total Pinfall

In this format, a team does not bowl directly against another team. Instead the team bowls against the whole field. The total pinfall for an expressed number of games determines the winner. This is a common format for tournaments that have hundreds, perhaps thousands, of participants.

Sweeper

This is a short-format tournament. There are no qualifying rounds, eliminations, or changes in format. Everybody in the sweeper squad bowls a set number of games. When all the squads scheduled for the event are done, the event is done. (A squad, by the way, is a set number of games bowled at a specific time by a group of bowler.) If there are fewer lanes available then can reasonable accommodate the number of bowler, the field may be split into multiple squads.

Many tournaments include smaller events within the format. The most common are singles, doubles, and team events. Players can participate in any of the smaller events, vying for that particular championship. If they bowl in all the scheduled events, the combined totals from all their games make them eligible for the *all-events* title. In many tournaments, the all-events champion is the most coveted title.

Almost all tournaments offer some kind of recognition for the champions. Money and trophies are the most common forms of recognition. In many smaller local tournaments, the financial reward is minimal. Many athletes bowl in tournaments for the challenge. The recognition they receive and the high regard in which their skills are held are reward enough.

Bowlers on the professional tour participate in events with national recognition. Certain amateur tournaments provide national recognition as well. The True Amateur Tournament, the Hoinke Classic, the Louisville Derby Tournament, the Petersen Classic in Chicago, and numerous others have been held for many years. A few of them have been conducted annually for well over 50 years. As of 2015, the USBC Open Championships has been held for over 110 years. Some of the larger amateur tournaments have total prize funds running into the hundreds of thousands of U.S. dollars. In the case of USBC national championship, the prize fund is into the millions of dollars.

The men's and women's national tournaments are held annually. Thousands of teams with tens of thousands of bowlers participate in these tournaments. In years where the events have been held at particularly large venues (such as the National Bowling Stadium in Reno, Nevada), participation has exceeded 100,000 bowlers. These tournaments take many months to complete. Based on the number of actual participants, they are the largest regularly scheduled sporting events in the world. Champions of these events enjoy considerable enhancement of both their bank accounts and reputations.

HANDICAP SYSTEMS

Almost all leagues and tournament bowlers participate in some sort of handicap system. The purpose of handicap is to level the playing field. Players with less experience have an opportunity to compete against more-skilled bowlers when a handicap is used. Handicap is quite simply bonus pins given to bowlers with a lower average to help make up the difference between their skill level and the skill level of players with a higher average. Because most league prizes do not involve large sums of money and many people participate solely for the camaraderie, it makes no sense to discourage new players. High averages get little handicap, while low averages get more. Success in a handicapped competition depends largely on whether players bowl at or near their average on a given day. It also depends on the kind of competitions and the use of percentages, as you will see.

Calculating Handicap

Three features contribute to a handicap system:

1. *Average*: the average score (bowled over a set number of games) that is representative of the bowler's current skill level
2. *Base*: the ceiling average to which all players are brought up to by the handicap system
3. *Percentage:* the difference between a player's average and the base being made up through the handicap

To calculate handicap: (base − average) × percentage

Example: Base of 200, using an 80-percent system and a 153 average

(200 − 153) × (.8) = 47

47 × 0.8 = 37.6 or 37 pins of handicap (Never use the decimals.)

When calculating any part of handicap, never round up. Instead, truncate the number at the decimal point. To truncate means to cut off anything that remains after the decimal. Pretend it doesn't exist. Truncate the average **before** calculating handicap. Truncate whatever remains from the handicap **after** the calculation

Using the earlier example (153 average, with a 200 base), what would the handicaps be using the three most common percentage systems of 80 percent, 90 percent, and 100 percent?

80-percent system: 47 × 0.8 = 37.6

90-percent system: 47 × 0.9 = 42.3

100-percent system: 47 × 1.0 = 47

Remember, drop digits after the decimal point. In these three percentage systems, the player has a handicap of 37 pins, 42 pins, or 47 pins. The larger the handicap percentage, the greater the difference in skill level being made up by the handicap system. With a 100-percent system, all of the difference is made up. Using percentages less than 100 percent for calculating handicap gives an advantage to the bowler with a higher average. The smaller the percentage used, the larger the advantage becomes.

Handicap is the number of pins players add to their game (or credit to their team's total) for every game of the competition. In other words, score + handicap = final total.

So, let's use the bowler from the earlier example, bowling in a typical league (one in which each bowler rolls three games in a series), and using a 90-percent system. If the bowler's actual game scores are 146, 168, and 156, their actual series total is 469. They receive 42 pins of handicap each game for all three games for a total of 126 pins of handicap. The series total would be 595 (469 actual pins + 126 pins total handicap).

By the way, when referring to a real score or total, the term *actual* is used. In the previous example, you would say, their series was a 469 actual and 595 with handicap. See the sample score sheet (figure 13.1) to see how a team sheet is properly filled out.

Name	Handicap	#1	#2	#3	Total	Name	Handicap	#1	#2	#3	Total
Karen	66	108	131	142	381	Steve	3	167	198	177	542
Bob	25	179	157	159	495	Larry	0	159	187	181	527
Dave	81	118	121	118	357	Sue	0	204	199	192	595
Betty	35	162	141	149	452	Jeff	0	225	181	192	598
Team actual		567	550	568	1685	Team actual		755	765	742	2262
Team handicap		207	207	207	621	Team handicap		3	3	3	9
Team total		774	757	775	2306	Team total		758	768	745	2271
		+18		+30	+35				+11		

Figure 13.1 Sample league scoring sheet, including handicaps.

Though one team seems better than the other (Steve has a 196 average and only gets 3 pins of handicap, whereas the other players on his team have averages high enough they don't receive any handicap at all), Dave had the best day on the lanes relative to his average. (Using 90% from a 200 base, he must have a 110 average in order to get 81 pins of handicap each game.) Though he only rolled a 357 series, his 81 pins of handicap each game gets him 243 total pins of handicap. Add those pins to his 357 actual total, and his final total was an even 600 for all three games. The team with the lower average bowlers won two of the games and had a higher team series as well.

High Handicap Percentages

Although it completely levels the playing field, I see the 100-percent system as a disincentive toward improvement. A 190-average bowler rolling a 190 game has demonstrated more skill than a 120-average bowler rolling a 120 game. Under a 100-percent system, these bowlers would tie. (Their respective handicaps plus their actual scores would bring them both up exactly to the base.) If all it takes to equal a better bowler is to merely bowl your average when they bowl theirs, what is the advantage of working toward a higher average?

If there is no advantage to having a higher average,
there is no incentive to improve.

In the classroom, I don't use a 100-percent system. Instead, I use a 90-percent system for in-class competitions. Bowlers with higher averages still have a slight advantage; thus, all students have an incentive to keep improving. Yet, the difference is not so great that the less-experienced bowlers feel overly disadvantaged during in-class competitions.

Handicaps and High-Average Bowlers

A bowler's handicap is calculated by using a specified percentage of the difference between a bowler's average and the base. As already mentioned, the lower the percentage used, the bigger the advantage to the higher average. Furthermore, a bowler whose average is higher than the base will always have an advantage.

This is because the handicap system only brings bowlers up toward the base; the system won't allow a bowler to catch up to bowlers whose average is over that base. It follows then that it would be best if the base average were higher than the averages of all the bowlers who are participating.

Usually, a bowler whose average is over the base receives no handicap. Unfortunately, not all competitions deal with the issue of high-average bowlers in the same way. Here are a few ways competitions deal with a situation in which bowlers have averages higher than the established handicap base.

RAISE THE BASE

This is the preferred method. Raise the base until it is higher than the average of any bowler in the competition. No rule says a base of 240, 260, or even 300 cannot not be used. The idea is not to bring one or two players down, but to bring everybody else up.

RAISE THE PERCENTAGE TO OVER 100 PERCENT

This method is not recommended because it would give an unfair advantage to a bowler with a lower average. In fact, the lower the average, the better off a player would be. So this system provides an incentive to intentionally bowl poorly. Intentionally misrepresenting ones skill in order to take advantage of a handicap system is called *sandbagging*. This is a heinous and all-too-real aspect of competitive bowling. Any handicap system that incentivizes bowlers to do less than their best is to be avoided. Using a percentage system greater than 100 percent is almost never implemented.

USE NEGATIVE HANDICAP

This method is not recommended because it takes pins away from bowlers whose average is over the base. Punishing a few bowlers for being more skilled than other players is another way to foster sandbagging. Occasionally, although relatively rare, one may come across leagues using this system.

USE A TEAM HANDICAP

The league rules establish a cap for the whole team. The team adds the averages of its players. The handicap is a percentage of the difference between the total of all averages on the team and the established team base (or cap). This moderates the advantage a single player has of being too high. Combining the relatively high average with the averages of the rest of the team raises the team's average and eliminates the advantage of having a bowler with a very high average on your team (see figure 13.1). This is the second most common format for calculating a team's handicap. While this is a better option than raising the percentage over 100 percent or using a negative handicap, this is not an optimal system either. The players on the team with lower averages lose handicap because of the influence (or skewing effect) of teammates with high averages. I don't know of a sport that punishes the weaker players on a team because of the skills of the team's better players.

Scratch Competitions

In some competitions, no handicap is used. Totals are based on actual, or scratch, scores. These competitions are largely for bowlers with higher averages. Frequently, the terms scratch league or classic league are used to describe leagues geared to these bowlers with higher averages.

ALTERNATIVE GAME AND PRACTICE GAME FORMATS

Many of the targeting and spare-shooting games described in earlier steps can be adapted for team practice situations. These are ways to bowl without following typical competitive formats. Some of these games may be part of a competitive event; others are strictly for skill development and team building.

Sometimes, it is useful to get away from concern for the individual score. Try to make practices fun, diverse, and challenging. Get teammates involved; one of the best ways to grow as a player is to grow with a team. Although bowling may be an individual sport, by no means does it have to be a selfish endeavor.

Scotch Doubles

Scotch doubles uses an alternating throw format. One person on the team throws the first ball. If pins remain, the partner tries to make the spare.

In some versions of the game, the leadoff bowler remains the first bowler for the entire game. If the leadoff bowler throws a strike, the partner doesn't play at all in that frame. In other versions of scotch doubles, bowlers alternate on every throw, no matter what. If the leadoff player throws a strike, the partner throws the first ball in the next frame. Scotch doubles is a popular social format; formal leagues and tournaments rarely use this system of competing. It is a fun way to get people to bowl together.

Best Ball

All players bowl their own game. In each frame, the best frame by a bowler is used as the frame for a fictitious extra teammate. The fictitious player's score is created using the best frames bowled by any of the real team members (figure 13.2). In this format, even less-skilled members of the team have a chance to contribute to a high score (even if that score is not their own).

		X	7	/		X		X	7	2		X		X	8	-		7	-		8	/	9
Tommy	20		40		67		86		95		123		141		149		156			175		
		X	9	/	6	/		X		X	8	1		X	9	-		9	/		7	2	
Jenny	20		36		56		84		103		112		131		140		157			166		
	7	/	6	2	8	/	6	3	9	/	7	2	9	-		X	6	/		9	-	
Darren	16		24		40		49		66		75		84		104		123			132		
Best frame		X	9	/		X		X		X		X		X		X	9	/		8	/	9
	20		40		70		100		130		160		189		209		227			246		

Figure 13.2 Best ball score sheet.

Worst Ball

This variation is played the same as in best ball, but the worst frame bowled by any individual is used in the game of the fictitious player (figure 13.3). This helps players understand how detrimental open frames can be. For instance, a player sees only two open frames during the game and thinks, that is not too bad. But, if every player on a five-person team did that, the team would have a cumulative total of 10 open frames. Ten open frames guarantees a score of 90 or less. In higher levels of competition, a team has little chance of success if, out every five games, one of them is equivalent to a player bowling under 100.

		X	7	/		X		X	7	2		X		X	8	-	7	-		8	/	9
Tommy	20		40		67		86		95		123		141		149		156			175			
		X	9	/	6	/		X		X	8	1		X	9	-	9	/		7	2	
Jenny	20		36		56		84		103		112		131		140		157			166			
	7	/	6	2	8	/	6	3	9	/	7	2	9	-		X	6	/		9	-	
Darren	16		24		40		49		66		75		84		104		123			132			
Worst frame	7	/	6	2	6	/	6	3	7	2	8	1	6	3	8	-	7	-		9	-	
	16		24		40		49		57		66		75		83		90			99			

Figure 13.3 Worst ball score sheet.

Although this format may be somewhat discouraging for inexperienced teams, it can help reinforce to higher-level players what is critical for team success. Open frames have a chance to hurt the team twice: once in the individual's game and again in the fictitious player's game. Under certain lane conditions, strikes come more easily for skilled players. So easy, they may get lackadaisical about spares. This practice keeps them on task concerning spares.

Baker System

The Baker system is named after Frank Baker, an American Bowling Congress (now USBC) official who devised this scoring system many years ago. In the Baker format, all bowlers combine for one game.

- For a typical five-player team, player one through five in the lineup bowl frames 1 through 5.
- After the 5th frame, the rotation starts over for frames 6 through 10.
- No bowler rolls more than two frames per game.
- Once a lineup is set, the order in which the players bowl is not permitted to change.
- For teams of fewer than five players, the order of bowling (or rotation) does not change. Because ten does not divide evenly by three or four, the leadoff player ends up bowling more frames in the game than others.
- Setting the correct lineup is critical to success; the goal is to have the strong frames of the better bowlers followed by other strong frames.

Under the Baker system, one player cannot dominate the competition. One player cannot carry the team. Unless all the team members are bowling well at the same time, it is difficult to produce high scores. One of the rarest feats in competitive bowling is a Baker 300, a perfect game bowled under the Baker format.

The Baker format is the truest form of team bowling, and it is a challenging format. All levels of bowling, from youth to national teams, use Baker games as part of the regular competition format. In the United States, Baker system bowling can be found in high school competitions and is very prevalent in college tournaments. In fact, some intercollegiate events (including sectional qualifiers and the Intercollegiate Team Championships) use Baker games exclusively. Occasionally, it is also featured in matches involving TEAM USA and professional bowling competitions. The Baker system is used frequently in collegiate competitions as well.

Jackpot Bowling

Jackpot bowling exists in a variety of formats. In one, the bowlers purchase tickets, and the funds collected from the sale of the tickets go toward the jackpot. Each night, one ticket (or more) is drawn. The person whose name is on the drawn ticket gets a chance at the jackpot.

This chance usually consists of throwing at a difficult spare or throwing a strike. If the bowler is successful, he or she wins the jackpot. If not, the jackpot rolls over to the next week and keeps growing until someone wins it.

Pot of Gold

Another form of jackpot bowling consists of throwing strikes in predetermined frames. In some bowling centers, you might notice a pot-of-gold board. On this board, particular frames are marked as a strike. These are the jackpot frames. Over the course of the night (usually a three-game series), the bowler must strike in all of the predetermined frames in order to win the jackpot. Some centers have a different pot-of-gold board for higher-average bowlers than for lower-average bowlers. The higher-average board will specify more frames than the one for the lower-average bowlers. Like other jackpot games, the prize fund keeps rolling over, week after week, until a bowler hits it.

Last Bowler Standing

In this simple elimination format, similar to a skins game, every bowler gets one throw at a full set of pins. All bowlers tying for the highest pinfall stay in; everybody else is out. The bowlers throw only at a full set of pins. Remaining pins are swept off; spare shooting is not usually part of the game. If all remaining bowlers tie on a throw, then everybody stays in. Play continues until only one bowler is left.

Last Bowler Standing 2

In this elimination format, bowlers have to exceed a predetermined pin count. All players whose roll equals or exceeds the pin count stay in; everybody else is out. As rounds progress, the target pin count increases. The last bowler in wins.

Last Bowler Standing 3

This game is a test of shot consistency as players move from lane to lane. The goal is to knock down at least eight pins on the first throw. The goal is to get the farthest in a set number of throws or amount of time.

If you knock down eight pins, move on to the next lane. If you knock down fewer than eight, there are two rule options; the second being the more challenging of the two.

1. Bowler stays on the current lane and only moves to next lane on throws of 8 or better.
2. Players rolling fewer than 8 go back to their starting lane.

Round the World

This is another type of game that tests a player's ability to adjust from lane to lane. In this version, though, spare shooting is critical for success. Each bowler has a starting lane. The goal is to reach a spot four lanes away (the first leg), and then during the second leg, get back to the starting lane.

1. Bowler can only advance to next lane by throwing a strike.
2. Bowler remains on current lane by making a spare.
3. Open frames send bowler back to starting lane.
4. Once a strike is rolled on the fourth lane, the first leg is finished. Bowler must strike on that lane again to start the second leg (the return trip).

The difficulty of this practice game is easily adjusted to accommodate different skill levels.

TO DECREASE DIFFICULTY

- Advance to next lane on both strikes and spares.
- Only go back one lane (or no lanes) after an open frame.
- Only go back to start by missing an easy (non-split or non-washout) spare.
- If on second leg, an open frame sends bowler back to start of second leg (instead of all the way back to initial lane of first leg).

Please note: If playing this game according to the most challenging format, allow ample time to complete game. Even skilled bowlers may not get all the way around the world in a reasonable amount of time.

Pin-Count Challenge

I first came across this game in the initial edition of *Bowling: Steps to Success* by Robert Strickland more 20 years ago.

> **Goal 1: Determine a strategy that results in the exact pin count of the current challenge level.**
>
> **Goal 2: Be the first to finish all boxes of the score sheet.**

Bowler is allowed to get the count in either one or two throws. For instance, if the bowler is on the 10s, the challenge can be met by either a strike or spare.

- Must get the exact pin count (in one or two rolls) to mark off a box
- Must finish all boxes of one level before moving on to the next level

The bowlers must be creative in their strategy (adjusting not just to where the ball makes contact, but also to how the ball works through the pins) to be successful. Adjusting angle and roll are almost as important as accuracy.

For some bowlers, this practice game is as much a test of patience as anything else. It's amazing how often a bowler strikes when only needing a nine count, or gets an eight when working on the sevens (or a seven when working on eights).

Some pin counts are difficult to get intentionally. The level I have found that gives bowlers the most trouble are the five counts. That is why the five-count level in both examples (see sample worksheet) requires the fewest number of attempts.